D0172242

Import/Export

Other Books by Carl Nelson

Nonfiction

Your Own Import/Export Business: Winning the Trade Game
Global Success: International Business Tactics of the 1990s
Managing Globally: A Complete Guide to Competing Worldwide
Protocol for Profit: A Manager's Guide to Competing Worldwide
International Business: A Manager's Guide to Strategy in the Age of Globalism
Exporting: A Manager's Guide to World Markets

Fiction

The Advisor (Cô-vân)
Secret Players

Import/Export

How to Get Started in International Trade

Third Edition
Expanded and Updated

Carl A. Nelson

McGraw-Hill, Inc.

New York San Francisco Washington, D.C. Auckland Bogotá
Caracas Lisbon London Madrid Mexico City Milan
Montreal New Delhi San Juan Singapore
Sydney Tokyo Toronto

Library of Congress Cataloging-in-Publication Data

Nelson, Carl A., 1930–
    Import export : how to get started in international trade / Carl A. Nelson.—3rd ed.,
expanded and updated.
       p.   cm.
    Includes index.
    ISBN 0-07-135871-4
    1. Trading companies—Handbooks, manuals, etc. 2. International trade—Handbooks,
manuals, etc. 3. Exports—Handbooks, manuals, etc. 4. Imports—Handbooks, manuals,
etc. 5. New business enterprises—Handbooks, manuals, etc. I. Title.

  HF1416 .N45 2000
  658.8'48—dc21

00-29204

McGraw-Hill

*A Division of The **McGraw·Hill** Companies*

Copyright © 2000 by Carl A. Nelson. All rights reserved. Printed in the United States
of America. Except as permitted under the United States Copyright Act of 1976, no part of
this publication may be reproduced or distributed in any form or by any means, or stored
in a data base or retrieval system, without the prior written permission of the publisher.

7 8 9 0 DOC/DOC 0 9 8 7 6 5

ISBN 0-07-135871-4

Printed and bound by R. R. Donnelley & Sons Company.

Materials in Chapter 12 of this book ("Doing Business in Africa") have been reproduced
or excerpted from pages 201–234 of Carl A. Nelson's book *Protocol for Profit: A Manager's
Guide to Competing Worldwide*, 1998, ISBN 1-86152-314-9, with the kind permission of
Thomson Learning Business Press, London.

McGraw-Hill books are available at special quantity discounts to use as premiums
and sales promotions, or for use in corporate training programs. For more information,
please write to the Director of Special Sales, Professional Publishing, McGraw-Hill,
Two Penn Plaza, New York, NY 10121-2298.

This publication is designed to provide accurate and authoritative information in regard
to the subject matter covered. It is sold with the understanding that neither the author
nor the publisher is engaged in rendering legal, accounting, or other professional service.
If legal advice or other expert assistance is required, the services of a competent professional person should be sought.
             —*From a Declaration of Principles jointly adopted by a Committee*
                of the American Bar Association and a Committee of Publishers.

This book is printed on recycled, acid-free paper
containing a minimum of 50% recycled, de-inked fiber.

This third edition is dedicated to my wife, Barbara,
who traveled Asia, suffered an often-absent
husband, and endured the painstaking labor of this
book through its life of almost two decades
and to
Guy Tozzolli, President
World Trade Centers Association, New York

Contents

List of Tables   *xi*

List of Figures   *xiii*

Foreword   *xvii*

Acknowledgments   *xix*

Introduction   *xxi*

The Book's Approach   xxiii
Who Is the Book For?   xxiii
What's in the Book?   xxv
What's New About This Edition?   xxvi
How to Use the Book   xxvi

Part 1   The Commonalities

1   Success and the Trade Game   *3*

International Trade   3
What Is an Import/Export Business?   3
Where Do Importers and Exporters Trade?   4
Global Opportunities   5
Why Get into Trade?   7
Is the Time Right to Get into the Market?   7
Success Stories:
   Serving the Golf Course Industry   7
   Sunglasses   8
   Old West Exports   8
   Introducing APT to the World   8
   Creative Tour Consultants   8
   Cirrus Logic   8
   Bicycles to Japan   9
   Ceiling Fans to Europe   9
   Avocados to Japan   9
   Frozen Waffles to Italy   10
   Surfboards to Japan 10
   German Crystal to the U.S.A.   10
   FTZ Success Stories   10
   Machinery to Mexico   11
   Harleys to France   12
   Importing Dresses from Mexico   12
   Golf Clubs to Sweden   12

Management Training Programs to New Zealand   12
Stuffed Toys to Japan   13
Peanut Butter to Australia   13
Rattan Furniture Imports   13
Software to Central and South America   13
Tax Advantage of an FSC   13

2   **Launching a Profitable Transaction**   *15*
Terminology   16
Homework   16
Four Questions   16
Choosing the Product or Service   17
Making Contacts   19
Conducting Research   21
Defining the Bottom Line   24

3   **Planning and Negotiating to Win**   *35*
The Market Plan   35
Negotiations   42
Tips and Traps of Culture   46
Intellectual Property Rights   52
Communications   54
Travel   59

4   **The Cyber Trader: Selling
with E-Commerce**   *65*
Background   66
Getting Started   67
Getting Out There   73
Pricing and Marketing Your Product   76
Further Reading   78

5   **Completing a Successful Transaction**   *81*
Financing   81
Avoiding Risk   86
Physical Distribution (Shipping and Packing)   105
Documentation   110

6   **How to Set Up Your Own
Import/Export Business**   *129*
The Mechanics of Start-Up   129
The 10 Commandments of Starting an Overseas
  Business   133
The Business Plan   134

Part 2   The Differences

7   Exporting from the United States   *151*
Government Export Counseling   152
Information Sources   156
Freight Forwarding   162
Export Controls   164
"Made in U.S.A."   169
Tax Incentives for Exporting   169
Relief from Unfair Import Practices   171

8   How to Import into the United States   *173*
Government Support   173
Import Information Sources   176
Customs House Brokers   177
Getting Through the Customs Maze   179
The Harmonized Tariff System   187
Import Quotas   195
Special Import Regulations   196
Free Trade Zones   198
Customs Bonded Warehouses   204

Part 3   Doing Business Worldwide

9   Doing Business Through World Trade Centers   *211*
What Is a World Trade Center (WTC)?   212
WTCA On-Line Services   212
WTCA Services and Benefits to Members   213

10   Doing Business in the Americas and an Expanding NAFTA   *215*
NAFTA   217
Maquiladora Implications   232
Other Existing Trade Arrangements   233

11   Doing Business in an Expanding Europe   *235*
The European Union   235
The European Free Trade Association (EFTA)   237
Trade Potential of the Newly Independent States   238
Enlargement of the EU   238

How to Do Business in the Single Market 240
Doing Business in Russia 247
Further Reading 249

12 Doing Business in Africa   251
African Trading Potential 251
American Partnership for Economic Growth 253
Useful Nation-by-Nation Business Information 256
Trade Blocs and Special Treaties 266
Funding Sources 267
Key Contacts and Web Sites 272

13 Doing Business in the Near East and Asia   275
Japan 275
People's Republic of China 277
Taiwan China 279
Pacific Basin 280
Helpful Publications and Information 281

14 20 Keys to Import/Export Success   283

Appendix A: ATA Carnet Countries and Their Customs Territories (2000)   289

Appendix B: U.S. Government Bookstores   291

Appendix C: Staging Codes   295

Glossary   297
Commonly Used Trade Terms 297
Internet Terms 326

Index   329

Tables

Number/Titles		Page
2-1	Making Contacts	22
2-2	Examples of Cost Elements	32
3-1	Intellectual Property Rights	53
5-1	Comparison of Various Methods of Payment	88
5-2	Typical L/C Charges	92
6-1	Categories of Expenses	132
6-2	Business Plan Outline	135
8-1	Commercial Entry Process	181
8-2	Formal vs. Informal Entry	189
8-3	Special Tariff Treatment Programs	194
8-4	Comparison of FTZ and Bonded Warehouse	206
10-1	The Americas	216
10-2	Trading Potential in the Americas	216
10-3	Examples of NAFTA Rule-of-Origin Types	226
11-1	Western European Trading Potential	236

11-2 The New Free Market Nations of Europe   *239*

11-3 VAT Rates in the 15-Member European Union   *245*

12-1 African Trading Potential   *252*

13-1 APEC (Asia-Pacific Economic Cooperation)   *282*

Figures

Number/Title		Page
I-1	Expansion of world exports	xxi
2-1	Typical letter of inquiry	25
2-2	Typical pro forma invoice	27
2-3	Where the risks and costs (obligations) begin and end	28
2-4	Market channel	29
2-5	Pricing model	31
2-6	Export costing worksheet	33
2-7	Import costing worksheet	34
3-1	Countertrade	44
3-2	Sample letter of introduction	56
3-3	International time zones	62
4-1	Typical Web site page	68
4-2	Example of HTML	70
5-1	Request to open a letter of credit	94
5-2	Sample letter of credit	96
5-3	The three phases of a letter of credit	97

5-4   Comparison of L/C risks   98

5-5   Transferable letter of credit   98

5-6   Assignment of proceeds   99

5-7   Typical letter of assignment   100

5-8   Back-to-back letter of credit   101

5-9   The intermodal concept   108

5-10   Example of markings   110

5-11   Certificate of origin   113

5-12   Commercial invoice   114

5-13   Consular invoice   116

5-14   Certificate of manufacture   118

5-15   Certificate of marine insurance   119

5-16   Inspection certificate   121

5-17   Packing list   122

5-18   Shipper's export declaration   123

5-19   Air waybill (bill of lading)   125

5-20   Ocean bill of lading   127

6-1   Pro forma sales projections   140

6-2   Pro forma income (profit/loss)
       statement   142

6-3   Pro forma balance sheet   144

6-4   Pro forma cash flow statement   146

7-1   Export license application form   *167*

8-1   Organization of U.S. Customs
        Service   *175*

8-2   Application for customs broker
        license   *180*

8-3   Special immediate entry permit
        (land)   *183*

8-4   Special immediate entry permit
        (ocean and air)   *184*

8-5   Sample entry summary   *190*

8-6   Sample page from Harmonized
        Tariff Schedule   *192*

10-1   NAFTA certificate of origin   *221*

10-2   NAFTA certificate of origin
        (continuation sheet)   *222*

10-3   NAFTA certificate of origin
        (instruction sheet)   *224*

13-1   Dispersement of potential
        Asian bloc   *280*

Foreword

Peace is something that everyone wants probably more than anything else. Yet since time began, the world has never known true peace. With all the technological advances that have profoundly changed the way we live, we still have not found a workable formula.

Yes, we can produce a long list of steps that can be taken to promote peace. The list includes education, communication, understanding, economic assistance, negotiation, statesmanship, treaties, protocols, and other government mechanisms to minimize friction and resolve disputes. However, we know from unfortunate experience that these approaches do not always succeed.

There is another major force for peace, and I am personally convinced that it offers civilization the best hope for a widespread and lasting accord around the globe. It's called world trade.

Virtually every society in the world depends on business to survive and prosper. Increasingly, success in business for most countries really means success in world business. Even businesses that sell only to a domestic market are affected by world trade. Why? Because other businesses in other parts of the world will be going after the same markets. Practically every country on earth realizes the importance of world trade and is working hard to develop international trade activities. This hard work has produced dramatic results for many countries, showing clearly the immense favorable impact that world trade can have on a nation's business and employment.

There is no question that as the number of business links between any two nations increases, the likelihood of war between those nations decreases proportionately. This is not simply a selfish issue of protecting profits. It is impossible to have effective business links without extensive communication, an understanding of cultural differences, and, above all, trust. These are the crucially important dividends for peace that result from the substantial and continuous exchange of commerce between nations. Alfred Nobel, noted philanthropist and champion of world peace, understood the concept completely.

This very successful businessman with operations in many countries said, "My factories may well put an end to wars sooner than your congresses." Events since then have completely validated Nobel's statement. His words have been a continual inspiration for those of us involved in world trade centers.

In my position as head of the World Trade Center in New York and as president of the World Trade Centers Association, I have had a unique opportunity over many years to witness the clear beneficial impact of world trade on world peace. I would like you to know that world trade centers and our association have built strong bridges for communications, understanding, and peace as well.

Today world trade centers are meeting all these needs, and they do so by creating shopping centers with representative offices of the many business and government organizations involved in trade. Many of these groups do business with one another on a daily basis, and their close proximity in a world trade center creates substantial operating efficiencies.

This includes educational programs, world trade libraries and other information services, exhibition facilities, trade mission programs, and special communications services. The combination of physical facilities and trade services makes a world trade center uniquely suited to stimulate a region's international business activities, attract new business to a region, and introduce world trade to firms that presently sell only to a domestic market.

To learn more about world trade centers and our association, I strongly recommend reading Chapter 9 of this excellent book.

Guy Tozzoli, President
World Trade Centers Association, New York

Acknowledgments

I am deeply indebted to the following people for their assistance in updating Chapter 7 of this edition: Julie Osman, Joe Burton, and Matthew Anderson of the Export Assistance Center, U.S. Department of Commerce, San Diego, California, for their help with the export services section; and John L. Bushnell, MPA, of the BXA Office, U.S. Department of Commerce, Orange County, California, for his assistance with the export controls section. I am also indebted to Mr. Herbert Ouida, Executive Vice President of the World Trade Centers Association; Frank Reynolds (contributor) and Peter Tirschwell (editor) of the *Journal of Commerce,* and to Griffin Hansbury, assistant editor, McGraw-Hill, as well as Janice Race, senior editing supervisor, McGraw-Hill.

Introduction

It's ".com" this and ".com" that, and before you know it you have opened a storefront on the Internet to sell your products and services electronically. It was just that easy. In this, the age of the Internet, convergence is not going to happen—it is happening. Things worldwide are flowing together. New connections are being created. E-commerce, Web sites, home pages—the face of international trade has changed and businesses all over the world are reaching cross-border customers using new communications and marketing techniques. According to a University of Texas study, since the introduction of the World Wide Web just five years ago, the Net economy in the United States has had a compound annual growth rate of about 175 percent. Internet sales in 1999 were up 300 percent from the previous year. Similar activity is reported in other nations. For instance, in Europe in 1998, the number of Internet retail sites stood at 4060, but by 2002, it is expected to exceed 22,000.

The result will be a new century that is even more prosperous than the past, because free and open international trade is the engine of economic development and everyone is going to be a part of it.

World exports of goods and services grew from less than $100 million shortly after World War II to well over $7 trillion today, pushing gross global product (GGP) to previously unthinkable levels. From less than $5 trillion in 1970, GGP is predicted to rise to as much as $100 trillion by the middle of the twenty-first century, and international trade could swell to as much as $40 trillion. Figure I-1 shows the indisputable expansion of world trade.

This is the third edition of *Import/Export: How to Get Started in International Trade,* a book that has continued its popularity as the best-selling book for its purpose. That purpose is to open the mysteries of international trade to everyone so that you too can get part of the action.

In order to keep the book vibrant and relevant, I have stayed with a practical format that explains the basics of the international trade transaction from A to Z—in terms anyone

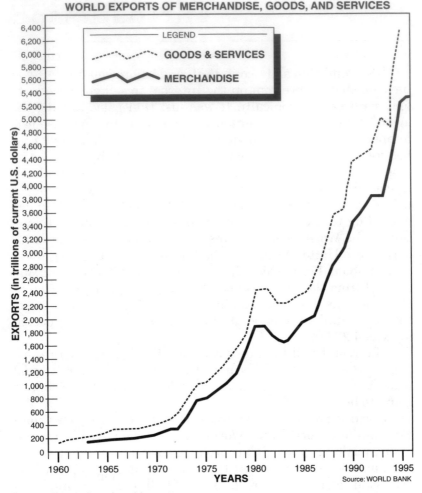

Fig. I-1. Expansion of world exports

can understand—while honing each edition to the cutting edge of the times.

This new edition *expands and updates* the basic material and adds the new "hot buttons" of international trade, such as information technology (IT), the Internet, and the Web sites that reside on the Net. This edition explains how to take advantage of e-commerce as a cyber trader (Chapter 4), how to do business in an expanding NAFTA (Chapter 10) as well as in Europe (Chapter 11), and how to profit from the growing opportunities in Africa (Chapter 12) and the Near East and Asia (Chapter 13).

The book deals with every aspect of exporting and importing, citing helpful details, examples, and success stories. Its overall message is that doing business across national borders is not difficult and can be *very profitable*.

Over the years *Import/Export* has had many printings and has enjoyed proven success, as have the thousands of people who have read it and put it to work.

The Book's Approach

From the beginning, the approach was to write a professional "how to" book that offers a small amount of theory with large portions of practical information in a tight, logical format that shows the details of the import/export *transaction*.

Unlike any previous book on international trade, *Import/Export* presents the basics by comparing and contrasting import and export. Other books on the subject separate importing from exporting, implying that the two are distinctly different. In fact, the mechanics of importing and exporting are basically the same. Importing is the mirror image of exporting. For example, terminology and communication for exporting and for importing across borders are identical.

The basics of *Import/Export* are not country-specific; that is, they work in any country and therefore give the book international appeal. Only Chapters 7 and 8 are U.S.-specific, and even those chapters are generic in the sense that the process applies to all nations.

Nothing about the approach to international trade has changed, and its basic treatment is as applicable today as it was when the book was first written. The focus is on the profitable business, and the underlying concept is that it is not enough to understand just exporting or importing—to be a successful trader, you must grasp your trading partner's problems. Therefore you must understand both.

Who Is the Book For?

Import/Export: How to Get Started in International Trade is for the owner of a small manufacturing or service firm, the person in search of a second career, or the entrepreneur who wants to know how to get into this $7 trillion worldwide market. The audience for the book will continue to be managers of firms who wish to expand internationally as well as students and entrepreneurs who see opportunity in the expanding global marketplace. It is especially valuable for small- and medium-size manufacturing and service firms that lack practical, hands-on experience and wish to learn the transaction mechanics of importing and exporting. A growing number of manufacturing and service companies worldwide are involved in international trade, yet as globalism sweeps across the land, to survive, more must get into the game.

The fact that this book is written by an American does not mean it is just for Americans. In every country of the world there are businesses that make things and sell them across borders. The process they use, except for a few differences in national rules, is exactly the same. This book describes that process and is a valuable tool for anyone in the world who wishes to profit from global trade.

Many people are intrigued by the challenge of starting a profitable business to market their own products, as well as others, across international borders. They see untapped markets and profits and want to know how to get into the growing business of international trade. An import/export business offers great opportunity to travel and enjoy the prestige of working with clients all over the world.

Many students (even those who have degrees in business) read this book to learn the practical application of their theoretical work as they embark on a career in one or more phases of international trade. Many teachers and professors have found it suitable as a classroom text that gives perspective and helps learners gain an appreciation of the total process and how their future fits into the big import/export picture.

The battle of the sexes has been fought and women have won their rightful place to participate as equals in global trade. From mailrooms to boardrooms, American women have become as commonplace as pinstripers with button-down collars. There's more opportunity and freedom for women in world business today than at any other time. In the United States more than 10 million businesses are owned by women—30 percent of all smaller firms—and they gross more than $200 billion annually. As the total number has increased, so have those businesses proportionately involved in international trade.

For new citizens of any country, many of the unexpected obstacles turn into advantages. For instance, in most of Africa it is an advantage to be a person of color. Most newcomers to any country have the advantage of speaking and understanding another language and culture. Getting off the ground in international trade is often easier because contacts are already in place.

What's in the Book?

This book is organized in an easy-to-understand anecdotal style and is intended for the entrepreneur as well as the decision-making executive.

Import/Export differs from other books on international trade in three ways:

1. It explains the import/export transaction in an entertaining way.
2. It reveals the fundamentals of importing and exporting in terms of their commonalities and differences.
3. It shows through anecdotes and specific cases how to put these fundamentals to work to earn big, untapped profits.

The Commonalities

This book cites 16 concepts common to both import and export: six in Chapter 3, six in Chapter 4, and four in Chapter 5.

The order in which these fundamental concepts are presented is designed to facilitate your understanding of them and also to parallel the order in which real world transactions generally occur. Please don't mistakenly assume that the order represents a hierarchy of importance or that each concept can truly stand alone. Each fundamental integrates with the other concepts in the process of international trade and each is equally necessary. Successful importers and exporters grasp the importance of the concepts and put them to work by setting up a firm as explained in Chapter 6.

The Differences

Some aspects of importing and exporting differ between or within countries. For example, controls (except for import quotas) apply only to exporting, whereas tariffs (duties) relate only to importing. These distinguishing features of exporting and importing are offered in Chapters 7 and 8, respectively. This treatment should clarify any differences and enable you to understand them easily.

What's New About This Edition?

This edition explains the import/export transaction process in many new ways:

- Enlarged and expanded coverage
- Extensive reference to Internet sources and addresses
- A new chapter on how to sell using e-commerce
- A new section on "success stories"
- New developments in product standards
- New developments in trade integration
- Tricks of using letters of credit

In addition, this edition has been organized with a new part, "Doing Business Worldwide," which explains how to conduct business in various nations and regions. For instance, Chapter 9 explains how to take advantage of world trade centers in most major cities. Because regionalism is a concept whose day has come, Chapter 10 is about doing business in the Americas and an expanded NAFTA, and Chapter 11 explains the basics of doing business in the expanding single market of the European Union. Of course, the book would be incomplete if it did not include new discussions of how to do business in Africa (Chapter 12) and the Near East and Asia (Chapter 13).

How to Use the Book

Whether you enter international trade through imports or exports, you should understand the basics of both. Therefore, the best way to use this book is to first master the concepts presented in Chapters 2 through 5. But it is unlikely that you will be ready to begin trading until you organize a business to do so. Therefore, Chapter 6 shows you how to set up and manage your company, then put the fundamentals to work profitably in the import/export business setting. This is where the fun really begins.

Import/Export answers these questions plus hundreds more:

What do I need to start my own import/export business?
How do I choose a product for import or export?
How do I make overseas sourcing contacts?
How do I make marketing contacts?
How can I sell over the Internet?
How do I get a Web site?
How do I design a home page?
How do I price a product for profit?
How do I prepare a market plan?
How do I negotiate a transaction?
How do I protect patents and trademarks?
What are the secrets of overseas travel?
How do I finance an import/export transaction?
How do I avoid risk?
What is a letter of credit?
To whom do I go for an export license?
What are the tax incentives for exporting?
How do I get through the customs maze?
How do I use the Harmonized Tariff Schedule?
How do I figure import duties?
How do I write a business plan for an import/export business?
What are the benefits of NAFTA?
How can I trade in Europe's single market?
Where do I go for information on doing business in Africa and Asia?

The final chapter of the book (Chapter 14) offers 20 secrets to import/export success. Obey them and enjoy big profits.

Part 1
The Commonalities

1
Success and the Trade Game

TRADE (COMMERCE) TAKES PLACE WHEN ONE PARTY PRODUCES and exchanges goods and services for currency or for the goods and services offered by someone else.

INTERNATIONAL TRADE

When an exchange of goods and services takes place across national boundaries, it is called *international trade*. Exports are the goods and service *sold* by individuals or nations. Imports are the goods and services *purchased*. By these methods, products valued at more than $7 trillion worldwide are exchanged every year. When we as consumers enjoy fresh flowers from Latin America, tropical fruits in the middle of winter, or a foreign car, we are participants in—and beneficiaries of—international trade, which is not a zero-sum game of winners and losers. It is a game in which everyone wins.

WHAT IS AN IMPORT/EXPORT BUSINESS?

What is an import/export business? What organizational methods do traders use? These are among the questions I'm most frequently asked, and they are explained in more detail in Chapter 6. Even so, the answers depend on whether you work for a manufacturer or are independent.

If you own or work for a manufacturer of an exportable product, that company can organize its own export department. But today many manufacturers outsource their export function to import/export companies.

An independent import/export business is an individual or company that acts as an international middleman (a unisex term). That is, it sells foreign-made products (import), sells domestic products (home country) in other countries (export), or does both. You see, every manufacturer not already exporting can be a potential client for you; all over the world there are many businesses that do not export. According to the U.S. Department of Commerce, less than 10 percent of all American manufacturers currently sell their products overseas.

Whether you run your business from your home or as an expansion of an existing domestic manufacturing firm, whether you work at it full or part time, an import/export business often requires little capital investment for start-up. Of course, the venture can grow into a giant business with billions of dollars in annual sales. An import/export business also offers great opportunity to travel and enjoy the prestige of working with clients all over the world.

WHERE DO IMPORTERS AND EXPORTERS TRADE?

The opportunity to conduct import/export is everywhere, because international markets have become much more interdependent. Trade conditions among nations have changed. Today, conditions favor importing and exporting from all countries.

Realistically, international trade involves both importing and exporting, not one at the exclusion of the other. Novices to international trade, whether companies or individuals, can get started through either importing or exporting. Once trade begins, opportunities spring out of nowhere. A person who successfully starts importing very soon learns of exporting opportunities and vice versa. In any case, a whole lot of money can be made. More than $7 trillion wouldn't be traded worldwide if it weren't profitable to do so.

GLOBAL OPPORTUNITIES

We are living in an era of profound changes in international trade. Called the age of interdependence, it is a time of increasing expectations brought about by worldwide distribution, the Internet, satellite communications, and speedy transportation systems. People all over the world seek the same luxuries and standards. They see things and, naturally, they want them.

Globalization is no longer a buzzword—it is a reality, and national governments have a stake in its outcome because the change affects their societies. Therefore, international trade is not a static process, and businesses that make things and attempt to sell them across borders must constantly adjust.

Globalism is a reality driven by changes in the marketplace as well as government policy. As the globalization process goes forward, the need for harmonizing interstate laws becomes a more serious reality. Major changes that took place in the late 1990s will have significant effect on international trade into the new century and provide unprecedented opportunity.

The World Trade Organization (WTO)

The creation of the World Trade Organization (WTO), with equal status alongside the World Bank and International Monetary Fund, has strengthened global trade. This organization, with over 120 national members, makes it easier to do business across borders by reducing tariffs and harmonizing laws and practices that are barriers to trade.

Cyber Trading

There is no president or congress of the Internet and it has no boundaries; therefore, cyber communication is the international trader's connection without barriers.

The World Trade Centers Association (WTCA)

Founded in 1970, the World Trade Centers Association (WTCA) is a not-for-profit, nonpolitical association dedicated to the establishment and effective operation of world trade centers as instruments for trade expansion. To date, the WTCA membership represents 336 centers in 101 countries.

World trade centers are dedicated to providing services to facilitate international trade and are located in over 170 cities with about 100 more in the planning stages. In other words, they are in virtually every major trading city in the world. To learn more about world trade centers, see Chapter 9.

Trade Integration

Trade integration is a preferential arrangement between two or more nations to facilitate commerce across borders. The North American Free Trade Agreement (NAFTA)—representing the world's largest trading bloc—is expanding to include many of the nations of the Caribbean Basin and South America.

The European Union (EU) formed a single internal market that has resulted in the removal of substantially all physical, technical, and fiscal barriers to the exchange of goods and services within the common market. The European Union is now enlarging to include some of the newly independent states of Central and Eastern Europe. Some of the changes agreed to are:

- A common value-added tax.
- Deregulation of transportation.
- Establishment of minimum industrial and safety standards.
- Broadening of the EU-wide bidding process for government procurement.

Asia

Importing and exporting from and to the Asian/Pacific Basin nations of Australia, New Zealand, China, Japan, and the Tigers (South Korea, Taiwan, Hong Kong, Singapore, and Thailand) presents the greatest new trade opportunity. This region has expanded faster than any other part of the world.

Africa

The latest world trade emphasis is on the African continent, particularly those nations south of the Sahara, where there are vast untapped resources and a need for modernization and economic development.

WHY GET INTO TRADE?

Three reasons exist for people to get into the trade game:

1. Imports bring big profits.
2. Exports make big profits.
3. People have awakened to reality. The economies of the world are interdependent—people of each nation rely on people of other nations to exchange goods, services, and ideas, and that free trade creates jobs.

IS THE TIME RIGHT TO GET INTO THE MARKET?

Those who are winning the trade game know that regardless of national deficits or surpluses, the time is always right for an import/export business to make profits. The winners simply swing with political and economic changes over which they have little or no control.

SUCCESS STORIES

This book does not guarantee financial success—there are too many variables such as management ability, financial capitalization, and determination; however, here are a few of the stories you might find interesting and stimulating. They may give you ideas about techniques that will work for you.

Serving the Golf Course Industry

Observing the growth and popularity of his favorite game, a young soils professional targeted a combination of agricultural *products and services* to serve the golf course industry throughout the world. The *products* he exported were bio-engineered organic fertilizers, pregerminated seed, and soil conditioners designed to maintain turf in the most ecologically responsible fashion. The *services* he offered included management and counseling for the most effective, cost-efficient, and environmentally sensitive golf courses.

Sunglasses

A young American retail store operator who specialized in sunglasses doubled his sales when he began offering his products over the Internet. Sales came from as far away as India, Brazil, and South Africa.

Old West Exports

Market research showed that Japanese imports of Western boots were growing at 4.6 percent per year. After answering the four preliminary questions asked in Chapter 2, he obtained $350,000 capitalization and successfully started Old West Exports, selling such products as Tony Lama boots into a very lucrative market.

Introducing APT to the World

A young Japanese student in the United States took on the additional task of importing APT, a new Japanese product that is supposedly better and safer than turpentine for cleaning oil- or water-based paint. He successfully introduced APT by focusing on a microsegment of 40 art stores in San Diego and 70 in Los Angeles.

Creative Tour Consultants

Creative Tour Consultants was founded by two women who took advantage of their knowledge of northern Europe and combined it with a background in the travel industry. Their market plan offered an introductory package called "Viking Tour" to a microsegment interested in touring Sweden. Soon they were booking all over Scandinavia.

Cirrus Logic

In 1989, California-based Cirrus Logic, Inc., which designs and provides software-rich integrated circuits for a range of applications, celebrated its fifth anniversary and took a major transpacific step, setting up a subsidiary in Japan. Today, global sales account for 20 percent of Cirrus Logic's total group sales.

Bicycles to Japan

Two of three people in Japan own a bicycle. When a young Japanese-American also learned that 36,630 all-terrain bicycles (ATB) were bought in 1989 and that number increased to about 500,000 by 1991, he decided to export high-grade bikes from the United States. He borrowed $160,000 from his family, established the International Express Bicycle Company, and began by sending 10 bikes a month, 5 to a retail shop in Tokyo and 5 to one in Osaka. By the summer of 1994 he had increased his sales of $1000 and $1500 bikes to 20 a month. His net profit for the first year was only $2440 on $150,000 sales, but the future looked very bright.

Ceiling Fans to Europe

A California woman opened Las Brisas Exports on an initial capitalization of $10,000, half from her Spanish business partner and half from her own Master Card line of credit. In her first year she sold 180 units of top-of-the-line ceiling fans and had profits of $24,000 on sales of $144,000. She sold 480 units in her second year with $69,256 net earnings on $395,520 sales. Conservative fifth-year projections show sales of over 600 units and net profits of $262,000 on sales of over half a million dollars.

Avocados to Japan

Most tropical fruits must be imported to Japan. Thinking through her business plan, a woman decided to start her business with avocados, and if that succeeded she would expand to other fruits such as wild cherry, mango, and papaya. She chose avocados because Mexican dishes are becoming popular in Japan. They are used in sushi because they taste like tuna and are very profitable. Her plan called for buying 4 tons (20,000 units) a month at $2.50 per unit and selling them at $3.50, and she did just that, making a whole lot of money.

Frozen Waffles to Italy

A young Italian gambled that Italy's younger generation was ready for an alternative to croissants. His import plan introduced frozen waffles from the United States into Italy's frozen food market. Market penetration was so successful that he opened a small production company in Genoa and has expanded sales to other cities in the European Community.

Surfboards to Japan

A San Diego, California, surfer and businessman knows a bargain when he sees it. He discovered that new major-brand surfboards sell for $1200 in Japan. He could buy boards from a new U.S. manufacturer at $120 and sell them to retailers at about half the going rate. That's when he got serious about international trade. First-year sales were $780,000, and he paid back his initial capital (borrowed from friends, parents, and relatives) in less than three years.

German Crystal to the U.S.A.

The opportunity came when a businesswoman discovered a market for German crystal tableware in California. Her new company, Crystal Treasures, grossed $85,000 the first year. The owner succeeded by buying at 5 percent below the wholesale price and gaining a 3 percent discount on the total sales price by making payment within 10 days. By ensuring that all shipments were above the $1000 threshold noted in the Harmonized Tariff Schedule (HTS) 7013.31.00, the businesswoman was able to take advantage of only a 3.4 percent ad valorem duty (tariff) rate. Thus she was able to become profitable by her second year in business.

FTZ Success Stories

Using a foreign trade zone (FTZ) is not to the advantage of every business, but those that do not take the time to do some simple calculations may find that they are paying significantly higher costs than their competitors. To learn more about how to take advantage of FTZs, see Chapter 8. The following success stories represent millions of dollars saved.

Leather Boots/Roller Skates.   An importer found very high quality boots manufactured in China, but the tariff at the time was too high. Cleverly, he shipped the boots into a foreign trade zone, attached wheels to the bottoms, and entered the boots as roller skates. Now at practically no duty, this businessman made a ton of money.

Maritime Subzone.   National Ship Building Company in San Diego, California, discovered a quirk in U.S. import laws that says a vessel is "an intangible" and not subject to tariff. The company applied for and received permission to become a subzone of the Long Beach Foreign Trade Zone. Foreign parts were brought into the zone duty free, incorporated into the hull of the vessel, then sailed away duty free. The company saved more than $1 million through this clever use of the law.

Computer Chips.   Computer chips were manufactured offshore in Singapore. Before they were entered into U.S. customs territory, they were brought into a foreign trade zone for quality assurance (QA) inspection. Chips found to be below standard were crushed, ground, and sorted. The gold used in the chips was reclaimed, but never entered into U.S. customs. It was shipped back to the plant in Singapore. The remainder of the waste materials was entered as trash, duty free. Only those chips that passed QA were entered for duty purposes. One savvy firm avoided the drawback, and thus kept its money working for the company, not Uncle Sam.

Machinery to Mexico

Taking note of Mexico's entry into the General Agreement on Tariffs and Trade (GATT) and then the potential success of NAFTA, a businessman intuitively saw opportunity for increased sales of heavy machinery. His research proved him right. The industry's growth rate was 15 percent, with most of the sales by U.S. manufacturers. He initially sold the popular Caterpillar tractors D5H and D6H to the Mexican states of Oaxaca and Chiapas, but soon he expanded into Guatemala, Belize, and Honduras.

Harleys to France

American products are very fashionable in France: Levis go for $80, Van's shoes for $100, Zippo lighters for $25, and so on. The Harley Davidson motorcycle is one of those very fashionable products. The price for a used Harley starts at $8000. One clever businesswoman started by buying used Harleys through the local city want ads at about $2000 to $3000 (depending on the model), and had a mechanic check them out. Her European import price was $3300 to $4500, with a retail price of $5700 to $7100. She sold 10 a month and was profitable in her first year.

Importing Dresses from Mexico

A mother of two, who grew up in Massachusetts, lived for many years in Mexico City, where she learned to speak fluent Spanish and understand the Mexican culture. This advantage helped her start a profitable business importing a line of women's dresses from Mexico City to Los Angeles.

Golf Clubs to Sweden

A Swedish exchange student started a lucrative business exporting American golf clubs to his home country. He played golf and knew that the sport was growing in Sweden. He already had contacts with sporting goods distributors, so he negotiated an exclusive contract with a San Diego golf club manufacturer and was quickly in business. It was a nice way to support his overseas education.

Management Training Programs to New Zealand

An American husband and wife team who specialized in management training programs made big profits exporting their service to New Zealand. Their research (homework) showed a growing market (need), little domestic expertise, but sufficient money to pay for management training services.

Stuffed Toys to Japan

When the value of the dollar fell in comparison to the yen, a Japanese-American who had contacts in Osaka and experience in the toy business saw an opportunity to export to Japan. He discussed it with his wife and his Osakan friends. They chose stuffed toys as their product, then they developed a well-defined market plan to penetrate the Japanese market. Why? Because there was a need—kids in Japan love stuffed animals—and the profit margin was excellent.

Peanut Butter to Australia

A woman in her sixties decided that she was too young to retire. She started a business exporting her special peanut butter to Australia, a country where she often vacations and has made many friends and business contacts. One of the first things she did was register her trademark, "Gone Tropo," in both the United States and Australia. From her investment came a lucrative business that allows her to travel Down Under several times a year.

Rattan Furniture Imports

A Filipino man who became an American citizen still had many island contacts. He started a successful rattan furniture import business by obtaining an SBA-guaranteed bank loan.

Software to Central and South America

A computer whiz in his early twenties studied the trade statistics at his local export assistance center and learned of the need for software in Central and South America. Now his business is booming as he markets by direct mail to several countries in that region.

Tax Advantage of an FSC

A construction engineering firm formed an export trading company (ETC) to supply Asia with the services of many smaller construction service companies (architects, engineers, etc.). To take advantage of the tax exclusion and deferral opportunities on increased profits, the firm set up a foreign sales corporation (FSC) on the island of Saipan in the western Pacific. To learn more about using FSCs for your tax advantage, see Chapter 7.

The next chapter will launch you into the first steps of an import/export transaction and speed you on your way to international trade success and profits.

2

Launching a Profitable Transaction

THE NEXT FOUR CHAPTERS EXPLAIN THE BASICS OF THE IMPORT/
export transaction. They apply to manufactured products as
well as growing service industries such as computer software,
construction engineering, and insurance.

These basics are "the bridge" from producer to buyer. They
have been in place for many years and are tested over time.
Nevertheless, it is possible to perceive the import/export
transaction process as an obstacle. Don't let it deter you.
Anyone can grasp the nuts and bolts of international trade.
Invest time and money in yourself by learning as much as you
can about the process before you commit to an import/export
project.

This chapter addresses the first six commonalities of the
import/export transaction. If you understand these steps, your
import/export business will get off to an excellent start toward
early profitability.

1. Learn the terminology.
2. Do your homework.
3. Choose the product or service.
4. Make contacts.
5. Conduct market research.
6. Define the bottom line.

Don't mistakenly assume that the order presented in this book represents a hierarchy of importance, or that these steps precisely parallel every import/export project. In reality sometimes things happen simultaneously.

TERMINOLOGY

Because of increasing international interdependency, trade literacy has become as important as Internet and computer literacy in modern business. As you progress in your reading, frequently refer to the extensive Glossary found at the end of this book. Many of these terms are also defined when they first appear in the text. Don't be frightened off by the new terminology—you can learn it!

HOMEWORK

Research is one of the keys to winning the trade game. Even if you have some experience in international trade, it's unwise to jump into an unresearched project. In fact, it's not unusual to spend several weeks learning about a product and its profit potential before getting serious. Think of it as an investment to reduce the number of inevitable mistakes.

FOUR QUESTIONS

Before deciding whether an import/export project merits further commitment of time and funds, you need to answer four preliminary questions:

Question 1: What Product or Service?   In what product or service are you interested or do you have some expertise? For the prospective importer/exporter, this decision is personal as well as technical. For the manufacturer of a product or provider of a service, this step is moot—you sell your own product or service.

Question 2: What Contacts?   To whom will you sell the product or service? And from whom will you obtain the product or service? Who are your contacts? Do you have more than one source for the product you intend to import or export? Choose very carefully the country where you intend to sell your product.

Question 3: What Research?   Must you do research? Yes! Are people and/or firms willing to buy this product or service? Although products and services that carry the label "Made in Country X" continue to be popular, they no longer sell themselves. But if a local product has a mature market, it very likely has a market in other parts of the world. On the one hand, the fact that many foreign goods cost less increases sales potential. On the other hand, if the product is unique to a given culture or the quality is cheap, many people will not buy it.

Question 4: What's the Bottom Line?   Do the rough calculations of price and quantity warrant undertaking the project? Determine whether the margin of profit makes the project worthwhile. What changes must you make to the product to ensure a profitable export or import? Bear in mind that just as much work goes into importing or exporting an unprofitable product or service as trading a profitable one. Don't waste time with losers.

CHOOSING THE PRODUCT OR SERVICE

The question asked most often is "What product should I select to import or export? Should it be rugs or machinery?"

Of course, if your firm already manufactures merchandise or provides a service, that product or service is what you sell. But for your own import/export business, your job will be to sell someone else's product or service. In other words, you will be the middleman.

The Personal Decision

Most people begin with a single product or service they know and understand or have experience with. Others begin with a line of products, or define their products in terms of an industry with which they are familiar. Above all, product selection is a personal decision, but the decision should make common sense. For example, if you aren't an engineer, don't begin by exporting gas turbine engines. Or if you are an electronics engineer, don't start with fashionable textiles.

A good example is the American house painter who began making excellent profits exporting a line of automated painting equipment to Europe. He knew the equipment before he began.

Start your business with a product or service that gives you an advantage. You can gain that advantage by having prior knowledge, by doing library research on a product, by making or using contacts, or by understanding a language or culture.

HOT TIP: Keep it simple in the beginning.

The Technical Marketing Decisions

Keep in mind that the product you select may have to adapt to the cultures of other countries.

Product Standards.   There is a movement toward harmonizing world product standards such as flammability, labeling, pollution, food and drug laws, and safety standards. ISO 9000 (product registration) and ISO 14000 (environmental management registration) are the international quality assurance series. They have been in effect for well over a decade and are unlikely to go away. Therefore it is important to check your products for compliance.

Technical Specifications and Codes.   Most of the world operates on 220 V, 50 Hz, but products in the United States use 120 V, 60 Hz. Similarly, most of the world uses the metric system of weights and measures. Determine how you can convert your product to meet these specifications and codes.

Quality and Product Life Cycle.   In the life cycle of product innovation, new products are typically introduced to developed countries (DCs), leaving an opportunity for sales of earlier models to less developed countries (LDCs). Assess the stage in the life cycle in which you find your import/export product.

Other Uses.   Different countries use products for differing purposes. For example, motorcycles and bicycles are largely recreation vehicles in the United States, but in many countries they are the primary means of transportation.

Developed countries: The more industrialized nations—including all member countries of the Organization for Economic Cooperation and Development (OECD)—as distinguished from "developing" or "less developed" countries.

Least developed countries: Some 36 of the world's poorest countries are considered by the United Nations to be the least developed of the less developed countries. Most of them are small in terms of both area and population, and some are landlocked or island countries. They are generally characterized by:

- Low per capita incomes, literacy levels, and medical standards
- Subsistence agriculture
- Lack of exploitable minerals and competitive industries

Many LDCs are in Africa (see Chapter 12), but a few, such as Bangladesh, Afghanistan, Laos, and Nepal, are in Asia. Haiti is the only country in the Western Hemisphere classified by the United Nations as "least developed."

MAKING CONTACTS

Importers and exporters need contacts to get started. The exporter must convince a domestic manufacturer of his or her ability to sell the manufacturer's product or service internationally. The importer, on the other hand, must find an overseas manufacturer or middleman from whom to buy the product or service.

Contacts are classified in two categories. By making these two groups overlap, you can expand your import/export network:

1. *Sourcing* (finding) a manufacturer or provider of the product or service you wish to import or export.
2. *Marketing* (selling) that product or service.

Sourcing Contacts

If you are an exporter, any product or service you select falls into an industry classification and that industry very likely has an association. Almost every industry has a publication—if not a magazine, at least a newsletter. Begin looking for manufacturers of your product or service in the appropriate industry publication. In Chapter 7 you will find other sources of information that may help you make contacts for products to export.

Contacts for importers are only slightly more difficult to obtain. Assuming you know in which country your product is manufactured, you need a contact in that industry in that country. Start with the nearest consulate office. Next, contact the International Chamber of Commerce in that country. You can also make contacts through your embassy or through a corresponding industry association. Furthermore, you can make direct contact with the government of the country in which you are interested.

Next, establish communications with the contact to seek further information or to ask for product samples and prices. You can make contact by letter, fax, or e-mail. (Communications are covered in Chapter 3.)

Eventually, take a trip to the country with which you intend to trade. It will make a big difference. (Travel is also explained in Chapter 3.)

Marketing Contacts

Marketing methods and channels of distribution are the same in most countries. Agents, distributors, wholesalers, and retailers exist everywhere, and you make marketing contacts through these channels.

For domestic marketing contacts, use trade shows, direct sales, direct mail, and manufacturers' representatives, as well as swap meets, flea markets, home parties, or wholesalers. Most governments will also help you find contacts.

> *Foreign sales representative:* A representative residing in a foreign country who acts as a sales agent for a U.S. manufacturer, usually for a commission. Sometimes referred to as a "sales agent" or "commission agent."
>
> *Distributor:* A firm that (1) sells directly for a manufacturer, usually on an exclusive basis for a specified territory, and (2) maintains an inventory of the manufacturer's goods.

The international marketeer (trader) also can make contacts through world trade centers (WTC) (see Chapter 9), trade shows, direct sales, distributors, or agents who serve as the equivalent of manufacturers' representatives. Trade fairs or shows are often the single most effective means to make contacts and to learn about products, markets, competition, potential customers, and distributors. The term *trade show* or *fair* includes everything from catalog shows through local exhibits to major specialized international industry shows. At these shows exhibitors offer literature and samples of the product.

Lists of worldwide trade shows and international conferences are available from most large airlines such as Lufthansa as well as from the U.S. Department of Commerce or Chamber of Commerce (COC). Your industry association will know when and where the appropriate trade shows take place.

Table 2-1 offers a range of ideas that should assist you, the importer or exporter, in making either sourcing or market contacts.

CONDUCTING RESEARCH

Market research is vital to the success of your import/export business. Is your product salable? Does anyone care? You must be able to sell enough of the product or service to justify undertaking the import/export project. If you are presenting a new product, you may have to create a market. But a good rule of thumb for the new import/export business is: "If the market isn't there, get out of the project and find another product."

International market research will save money and time. Unfortunately, too many newcomers plunge into import/export *without* determining whether they can sell the product at a profit. Following are checklists of research items for importers and exporters.

Exporter Checklist

☑ Is there already a market for the product?

☑ What is the market price?

☑ What is the sales volume for that product?

☑ Who has market share, and what are the shares?

☑ What is the location of the market, including its size and population? People in major urban areas generally have more money than people elsewhere.

☑ What are the climate, geography, and terrain of the market country?

Table 2-1. Making Contacts

	Source	Market
Import	Consulate offices International COC Industrial organizations Foreign governments WTCA The WEB (Internet)	Swap meets Direct mailers Mail orders Home parties Trade shows Wholesalers Associations Representatives Retailers U.S. government WTCA The WEB (Internet)
Export	*Thomas Register* *Contacts Influential* *Yellow Pages* U.S. Dept. of Commerce Trade journals Trade associations WTCA The WEB (Internet)	Distributors Trade shows Retailers Foreign governments U.S. Dept. of Commerce Direct mailers United Nations USAID Sell Overseas America *Business America* State trade promotion offices *Journal of Commerce* WTCA The WEB (Internet)

☑ What are the economics of the country, including its GNP, major industries, and sources of income?

☑ What is the local currency? How stable is it? Is barter commonplace?

☑ Who are the employees of the country? How much do they earn? Where do they live?

☑ Is the government stable? Do they like Americans? Does the country have a good credit record?

☑ What are the tariffs, restrictions, and quotas?

☑ What are the other barriers to market entry, such as taxation and repatriation of income?

☑ What language is spoken? Are there dialects? Does the business community speak English?

☑ How modern is the country?

☑ Do people use the Internet?

☑ Is there electric power?

☑ How do businesses move their goods?

☑ How good is the hard infrastructure (roads, trains, etc.)?

☑ What about the soft infrastructure (schools, etc.)?

☑ Does the country manufacture your product? How much does it produce? How much is sold there?

☑ What kind of and how much advertising is generally used? Are there local advertising firms? Are there trade fairs and exhibitions?

☑ What distribution channels are used? What levels of inventory are carried? Are adequate storage facilities available?

☑ Who are the customers? Where do they live? What influences a customer's buying decisions? Is it price, convenience, or habit?

☑ What kinds of services are expected? Do customers throw away or repair? Can repair services be set up?

☑ What about competition? Are there sales organizations? How do they price?

☑ What are the property right implications?

Importer Checklist

☑ Is there already a market for the product?

☑ What is the market price?

☑ What is the sales volume for that product?

☑ Who has market share, and what are the shares?

☑ What is the location of the market, including its size and population? People in major urban areas generally have more money than people elsewhere.

☑ Who are the wholesalers?

☑ What kind of and how much advertising is generally used? Are there local advertising firms? Are there trade fairs and exhibitions?

☑ What distribution channels are used? What levels of inventory are carried? Are adequate storage facilities available?

☑ Who are the customers? Where do they live? What influences a customer's buying decisions? Is it price, convenience, or habit?

☑ What kinds of services are expected? Do customers throw away or repair? Can repair services be set up?

☑ What about competition? Are there sales organizations? How do they price?

☑ What are the property right implications?

The answers to these questions are available through most good libraries, the U.S. Department of Commerce or Chamber of Commerce, or private market research companies. (See Chapters 7 and 8 for export and import information sources.)

DEFINING THE BOTTOM LINE

Profit is an internal, individual decision that varies from product to product, from industry to industry, and within the market channel. Desirable profit relates to the goals you plan for your import/export business. For instance, one person's goal might be to cover expenses, take a small salary, and be pleased if the business supports occasional travel to exotic places. Another person might seek to expand the business into a major trading company. Yet another might decide to work for only five or six years, sell the business at a profit, and retire on the capital gain.

This segment of the chapter discusses the profit aspects of international trade, beginning with initial quotations, terms of sale, the market channel, and pricing.

Initial Quotations

Initial quotes begin either with a request for quotation (RFQ) sent by the importer to the exporter or with an unsolicited

Our Company, Inc.
Hometown, U.S.A.

Ref:
Date:

Your Company, Ltd.
2Λ1 Moon River
Yokohama, Japan

Our company is a medium-size manufacturing company. We are interested in your products.

Please send us a pro forma invoice for five of your machines, CIF Los Angeles. Please indicate your payment terms and estimated time of delivery after receipt of our firm order.

Sincerely,

W. T. Door
President

Fig. 2-1. Typical letter of inquiry

offer from the exporter. A simple letter or fax can be a request for a quotation. Figure 2-1 shows a sample letter of inquiry.

The pro forma invoice, a normal invoice document visibly marked "pro forma," is the method most often used to initiate negotiations. This provisional invoice is forwarded by the seller of goods, prior to a contemplated shipment, advising the buyer of the kinds and quantities of goods to be sent, their value, and important specifications (weight, size, etc.). Its purpose is to describe in advance certain items and details. The invoice contains the major elements of a contract that will be used later in shipping and collection documents such as letters of credit (discussed in Chapter 5).

Keep in mind that everything in a pro forma invoice is negotiable, so carefully think through any terms entered on this document. Once accepted by the purchaser, it becomes a binding sales agreement or legal contract, and the seller is bound to the terms stated. Figure 2-2 is an example of a pro forma invoice, showing the key elements of the contract:

- Product description and specifications
- Material costs
- Price
- Quantity
- Shipping costs
- Delivery terms
- Procedures

Terms of Sale

In international business, suppliers use pricing terms, called *terms of sale.* These pricing terms quite simply define the geographical point where the *risks* and *costs* of the exporter and importer *begin* and *end.*

The International Chamber of Commerce (ICC) has, over time, developed a set of international rules for the interpretation of the most commonly used trade terms, called IN-COTERMS. If, when drawing up the *contract,* both buyer and seller specifically refer to INCOTERMS, they can be sure of defining their respective responsibilities. In so doing, buyer and seller eliminate any possibility of misunderstanding and subsequent dispute. A copy of INCOTERMS 2000 (effective January 1, 2000) can be ordered from: ICC Publishing Corporation, Inc., 156 Fifth Avenue, Suite 417, New York, NY 10010; phone: (212) 206-1150; fax: (212) 633-6025; e-mail: iccpub@interport.net; Web: www.iccbooks.com.

There are many variant terms of sale. INCOTERMS organize them into four groups; "E group" for EXW points of origin; "F group" for FCA, FAS, and FOB; "C group" for terms in which the seller has to contract for carriage (CFR, CIF, CPT, CIP); and "D group" for terms in which the seller has to bear all costs and risks to bring the goods to the place of destination (DAF, DES, DEQ, DDU, and DDP).

Among all these terms there are four—EXW, FAS, CIF, and DAF—that are most commonly used. Figure 2-3 shows how these terms function.

XYZ Foreign, Co.
2A1 Moon River
Yokohama, Japan

Our Company, Inc.
Hometown, U.S.A.

Purchase Order Date:
Invoice Date:
Invoice Ref. No.:
PRO FORMA 00012

Terms of Payment:
Confirmed
Irrevocable Letter of Credit
Payable in U.S. dollars

Invoice To:
Ship To:
Forwarding Agent:

Via: Country of Origin:

QUANTITY	PART NO.	DESCRIPTION	PRICE EACH	TOTAL PRICE
10	A2Z	Machines	$100.00	$1,000.00
Inland freight, export packing & forwarding fees				$ 100.00
Free alongside (FAS) Yokohama				$1,100.00
Estimated ocean freight				$ 100.00
Estimated marine insurance				$ 50.00
CIF Long Beach				$1,250.00

Packed in 10 crates, 100 cubic feet
Gross weight 1000 lbs.
Net weight   900 lbs.
Payment terms: Irrevocable letter of credit by a U.S. bank.
Shipment to be made two (2) weeks after receipt of firm order.
Country of Origin: Japan
We certify this pro forma invoice is true and correct.

Issu A. Towa
President

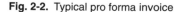
Fig. 2-2. Typical pro forma invoice

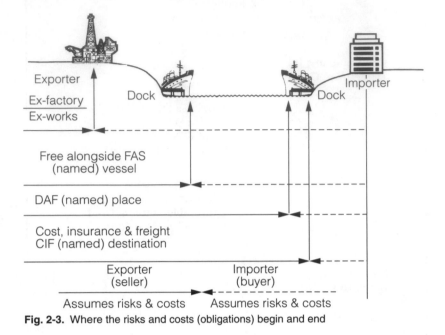

Fig. 2-3. Where the risks and costs (obligations) begin and end

EXW is used with a named place or point of origin. Examples are Ex-Factory (named place) and Ex-works (named place). This term represents minimum seller responsibility. Seller covers all charges to the agreed to "specified delivery point." The buyer pays all costs and accepts all risk from the point where the goods are made available, including export clearances.

FAS (*free alongside a ship*) is usually followed by a named port of export. A seller quotes this term for the price of goods that includes charges for delivery alongside a vessel at the port. The buyer is responsible thereafter.

CIF (*cost, marine insurance, freight*) is used with a named overseas port of import. The seller is responsible for charges up to the port of final destination.

DAF (*delivered at frontier*) is used with a named place of import. The seller delivers when the goods are placed, unloaded, at the disposal of the buyer on the arriving means of transport. The goods are cleared for export, but not cleared for import at the frontier—that is, they must still pass the customs border of the named country.

Marine insurance: Insurance that will compensate the owner of goods transported on the seas in the event of loss if such loss would not be legally recovered from the carrier. Also covers overseas air shipments.

Specific delivery point: A point in sales quotations that designates specifically where and within what geographical locale the goods will be delivered at the expense and responsibility of the seller (e.g., FAS named vessel at named port of export).

The Market Channel

In general, the international market channel includes:

- The manufacturer
- The foreign import/export agent
- Any distributors (wholesalers)
- Any retailers
- The buyers or customers

Figure 2-4 shows how the market channel might look.

Fig. 2-4. Market channel

Pricing for Profit

The price of your product should be high enough to generate a suitable profit but low enough to be competitive. Ideally, the importer or exporter strives to buy at or below factory prices. This can be done by eliminating from the overseas price the manufacturer's cost of domestic sales and advertising expenses.

Each step along the market channel has a cost. If a product is entirely new to the market or has unique features, you may be able to command higher prices. On the other hand, to gain a foothold in a very competitive market, you can use *marginal cost pricing*. In marginal cost pricing, you set the market entry price at or just above the threshold at which you would incur a loss. (Under WTO rules it is illegal to dump—that is, gain market share—by incurring a loss.)

Most new importers and exporters simply use the domestic factory price plus freight, packing, insurance, and so on. Prices may be quoted in U.S. dollars or in the currency of the buyer. In general, pricing should be based on long-run profit-maximizing objectives. Market share and volume should be targeted for the long-term export commitment.

It is important that you understand not only the elements that make up your price but also those of your overseas trading associate. Remember there are no "free lunches"; everything has a cost.

Figure 2-5 illustrates how an importer or exporter might move a product from one country to another. In particular, it shows how the selling price in one country becomes the buying price in the other. Typical commissions are between 7 and 20 percent for an export middleman and between 5 and 20 percent for an import middleman (foreign distributor or agent), although commissions may be as low as 1 percent and as high as 40 percent. The key issues are the price of the product and the number of units (sales volume) that you can sell. If, for instance, the product is a big-ticket item (high sales price), the commission percentage may be quite low, but a small percentage of a million-dollar sale can be very good business.

Table 2-2 shows a set of fictitious cost elements associated with a CIF quotation, corresponding to the steps shown in Figure 2-5. Figures 2-6 and 2-7 are worksheets to aid you in accurate costing of your product.

Is there sufficient profit at the *volumes* (number of units) you can sell to make it worth your while and meet your personal profit goals? Recall that the same amount of work goes

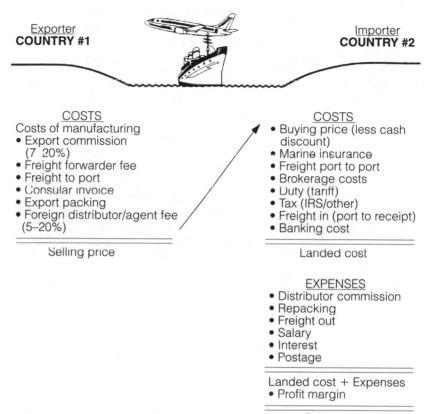

Fig. 2-5. Pricing model

into importing or exporting a product that makes no profit as goes into one that makes a good profit.

> **HOT TIP:** A word of caution for manufacturers. If at first exporting doesn't appear profitable, check your manufacturing costs. It may be necessary to import less costly components in order to compete internationally.

Now that you are satisfied that you have a viable project, the next step is to lay out a written long-range market plan. The next chapter explains how to develop that plan, then how to put it into action to make a transaction.

Table 2-2. Examples of Cost Elements

Terms of Sale: CIF

Export		Import	
Cost elements	*Cost*	*Cost elements*	*Cost*
Factory cost of 100 units @ $100/unit	$10,000	Landed cost CIF	$14,105
Expenses:		Duty @ 5.5%	$ 776
		Tax (IRS or other)	$ 150
Brokerage costs	$ 100	Brokerage	
Export packing	$ 150	clearance fees	$ 50
Freight to port	$ 500	Reforwarding	
Consular invoice	$ 50	from broker	$ 100
Freight forwarder		Banking charges	$50
fee	$ 150	Letter of credit	
		@ $1/4$%	$ 75
*Export agent commission			
@ 15% of cost	$ 1,500	Total landed cost	$15,306
**Foreign agent commission		Expenses	
@ 5% of cost	$ 500		
		Warehouse	$ —
		Repacking	$ 100
		Freight out	$ 100
		Advertising	$ 500
		*Salary	$ 1,410
		Interest	$ —
		Postage	$ 100
Marine insurance			
($12,950 @ $1.20		Total landed	
per $100 value	$ 155	plus expenses	$17,516
Transportation			
(ocean)	$ 1,000	Unit cost	$175.16
Landed cost (CIF)	$14,105	Suggested selling	
		price @ 100%	
		markup	$350.32
		Profit on 100 units	$17,516

*Only if an export middleman or import agent is used.
**Calculated at a commission of 10% of buying price:
Markup (%)=Sell cost\Cost×100

Reference Information
Our Ref _____   Customer Reference _____

Customer Information
Name _____   Cable Address _____
Address _____
_____   Telex No. _____

Product Information
Product _____   Dimensions _____ x _____ x _____
No. of Units _____   Cubic Measure _____ (sq. in.)
Net Weight _____   Total Measure _____
Gross Weight _____

Product Charges
Price (or cost) per unit _____ x units _____ Total _____
Profit (or markup)   _____
Sales Commissions   _____
FOB Factory   _____

Fees–Packing, Marking, Inland Freight   _____
Freight Forwarder   _____
Financing Costs   _____
Other Charges   _____
Export Packing   _____
Labeling/Marking   _____
Inland Freight to
FOB, Port City (export packed)   _____

Port Charges
Unloading (heavy lift)   _____
Loading (aboard ship)   _____
Terminal
  Consular Document (check if required) _____
  Certificate of Origin (check if required) _____
  Export License (check if required) _____
FAS Vessel (or airplane)   _____

Freight
Based on _____ Weight _____ Measure _____
Ocean _____ Air _____
Rate _____ Minimum _____ Amount _____

Insurance
Coverage required _____
Basis _____ Rate _____ Amount _____
CIF, Port of destination

Fig. 2-6. Export costing worksheet

Reference Information
Our Ref _____   Customer Reference _____

Customer Information
Name _____   Cable Address _____
Address _____
         _____   Telex No._____

Product Information
Product _____   Dimension _____ x _____ x _____
         _____
No. of Units _____   Cubic Measure _____ (sq. in.)
Net Weight _____   Total Measure _____
Gross Weight _____

NOTE: IF QUOTE IS FOB FACTORY USE EXPORT
COSTING SHEET TO DETERMINE PRICE AT
CIF, PORT OF DESTINATION

Landed Cost (CIF, Port of destination)   _____
Customs Duty   _____
Customs House Broker Fees   _____
Banking Charges   _____
Taxes: Federal   _____
       State   _____
       Other   _____
Total landed   _____

EXPENSES:
Inland Freight (from port city)   _____
Warehouse Costs   _____
Repacking   _____
Inland Freight (from warehouse)   _____
Advertising/promotion   _____
Overhead (% of annual)   _____
Salary (% of annual)   _____
Loans (principal/interest)   _____

Total landed plus expenses   _____

Unit cost   _____

Selling price   _____
Margin _____%

Profit   _____

Fig. 2-7. Import costing worksheet

3

Planning and Negotiating to Win

IF THE HOMEWORK YOU DID FOR THE LAST chapter shows you have a marketable and profitable product that will sell in sufficient volumes, you now are ready to commit resources (time and money) to the project. But before you do, make sure you address the next six commonalities of the import/export transaction:

- Develop a market plan.
- Prepare for negotiations.
- Understand the tips and traps of culture.
- Consider intellectual property rights.
- Learn about communications.
- Get ready to travel.

THE MARKET PLAN

You have determined that your project is viable. Now write a long-range market plan, then execute it.

A *market plan* is simply a process recorded on paper that allows you to think through the many logical ways to reach buyers and convince them to say yes to a sale. It is important to integrate the international market plan with the firm's overall strategic business plan. (See Chapter 6 for details about how to write a business plan.)

Use the following logical, step-by-step process to write your market plan:

1. *Objectives*
   Examples:
   - Sales of $XXX,XXX by the end of the second year.
   - Expansion into countries A and B by the end of the third year.

2. *Specific tactics*
   Examples:
   - Radio advertising in two cities.
   - Three direct mailings to each company or person on a specific list.
   - An Internet Web site that advertises the address.

3. *Schedule of activities or action plan*
   Examples:
   - A list of trade shows indicating which you will attend, including dates and duration of trips to visit overseas distributors, with their names, addresses, and phone numbers.
   - Specific assignments of responsibility (an essential feature of an action plan).

4. *Budget for accomplishing the action plan*
   A list of every conceivable cost associated with marketing the product.

Don't scrimp on the budget, because this is where most start-up firms underestimate. Initial marketing costs will be high.

Segmenting the Market

Marketing segmentation enables an import/export organization to choose its customers and fashion its marketing strategy on the basis of (1) identified customer wants and requirements and (2) the response to the firm's specific desires and needs. You should visualize segmentation on both a macrolevel and a microlevel.

Macro: From the Greek *makros,* long. It is a combining form meaning large.

Micro: From the Greek *mikros,* small. It is a combining form meaning little, small, microscopic.

Macrosegmentation. Macrosegmentation divides a market by such broad characteristics as industry shipments, location, and firm size. An import macrosegment might be the dividing of a city into marketing segments. On a larger scale, it might involve dividing the United States into regions, prioritizing those regions, then developing a microplan for each region.

Export macrosegments might include prioritizing continents or countries within a continent; better yet, export macrosegments might sort by language, purchasing power, or cultural preference.

Microsegmentation. Microsegmentation finds the homogeneous customer groups within macrosegments. Microsegmentation therefore seeks to find out who makes the decisions for each homogeneous group. It pinpoints where (by address) potential customers (by name) can say yes to a buying decision. From this analysis, a promotional strategy can be designed to target the decision-making units (DMUs).

An import microsegmentation might take the data from your market research effort and identify where the wholesalers are located. If you list and prioritize these decision makers by name and address, you will have a very logical specific plan of attack for your marketing effort.

Your marketing plan and schedule should cover a three- to five-year period, depending on the kinds of products you market, your competitors, and your target markets. Be sure to write this plan no matter how small the import/export project. Only when the plan is in writing will it command proper attention and receive adequate allocation of funds.

Executing the Market Plan

Next comes the fun—putting the plan into action by actively marketing the product through trade shows, advertisements, television promotions, and direct mail, all in accordance with your budgeted plan. Remember, nothing happens in a business until something is sold.

Personal Sales

The two basic approaches to selling internationally, for both imports and exports, are direct and indirect sales. In the *direct sales method,* a domestic manufacturing firm has its own marketing department that sells to a foreign distributor or retailing firm and is responsible for shipping the goods overseas. In the *indirect sales method,* the firm uses a middleman, who usually assumes the responsibility for moving the goods.

This is where your import/export business fits into the picture. You may sell directly to retailers or to distributors/wholesalers. Regardless of where your targeted DMU is in the market channel, keep in mind that international sales are just like domestic sales: someone makes personal contact and presents a portfolio, brochures, price lists, and/or samples to decision makers (potential buyers) who can say yes.

HOT TIP: Making sales requires persistence and determination. Follow up, then follow up again.

Trade Shows (Fairs)

If you are attending a trade fair or show for the first time, consider using it as the keystone of your sales trip. Allow time afterward to visit companies you meet at the fair.

The international trader attends trade shows for five basic reasons:

1. To make contacts
2. To identify products for import or export
3. To evaluate the competition (often done without exhibiting)
4. To find customers and distributors for import or export
5. To build sales for existing distributors

HOT TIPS ON TRADE FAIRS
- If you are exhibiting to sell, don't overcommit. You may get more business than you can handle reasonably.

- If you are searching for products to import, don't buy until you have done your homework.
- Take more business cards to the trade show than you think you will need. Have your fax number, Web site, and e-mail address on your card.
- Obtain translation/interpreter assistance from a local university or college.
- If you are exhibiting to sell, consider prior advertisement to let potential customers know you will be there.

Trade Missions.   Trade missions are trips made for the express purpose of promoting and participating in international trade. State and local governments organize several kinds of trade missions for exporters.

Special Missions.   These are organized and led by government officials with itineraries designed to bring you into contact with potential buyers and agents. You pay your own expenses and a share of the costs of the mission.

Seminar Missions.   Similar to the specialized trade mission, seminar missions add several one- or two-day technical presentations to the trip by a team of industry representatives.

Industry-Organized, Government-Approved Trade Missions.   Though these missions are organized by chambers of commerce, trade associations, or other industry groups, government officials often provide assistance prior to and during the trip.

Catalog Shows and Video/Catalog Exhibitions. These are the least expensive ways to develop leads, to test markets, and to locate agents—because you don't have to be there. You simply send along product catalogs, brochures, and other sales aids to be displayed at exhibitions organized by government officials and consultants.

Video/catalog exhibitions are ideal for promoting large equipment or machinery, which is costly to ship.

Trade Show Central. This free Internet service (www.tscentral.com) provides information on more than 50,000 trade shows, conferences, and seminars as well as 5000 service providers and 8000 venues and facilities around the world.

Advertising

All companies advertise to communicate with customers. Exporters and importers must ask themselves whether advertising is both important to sales and affordable. The assistance of an agency familiar with the market environment you wish to target could be critical to the success of your advertising campaign. Some countries do not carry television and radio advertising. In addition, cultural differences often require more than a simple translation of promotional messages.

In countries with low literacy rates, you may prefer to avoid elaborate print vehicles such as magazines, concentrating instead on outdoor advertising such as billboards, posters, electric signs, and streetcar/bus signs. These reach wide audiences in most countries.

Distributors

A *distributor* is a merchant who purchases merchandise from a manufacturer at the greatest possible discount and resells it to retailers for profit. The distributor carries a supply of parts and maintains an adequate facility for servicing. The distributor buys the product in its own name, often arranging payment terms on a credit basis. A written contract usually defines the territory to be covered by the distributor, the terms of sale, and the method of compensation (see "Avoiding Risk" in Chapter 5). The work is usually performed on a commission basis, without assumption of risk, and the representative may operate on either an exclusive or a nonexclusive basis. The contract is established for a specific time frame such that it may be renewable with satisfactory performance.

As with domestic sales, foreign retailers usually buy from the distributor's traveling sales force, but many buy through catalogs, brochures, or other literature.

Importers and exporters seldom sell directly to the end user. The practice is not recommended, because (1) it is time-consuming and (2) it leads to goods being impounded or sold at auction when the buyer doesn't know his or her own trade regulations.

Overseas Trader's Checklist

Here's what you want from a foreign representative:

- ☑ A solid reputation with suppliers and banks.
- ☑ Financial strength.
- ☑ Experience with the product or a similar product.
- ☑ A sales organization.
- ☑ A sales record of growth.
- ☑ Customers.
- ☑ Warehouse capacity.
- ☑ After-sales service capability.
- ☑ Understanding of regional culture and business practices.
- ☑ Knowledge of both English and the language of the country.
- ☑ Knowledge of marketing techniques (promotion, advertisement, etc.).

Trading Partner's Checklist

Here's what the foreign representative wants from you:

- ☑ Excellent products.
- ☑ Exclusive territories.
- ☑ Training.
- ☑ Parts availability.
- ☑ Good warranties.
- ☑ Advertising and merchandising support.
- ☑ Credit terms, discounts, and deals.
- ☑ Commissions on direct sales by the manufacturer in the distributor's territory.
- ☑ Minimum control and/or visits.
- ☑ Freedom to negotiate price.
- ☑ Ability to deal with one person.
- ☑ Security that the product will not be taken away once it is established in the territory.

☑ Right to terminate the agreement when the representative pleases.

NEGOTIATIONS

Bargaining is a custom in many societies. But culturally nothing comes less naturally to Americans. The United States operates on a fixed-price system, and most buyers have grown
up with the notion of purchasing off the shelf at the offered
price or not buying at all. Of course, comparative shopping is
native to everyone's buying psyche, so when the international
stakes increase and foreign competitors (often born cultural
negotiators) begin to force your hand, your instincts should
give you some basis for taking the right action. You can make
the right moves if you prepare.

Preparations

Unfortunately, too many people wander into international
bargaining situations with no plan and no idea how to proceed. For them, it's an ad lib and ad hoc operation all the way.
For some, lack of preparation is the result of a sense of supe-
riority, but for most it's pure ignorance of the number and
competence of the ferocious competitors out there scouring the
world for scraps of business.

The first step in preparing for international negotiations
is to develop a complete assessment of your firm's capabilities.
Analyze your strengths and weaknesses, particularly in terms
of managerial skills, product delivery, technical abilities, and
global resources.

Next, analyze your target—the company or country you
intend to sell your product to. Keep in mind that the human
and behavioral aspects of your negotiations will be vital.

- Understand the place in the world where you will be
  traveling.
- Know the target area's culture, history, and political
  processes.
- Pay particular attention to the importance of face saving to the people of the country where you will be negotiating.

- Assess the host government's role in country negotiations.
- Determine the importance of personal relations.
- Learn how much time you should allow for negotiations.
- Be sure the final agreement specifies terms for the cost, quality, and delivery of the product. Quality can be assured only by seeing the product, but cost and delivery terms are the result of a quote agreed to by the seller.

In Japan, young executives role-play negotiations before they make an initial quote. They form teams, sit around a table with a chalkboard nearby, and pretend to negotiate the deal. Each team has a set of negotiating alternatives related to the country it is pretending to represent. Sometimes the players cut their offer price by 10 percent; if that doesn't work, they cut it another 5 or 10 percent. Other ploys are (1) offering lower-interest-rate loans than competitors, (2) offering better after-sales service warranties, and (3) providing warehouses for parts. Sometimes, even the cost of advertising can make the difference in the sale.

Agreeing to a Contract

After you obtain the initial quotations as explained in Chapter 2, the next step in any international business arrangement is to reach an agreement or a sales contract with your overseas partner.

Negotiating is integral to international trade, and an importer/exporter should be ready to offer or ask for alternatives by letter, fax, or e-mail. In the highly competitive international business world, a trader's ability to offer reasonable terms to customers may mean the difference between winning and losing a sale.

Exporters are finding it increasingly necessary to offer terms ranging from cash against shipping documents to time drafts and open accounts, and even installment payments spread over several years. More sophisticated business arrangements such as countertrade—which includes barter, product buyback, counterpurchase, and after-sales service—are also negotiable. Figure 3-1 illustrates the concept.

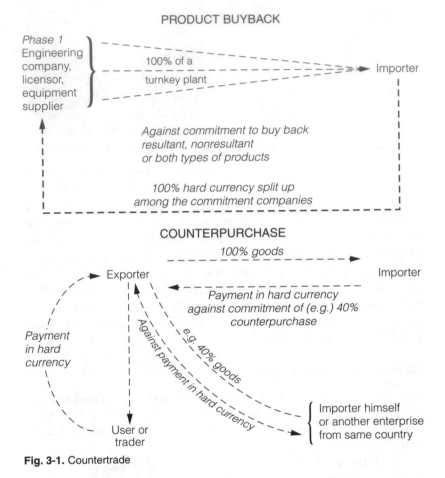

Fig. 3-1. Countertrade

Countertrade: A general international trade term for a variety of methods to conduct reciprocal trade in which the seller is required to accept goods or other instruments of trade, in partial or whole payment for its products.

Barter: Trade in which merchandise is exchanged directly for other merchandise without use of money.

Product buyback: Principally applicable for the construction and supply of plant and equipment. The major characteristic is its long-term aspect.

> *Counterpurchase:* A common form of countertrade in which the seller receives cash but contractually agrees to buy local products or services as a percentage of cash received and over a stated period of time.

The trader must have a list of alternatives ready. Keep negotiations open and don't firm them up on paper until a general agreement has been reached. The following is a partial list of alternatives and conditions you may wish to consider during negotiations:

- Quantity price breaks (don't offer just one price)
- Discounts for cash deals or even down payments
- Countertrade offers to those countries short on foreign exchange
- Guaranteed loans
- Low-interest loans
- Time payments
- Home factory trips for training

Let your banker, freight forwarder, or customs house broker review the final offer or quotation. A second pair of experienced eyes can save you money. (See Chapters 7 and 8 respectively for an explanation of the freight forwarder and customs house broker.)

Foreign Corrupt Practices Act (FCPA)

During your negotiations make sure you stay on the right side of the Foreign Corrupt Practices Act (FCPA) of 1977. In essence, this act makes it illegal for companies to bribe foreign officials, candidates, or political parties. Make certain that everything is in the contract and has a price. Don't get caught making illegal payments or gifts to win a contract or sale. The penalties are severe—subject to a five-year jail sentence and a fine of up to $15,000.

The law does not address itself to "facilitating payments," those small amounts used to expedite business activities. These payments are euphemistically referred to in various countries as "mordida," "grease," "bakshish" (small amount of money), "rashoa" (big amount of money), "cumsha," or "squeeze." Nevertheless, great care should be exercised in this regard as well.

TIPS AND TRAPS OF CULTURE

The very thought of doing business in a foreign culture can be a major barrier to negotiations, but it shouldn't be. After all, traders are known for their spirit of curiosity, inquisitiveness, and risk taking.

Developing overseas alliances does present new elements of risk and due diligence, along with the inherent challenges brought by distance, differing cultural motivations and priorities, and effective integration of differing approaches and objectives. But that's what brings the rewards.

Can one culture be superior to another? Political systems, armies, navies, and even economic systems may be superior, but cultures are not.

The best way to appreciate another culture is to "walk in the other person's shoes"—that is, visit or live in the country and get a feel for the similarities and differences. Short of that, this section of the chapter is the next best thing, because its purpose is to help you break through cultural barriers. You are cautioned that to be effective in your business dealings it is essential to be prepared. Do your homework before you interact in a new country, and then get on with doing business.

Does understanding foreign cultural values really make a difference? You bet it does!

One person who had traveled overseas regularly and had made friends in many countries, said, "They're more like us than they're different." What the visitor meant was that they like kids, they want children to be educated, they understand business, and they work hard. What he didn't say was that the differences are what affect attitudes—so much at times that some managers won't even consider entering the market to do business with "them."

What Is Culture?

Culture is a set of meanings or orientations for a given society, or social setting. It's a complex concept because there are often many cultures within a given nation. For an international businessperson the definition is more difficult, because a country's business culture is often different from its general culture. Thus the environment of international business is composed of language, religion, values and attitudes, law, education, politics, technology, and social organizations that are different.

Whatever a nation's culture is, it works for that society. In order to function within it, you must get on the bandwagon.

The Japanese do it very well. They learn how to penetrate foreign markets by sending their managers to live and study in "the other person's shoes." Their mission is to develop relationships with contemporaries that will last for years. The Japanese don't try to change the way of life in the other country; they learn about it. When they go home, they are specialists in marketing and production in the country that they researched.

It's a country's culture that regulates such things as sexuality, child raising, acquisition of food and clothing, and incentives that motivate people to work and buy products. All these things are of course major factors in marketing products.

The Nine Elements of Business Culture

Business culture is secondary to a country's general culture, but it provides the rules of the business game and explains the differences and the priorities.

Relationships.   Mistrust is reduced when relationships are developed over a long period of time. To meet this challenge, you need to understand the countries, people, and cultures where you intend to do business.

Language.   Ask international traders what language they speak, and they will say the language of the customer.

Language is the thing that sets humans off from other forms of life. It is the way you tell others about your history and your intentions for the future. Language is the means of communicating within a culture. For people in a given culture, their language defines their socialization.

Body Language.   Body language is the subtle power of nonverbal communication. It's the earliest form of communication you learn, and you use it every day to tell other people how you feel about yourself and them.

This language includes your posture, gestures, facial expressions, and costumes, the way you walk, and even your treatment of time, material things, and space.

Religion.   Religion plays a major part in the cultural similarities and differences of nations. In itself religion can be a basis of mistrust and a barrier to trade.

Religion is often the dominant influence for the consumer of products. Such things as religious holidays determine buying and consumption patterns. Knowing what is forbidden and what a society expects as a result of various religious beliefs affects market strategy.

Values and Attitudes.   The role of values and attitudes in international business is difficult to measure, but vital to success. Work ethic and motivation are the intangibles that affect economic performance.

The values of a society determine its attitudes toward wealth, consumption, achievement, technology, and change—and you must evaluate all of them in terms of the host culture. Researching attitudes about openness and receptivity to new technology is essential to marketing.

Laws and Legal Environment.   The laws of a society are another dimension of its culture. They are the rules established by authority and social interaction. On the one hand, laws provide an opportunity to handle the mistrust of doing business across international boundaries; on the other hand, they can become barriers and constraints to operations. The laws of nations are often greatly different. About half the nations of the world are under a form of either Napoleonic code or common law; the other half are under Muslim, Communist, or indigenous laws. None of the world's legal systems is truly pure. Each nation has its unique laws; nevertheless, similarities and mixtures abound within each classification.

For most dealings, you will be chiefly interested in the law as it relates to contracts, but you should always consider litigation as a last resort. Settle disputes in other ways if possible. Litigation is only for the stupid or the rich, because it usually involves long delays, during which inventories are tied up and trade is halted. Lawsuits are costly, not just because of the money, but also because of the broken relationships that result. Most international commercial disputes can be solved by conciliation, mediation, and arbitration. The arbitration service provided by the International Chamber of Commerce can often be written right into a sales contract, just in case the unspeakable should happen.

Education.   Culture shapes your thoughts and emotions. Motivation is influenced by your education as well as by other things such as values and religion, as already discussed. The biggest international difference is the educational attainment of the population. The next biggest difference is the educational mix. In some countries such as the United States there is little difference in the mix. Practically all Americans are educated through twelfth grade, making education no longer a function of wealth. This is not so in many other countries. It is not unusual to find only the elite of some nations educated to the levels that Americans assume for all people. The impact of education is therefore profound for marketing products as well as for establishing relationships, because good communications are often based on relative education capacities and standards.

Technology.   The most recent change in technology is our growing control over energy and information. The word *technology* begets concepts such as science, development, invention, and innovation. Some languages lack precise words to express these concepts. Understanding the technological gap among nations is an essential element to exporting products across borders. Wide gaps still exist between the most advanced nations and those we call "traditional societies." It is clear that training is needed to transfer technology, and the impact of that transfer on social environments must be considered. You should always look at technology from the importing country's point of view.

Social Organization.   Social stratification is the hierarchy of classes within a society—the relative power, social priorities, privilege, and income of those classes. Each class within a system has somewhat different and distinct tastes, political views, and consumption patterns. Many countries have a socioreligious ideology that allows rank to be intrinsic and inherited biologically. This implies that different categories of humans are culturally defined as if consisting of different worth and potential for performance. Regardless of how you react to such noncompetitive socialization, such ideas are predictable in some countries. Faced with such a system of socioreligious rank, you need to learn how to deal with it—not attempt to change it.

Practical Applications

Now that you have an appreciation of culture, let's take a look at the practical side.

It's important to understand as much about the culture of a country as possible, even when just visiting on business trips. To begin, let's look at some generalities—ideas that will help you make a good impression no matter where you're doing business.

Saving face is not just an Asian concept, although it is particularly sensitive in those countries. Avoiding embarrassment to others, particularly ranking persons, is essential wherever you are in the world.

People of any country like to talk about their own land and culture. If you ask questions that show genuine interest, you will cultivate people's respect. But no one likes critical questions, such as "Why don't you do it this way?" Or "How come you do it that way?" Above all, people don't want to hear how much better it is where you come from.

First impressions do count, and the wrong first impression can stop your business deal in its tracks. Bad first impressions are all but impossible to overcome.

Tips for Business Travelers

1. Smile! It's the universal business language and overcomes many problems.
2. But smile right. A tight smile with lips parted in an ellipse around the teeth comes across as phony and dishonest. Smile easily—with your full teeth exposed and the corners of your mouth pulled up. This kind of smile says, "Hi, I'm sure pleased to meet you!"
3. Look the part. Grooming is important all over the world. Studies indicate that most people are more attracted to others who are neat, well groomed, and crisply dressed.
4. Flash your eyebrows. In most cultures raising the eyebrows almost instinctively in a rapid movement and

keeping them raised for about half a second is an unspoken signal of friendliness and approval.

5. Lean forward. Liking is produced by leaning forward.

6. Look for similarities. People tend to like others who are like them, so common experiences and interests are often a starting point for producing liking.

7. Nod your head. People like other people who agree with them and are attentive to what they are saying.

8. Open up. Closed hands and arms crossed in front of the chest may give the impression that you're resisting the other person's ideas. Open, frequently outstretched arms and open palms project the opposite.

Tips for Women

1. Never give a man a gift, no matter how close the business relationship. A small gift for his family might do.

2. Give gifts from the company, never from you.

3. If you are married, use Mrs. when overseas, even if you don't at home.

4. Avoid eating or drinking alone in public. Use room service, or invite a woman from the office where you are doing business to join you at a restaurant.

5. If the question of dinner arises and is useful to cement the deal, avoid any doubts by inviting your counterpart's family.

6. Make a point to mention your husband and ask about your male counterpart's family. Some businesswomen who are not married invent a fiancé or steady back home.

7. Try not to be coy about flirtations. Turn them off immediately with a straightforward no.

8. Be aware of the culture, and dress to fit as closely as your wardrobe will permit. Conservatism works.

About Jokes

The people of every country enjoy humor and they all have their funny stories, but explaining complicated jokes to businesspeople who don't share your culture can be very tricky. Here are a few tips and traps:

1. Do remember that each culture reacts differently to jokes.
2. Don't tell foreigners a joke that depends on word play or punning.
3. Do be careful of the subject of your joke. It could be taken seriously in a culture different from your own.
4. Do be informed about the sensitive issues in the country where you are visiting.
5. Do ask to hear a few local jokes. They will give you a sense of what's considered funny.
6. Do tell jokes. Everyone enjoys a good laugh.

INTELLECTUAL PROPERTY RIGHTS

"The Chinese stole our stuff! They just drove down the road, passed our factory, and copied our trademark. It took us two and a half years and $5000 to get it back," said one executive. On the other hand, because this company had the trademark registered, no one else in the United States could use it, and the litigation against the guilty Chinese firm was considerably easier than it would have been without proper registration.

Intellectual property is a general term that describes inventions or discoveries that have been registered with government authorities for sale or use by their owner. Such terms as *patent, trademark, copyright,* and *unfair competition* fall under the domain of intellectual property.

You can obtain information about patents and trademarks from: U.S. Patent and Trademark Office, Crystal Plaza 3, Room 2C02, Washington, DC 20231; phone: (800) 786-9199; Web: uspto.org.

The booklet *General Information on Patents* can be ordered from the Government Printing Office, Washington, DC 20402. Table 3-1 summarizes the basic elements of intellectual property in the United States.

You should recognize that registration in the United States does not protect your product in a foreign country. In general, protection in one country does not constitute protection in another. The rule of thumb is to apply for and register

Table 3-1. Intellectual Property Rights

	Patents	Copyrights	Trade and service marks	Trade name	Trade dress	Trade secrets
Duration (years)	14–17 years	Life + 50 years	As long as in use	As long as in use	As long as in use	Until public disclosure
How	Apply to Patent Office	By original creation in permanent form	By use	By use	By use	By security measures
Requirements	Useful/novel	Nonfunctional original creation	Fanciful and distinguishing	Nonconfusion with others	Fanciful, nonfunctional	Not known
Prevents	Manufacturer use or sale	Copying or adapting	Confusing or misleading use	Confusing or misleading use	Confusing or misleading use	Disclosure
Protects	Utility and design attributes	Authorship	Reputation and goodwill	Goodwill	Reputation	Info for competitive advantage
Examples	Product/ mechanism/ process/style	Label design/ operating manual	Coca-Cola	Computer-land, Inc.	Container shape	Formula
Legal costs	$1500–$3000	$10–$100	$100–$400			

all intellectual property rights in each country where you intend to do business. Because registration can be expensive, several multilateral organizations have been formed to make registration possible in all member countries. Your first step is the World Intellectual Property Organization (wipo.org).

Patent Registration

Patent registration is covered by the following agreements.

1. The European Patent Convention (18 European area countries).
2. The European Patent Organization (19 EC countries).
3. The Patent Cooperation Treaty, which gives by far the greatest international coverage (more than 25 signature countries, including Russia).

Trademark Registration

Trademark registration is less costly and time-consuming than patents and is covered by the following agreements.

1. The International Convention for the Protection of Industrial Property. Better known as the Paris Union, this organization is 90 years old, and it covers patents as well as trademarks. Under this convention, six-month protection is provided the firm, during which time the trademark can be registered in the other member countries.
2. The Madrid Arrangement for International Registration of Trademarks. With 46 members, this agreement offers the advantage that registration in one country qualifies as registration in all member countries.

COMMUNICATIONS

Although nothing substitutes for personal contact when developing an international marketing structure, this may not always be possible. Therefore, the tone of initial written communications is critical. It often makes the difference between a profitable long-term arrangement and a lost opportunity.

The Introductory Letter, Facsimile (Fax), or E-Mail

Your introductory letter, fax, or e-mail most often can be written in English. Outside Latin America, English has become the language of international business. Even so, always use simple words. If your message must be translated and transmitted into a foreign language, make sure you have it translated back to English by a third party before sending it. However proficient a person is in the other language, funny things can happen in translation.

From the beginning, establish your company's favorable reputation and explain the relationship that you seek. Describe the product you want to market (export) or to purchase (import). Propose a personal meeting and offer the buyer a tour of your firm during the person's next visit to your country. Ask for a response to your letter. Figure 3-2 shows a sample letter of introduction.

Follow-Up Communications

As technology improves, alternative forms of communication become available, and choosing the best alternative may result in the competitive difference. Successful importing or exporting depends on reliable two-way communication. It is critical in establishing and running an import/export marketing network.

Telephone

Speech is the fastest way to convey ideas and receive answers. Voice communications allow for immediate feedback—quick response to fast-breaking problems or opportunities. Most countries can be dialed directly, and the rates for international telephone service depend on the time of day. Although international telephone can be expeditious, it can be expensive if you have a lot to say.

Facsimile

Facsimile (fax), or telecopier service, is one of the fastest-growing means of business communication. The advantage of fax is that any image up to $8\frac{1}{2} \times 14$ inches can be transmitted

Our Company, Inc.
Hometown, U.S.A.

Ref:
Date:

Your Company, Ltd.
2A1 Moon River
Yokohama, Japan

Gentlemen:

Our Company, Inc. markets a line of highway spots. When secured to the centerline of highway, these spots provide for increased safety for motorists. We believe that these spots might interest foreign markets, especially the Japanese market. Our major customers include highway contractors and highway departments of the states of ABC and DEF.

Our Company, founded in 1983, has sales of $1.5 million. Further details are given in the attached brochure. The attached catalogs and specification sheets give detailed information about our products.

We are writing to learn whether: (1) Your Company has a requirement to purchase similar products for use in Japan; and (2) Your Company would be interested in representing Our Company in Japan.

Don't hesitate to telephone if you need further details. We look forward to meeting with representatives of Your Company about our highway spots.

Sincerely,

W. T. Door
President

Fig. 3-2. Sample letter of introduction

directly to the receiving unit. Letters, pictures, contracts, forms, catalog sheets, drawings, and illustrations—anything that will reproduce in a copy machine—can be sent.

HISTORY NOTE: Facsimile is not new. It was invented over a century ago, in 1842, by Alexander Bain, a Scottish clockmaker. His device used a pendulum that swept a metal point over a set of raised metal letters. When the point touched a letter, it created an electrical charge that traveled down a telegraph wire to reproduce on paper the series of letters that the pendulum had touched. Wire service photos were transmitted by fax machines as early as 1930. The U.S. Navy used them aboard ship during World War II for the transmission of weather data.

The earliest fax machines were very expensive clunkers, costing more than $18,000 and taking more than 10 minutes to send a single page. Today, there are more than 5 million machines, and dedicated facsimile terminals now cost as little as $150. Their speed equates favorably with telex. Fax transmits over the ordinary voice-phone network. Several private bureaus manage the worldwide service. On the downside, there is no effective proof of delivery of a fax document.

The Internet

It wasn't that long ago that the Internet was just a public, amorphous collection of computer networks—a techno-fad made up of blending a few personal computers and citizens band radio enthusiasts.

Today the Internet is the fastest-growing and most exciting place to do business (see Chapter 4). Dedicated servers and high-speed circuits, combined with new cross-indexing software and imaginative services, have connected the home computer masses to electronic commerce through the World Wide Web.

As the concept matures, the linking of buyers and sellers and elimination of paperwork will drive down the cost of transactions. The Internet has become the low-cost alternative to fax, express mail, and other communications channels such as 1-800 telephone sales.

The Internet knows no international boundaries. Internauts are logging on from Bangkok to Broadway. Already the network extends to all countries, and the most interesting part is that no-body owns the Internet. It is not guided by a single company or institution. The Internet Protocol (IP) allows any number of computer networks to link up and act as one.

HISTORY NOTE: The Internet is not a new concept. It began in the late 1960s, when the Pentagon asked computer scientists to find the best way for an unlimited number of computers to communicate—without relying on any single computer to be traffic cop. That way the system would not be vulnerable to nu-clear attack. The outcome was the decision to fund an experi-mental packet-switching communications using a Transmission and Control/Internet Protocol (TCP/IP) called ARPAnet that quickly expanded to dozens of universities and corporations. Programs were written to help people exchange e-mail and tap into remote databases. In 1983 ARPAnet was split into two net-works—ARPAnet and Milnet—and the Pentagon mandated TCP/IP as the standard protocol. These two networks evolved into the Internet.

HOT TIP: Though print lacks speed (compared with voice), it provides written documentation that can be read and reread at the reader's pace and schedule.

Cables and Telexes

International mailgrams, telegrams, or cables can still be sent anywhere mail goes and require a complete mailing address, including postal codes.

Cables are sent electronically to the major city nearest the recipient. There, the message may be telephoned and mailed, mailed only, or (in a few locations) delivered by messenger. Cables don't offer proof of delivery the way a telex message does, and because of the extra handling, cables are signifi-cantly more expensive than telex messages. But a cable can be sent to anyone, anywhere.

There are still some telex terminals in government and business offices around the world, but with the advent of fac-simile and Internet the process is becoming obsolete. Their advantage is they can receive information automatically, even when unattended.

Communications Equipment

Electronic data transmission grew rapidly throughout the 1990s. In the new century data must flow back and forth among the import/export business and agencies, distributors, and customers. Electronic mail is now commonly delivered over international phone lines. Practically any computer can be interfaced by a modem via a cable, ordinary telephone, satellite, or microwave to any other computer or word processor anywhere in the world—so long as the receiving country does not restrict or prohibit transborder data flows. If you have a personal computer, a modem and software package can cost you less than $300 for data communications.

HOT COMMUNICATIONS TIPS

1. Write out your message and check it by reading it aloud.
2. Some situations in international business can be frustrating, so take care not to lose your temper and send a "zinger" that you'll regret later. Develop a cordial and professional style, and stick to it at all times. Try to draft replies in the morning when you are fresh. Whenever possible, let a second party read each message.
3. Send messages earlier in the day and earlier in the week to avoid the heavy calling periods and possible delay of your message.
4. Keep your messages brief, but avoid any abbreviation that might not be understood.
5. Try to reply to every fax/telex/Internet message the same day it is received, even if only to give a date when a more complete reply will be sent.
6. Use "ATTN: Name" rather than "Dear Name." Almost all fax/Internet messages, by customer, end with "Regards," "Best Regards," or occasionally "Cordially."

TRAVEL

Mistrust across international borders can be a barrier to a successful import/export business. Therefore visiting the country and the people who offer goods for your importation or the agents or distributors who market your export products is essential. These personal contacts remind you that you have more in common with people from other nations than differences. Travel to exotic places is not only fun; it is a tax-deductible expense of international trade as well.

> **HOT TIP:** The Internal Revenue Service will look closely at travel expenses to make sure you are actually doing business, and not indulging your travel hobby. For this reason, keep a good record during your travels and make sure you profit from your trips.

Planning a Trip

You alone know your itinerary, how long you can stay in each place, and what you expect to accomplish, so lay out your own trip before turning it over to the travel agent. Make certain your local arrival time allows for time zone changes and scheduled business meetings. Factor in time for rest prior to negotiating.

After you have laid out your trip, take it to the travel agent for booking. Allow three to five days, and expect some changes. You may need to go through country B in order to get to country C.

Foreign Travel Information

To stay alert to any possible danger areas in the world, contact: Citizens Emergency Center, U.S. Department of State, Washington, DC 20520; phone: (202) 647-5225.

Packing for a Trip

Travel light. The usual arrival sequence is immigration followed by customs. Be ready to open your luggage and sometimes declare each item.

Transportation

Request business class to most countries; it's more comfortable than coach and less expensive than first class.

Hotels

Unless you are familiar with the better hotels in a country, you are usually better off staying at one that is internationally recognized. Most major travel companies, agents, or your local library can supply the names of the best hotels.

Food and Drink

Are you a bit overweight? Now is the time to drop a few pounds. The food may be the best in the world, but eat light and drink only sterilized water.

Time Changes

Plan for the changing time zones. Think ahead and figure the local time of arrival for the plane you have booked. Remember that time is reckoned from Greenwich, England, and watches are normally set to some form of zone time. Time is changed near the time of crossing of the boundary between zones, usually at a whole hour. If you know the time zone, you can calculate the local time. Figure 3-3 depicts international time zones as they appear at noon Eastern Standard Time.

Passport

A key travel document, the *passport* identifies the holder as a citizen of the country by which it is issued. In the United States, the Department of State issues passports. You can apply at your local U.S. post office. The cost is about $60. You should allow two to three weeks for processing.

Visa

The *visa* is an official endorsement from a country that a person wishes to visit. You must receive it before entry into that country is permitted. Some nations don't require a visa. Check with your travel agent or local consul/embassy. You may prefer to give your passport, and three photos, to a "visa service" and let the agency make the rounds of embassies. Count on waiting a week for the completion of this service.

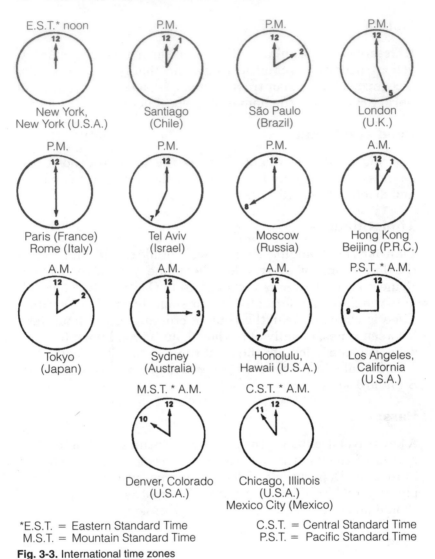

New York,
New York (U.S.A.)

Santiago
(Chile)

São Paulo
(Brazil)

London
(U.K.)

Paris (France)
Rome (Italy)

Tel Aviv
(Israel)

Moscow
(Russia)

Hong Kong
Beijing (P.R.C.)

Tokyo
(Japan)

Sydney
(Australia)

Honolulu,
Hawaii (U.S.A.)

Los Angeles,
California
(U.S.A.)

Denver, Colorado
(U.S.A.)

Chicago, Illinois
(U.S.A.)
Mexico City (Mexico)

*E.S.T. = Eastern Standard Time   C.S.T. = Central Standard Time
M.S.T. = Mountain Standard Time   P.S.T. = Pacific Standard Time

Fig. 3-3. International time zones

Arrival/Departure

When you arrive in a country you have never visited before, ask the airline crew or counter personnel for such tips as normal taxi fare from the airport to the hotel, sights to see, and local travel problems. Exchange your currency at the best rate. On departure, use any excess local currency to pay your hotel bill. Be sure to save enough local currency for taxi fare and airport departure tax.

Smile and be cheerful as you pass through immigration and customs. A smile can head off a lot of problems.

Carnets

In some countries you can transport goods duty free and avoid extensive customs procedures if you have an ATA (admission temporaire) carnet. The ATA carnet is a standard international customs document used to obtain duty-free temporary admission of certain goods on an annualized basis into the countries that are signatories to the ATA Convention. Under the ATA Convention, commercial and professional travelers may take commercial samples, tools of the trade, advertising material, and cinematographic, audio-visual, medical, scientific, or other professional equipment into member countries temporarily without paying customs duties and taxes or posting a bond at the border of each country to be visited.

Applications for the ATA carnet are made to the Council for International Business in your country. In the United States, contact www.uscib.org or call (212) 354-4480. Since countries are continuously added to the ATA carnet system, you should contact the Council for International Business regularly to learn if the country to be visited is included on the list. A list of nations where the ATA carnet can be used (current as of 1998) may be found in Appendix A.

The fee charged for the carnet depends on the value of the goods to be covered. A bond, letter of credit, or bank guarantee of 40 percent of the value of the goods is also required to cover duties and taxes that would be due if the importer of goods into a foreign country were not a carnet holder. Typical processing fees are:

Shipment value	Basic processing fee
Under $5000	$120
$5000–14,999	$150
$15,000–49,000	$175
$50,000–199,999	$200
$200,000–499,999	$225
$500,000 and over	$250

Further information can be found in the informative book published by the council titled *Carnet: Move Goods Duty-Free Through Customs.*

If you don't get a carnet, check your samples at the airport with customs, but allow plenty of time to get them before the next flight.

The next chapter is new with this revision. It explains how to do international business over the Internet, including how to get started, how to establish a home page presence, and how to find foreign markets.

4

The Cyber Trader: Selling with E-Commerce

NO ONE NEEDS TO BE TOLD THAT THE INTERNET IS REDEFINING modern business, communications, and research. Virtually every newspaper and television station, every day in every country, tells the story of how millions of computer users tap the global network for unparalleled access to information.

In its many forms, e-commerce may be defined as any commercial transaction carried out, facilitated, or enabled by the exchange of information electronically. The true value of the Internet, and the World Wide Web that resides therein, is that it is borderless.

Think of countries as if they were lakes without connecting canals. With the Internet the people from one lake can swim easily to the other lake, where they can sample food, wares, and culture that they never before had access to.

The second edition of this book, updated only five years ago, spoke simply of the potential of the Internet for international e-commerce. Since then, that prophecy has been more than realized—big, crossborder business is being conducted over the Web. The benefit to business is the capability to leverage the Internet to bring customers, vendors, and suppliers closer together, thus getting maximum results. Economies of scale, operational costs, and customer service are improved by communicating directly with the client.

BACKGROUND

Once the exclusive province of government and university researchers, the Internet has become an information Nirvana for the common business and is growing at a rate of about 10 to 20 percent a month.

Created in 1989 at CERN, a huge Swiss research laboratory, the World Wide Web began simply as a project to link scientists worldwide. But its intuitive, easy-to-use hypertextual design caused the Web to spread beyond its original user community. By accessing the Web with a browsing program, you can now tap a graphical environment in which you move among millions of Web sites that offer everything from sunglasses to Silly Putty. Most Web pages integrate images, sounds, and text to advertise their products and services.

In the 1950s the world sold things on Main Street; in the 1980s it was the mall; in the 1990s it was the superstore; but in the 2000s it will be at www.com. Why? As Bill Gates, the founder of Microsoft, says, "The Net represents frictionless capitalism."

The Global Marketing Opportunity

No supranational organization or head of state has been able to bring continents together, but the Web is uniting the world! There is no president or king of the Internet, so small businesses can sell anywhere in the world.

The obvious advantage of the Internet is the ability to bypass the middle of the supply chain—that is, the many distributors, wholesalers, and storefronts of traditional business—to reach directly to the consumer. Now customers (users and buyers) can be served directly, just like the old direct-mail marketing process, but without the high cost of printing and postage. More important, the Internet knows no boundaries—it can reach the potential customer in every nook and cranny of the world, wherever a person can surf the Web.

In 1998 there were $6.1 billion consumer purchases over the Net and about $15.6 billion business-to-business sales. By 2001 the increase is expected to move to more than $25 billion consumer purchases and more than $200 billion business-to-business sales. Yet today e-commerce is only 1 percent of total American gross domestic product (GDP) and only 0.02 percent of total retail sales. However, by 2003 it is expected to reach as much as 6 percent of GDP.

Changing Competition

The Web is also changing competition. On-line businesses have an easier time locking in their customers with plenty of room for further growth. Consider geography. As retailers expand, they must build storefronts and organize distribution networks, settling for smaller and smaller markets after hitting the larger ones. The on-line competitor has the advantage because the business has instant reach. The cost of acquiring a customer in another city or country is the same as finding one locally.

Price is another way that the on-line business wins in the ever-changing competitive world. An on-line seller can undercut the non-Web player. In fact, some Web businesses are even offering products and services for free while gaining their income through outside advertising.

GETTING STARTED

The Internet is not just hype. Companies are making sales on the Net right now, so why not get started? A special section on Internet terms is included in the Glossary at the end of this book.

Requiring the least amount of financial capital, a Web business can be started simply by setting up a virtual office—that is, a computer or television, proper software, and a modem. This virtual office, which could be in the back room of your business, in your home, or on your lap when traveling, gives you the adaptability and flexibility to enter your business environment on an equal footing with the largest companies. In other words, your business is no longer tied to a physical storefront or a desk—your Web page is your storefront. As long as you can plug into a telephone or cable line (even a satellite), you can do business. You can even get faxes through your e-mail system by using services such as efax.com.

The Home Page Presence

The first step in obtaining a presence on the World Wide Web is designing a Web site, which is made up of a home page and several supplemental pages of information (see Figure 4-1). The home page is to the rest of your Web site as a book cover is to its contents. Because your business is international, you should consider allowing the user to click on a choice of language—say, English, French, Italian, or Mandarin. Similarly, you'll need to decide in how many countries you will have home page presence. For instance, Dell Computers has crossed national boundaries by having Web sites all over the world.

The home page design should be bold and visual but lean and mean, so that it can quickly capture attention yet be understood at a glance and lead the reader to the other pages of the site. Keep the home page simple. Don't clutter. Make it easy to navigate. The prospective customer who gets lost or confused while reading quickly is gone. Use your home page to

Fig. 4-1. Typical Web site page

make a few essential points like who you are, what you offer, and what's on the rest of the pages. Don't be too commercial. Internet protocol dictates that you offer free information and entertainment first, then ask for the sale.

No matter what you are selling, there are already many sites devoted to the same products or services. Know your competitors by searching them out. Learn what they have emphasized and what is working for them.

All too many businesses rush into this project without thinking it through. It is essential to plan ahead by identifying and honing your key messages and organizing them in a logical structure, developing a prototype page design, testing it on representative users, and refining it through successive iterations. Even after your Web site is up and running, revisit it often—keep it fresh by giving users something new, a reason to return.

KEYS TO SITE DESIGN
- Start slowly.
- Place emphasis on content.
- Make the site easy for consumers to get around.
- Avoid using too many graphical elements.
- Be entertaining.
- Make your site graphically pleasing.
- Reach sight-impaired readers.
- Design for overseas markets with multiple languages.
- Add pages to your site.
- Accept credit cards.
- Give payment options.
- Make it easy to order.
- Provide a shopping cart.
- Provide links.

Do It Yourself

Can you design your own Web site? Of course! Many people do. Learning HTML code is not difficult (see Figure 4-2). What is difficult is designing a Web page that captures the attention of customers. The technology of design is easy enough to learn but the art of getting attention is not, so you might want to consider getting professional help. Why? Too many firms turn this task over to a marketing director of the old school who never got past e-mail. What you need is a modern Internet "geek" who can design an entire on-line transaction from first look to showroom tour to a final handshake deal.

Software Guide

There are many software tools available to allow you to get your e-commerce project off the ground. Here is a list of

Partial List of HTML Markup Tags

Markup Tags	Use of Tag
<A HREF="pagename.htm"> ... </A>	Create a link to another document
<A HREF="http://www.abc.com"> ... </A>	Create a link to another Web site
<A HREF="MAIL TO:you@xyz.com"> ... </A>	Create a link in order to send an e-mail message
<B> ... </B>	Boldface text
<BLOCKQUOTE> ... </BLOCKQUOTE>	Indents text from the left and right margins
<BODY> ... </BODY>	Encloses the body of the HTML document which is displayed by the browser
 	Creates a line break without extra space
<CENTER> ... </CENTER>	Centers text
<FONT COLOR = "X"> ... </FONT>	Allows use of different font colors eg: <FONT COLOR = "red">
<FONT FACE = "X"> ... </FONT>	Allows use of different font styles eg: <FONT FACE = "arial">
<FONT SIZE = "X"> ... </FONT>	Allows change of font size in running text eg: <FONT SIZE="+2">
<H1> thru <H6> ... </H1> thru </H6>	First- through sixth-level headings
<HEAD> ... </HEAD>	Encloses the heading of the HTML document
<HR>	Creates a horizontal rule line
<HTML> ... </HTML>	Encloses the entire HTML document
<I> ... </I>	Italic text
<IMG SRC="xxx">	Used to insert an inline image eg: <IMG SRC="pic.gif">
<LI>	Used to create list items
	Used in place of a space to create a nonbreaking space so line doesn't overflow line
<OL> ... </OL>	Used to create a numbered or ordered list
<P>	Creates a line break with extra space before start of next text block
<PRE> ... </PRE>	Retains the spacing that is keyed in the text within the tags
<TITLE> ... </TITLE>	Indicates the title of the HTML document
<U> ... </U>	Underlined text
<UL> ... </UL>	Used to create a bulleted or unordered list
<!-- ... -->	Used to insert nondisplayed comments in the HTML document

Note: For a complete listing of HTML codes, check the following Web site: http://www.willcam.com/cmat/html/crossname.html

Fig. 4-2. Example of HTML

Sample of Markup Tags

```
<HTML>
<HEAD>
<TITLE>My Home Page</TITLE></HEAD><BR>
<BODY>
<FONT SIZE="+2"><B><I>Welcome to...</B></I></FONT><BR>
<FONT SIZE="+3"><B><I>My Home Page</B></I></FONT><P>
<IMG SRC="4bird.gif"><P><P><P>
<FONT SIZE="+1">I'm<B>glad</B>you are visiting my home page.
<BR><BR>
<H1>Example of first-level heading</H1>
<H3>Example of third-level heading</H3><P>
<!--This comment will not print on the Web page-->
Following are list items:<BR>
<UL>
<LI>List item #1<BR>
<LI>List item #2<P>
</UL>
<PRE>      A PRE tag allows you to control placement
</FONT></PRE><P>
Send an e-mail message to:
<A HREF="mailto:me@my-isp>me@my-isp</A>
<BR><BR></FONT>
<HR>
<CENTER>
<FONT SIZE="2">Copyright &#169 1996-97.companyname
</CENTER>
</BODY>
</HTML>
```

Essential Web Page Tags

```
<HTML>
<HEAD>
    Between the HEAD tags you put the title, meta
    tags, and other nonprinting information
<TITLE>Title of your page goes here</TITLE>
</HEAD>
<BODY>
    Between the BODY tags is where you put all
    information that will be visible on your Web page.
</BODY>
</HTML>
```

Fig. 4-2. Example of HTML home page (*Continued*)

Internet software suppliers; however, neither quality nor rank is implied—be aware that the market is changing rapidly so these may not be around next year.

Oracle Applications, (650) 506-7000, www.oracle.com
Peoplesoft, (800) 380-7638, www.peoplesoft.com
MySap.com, (610) 355-2500, www.sap.com

Broadbase EPM, (650) 614-8301, www.broadbase.com
BroadVision One-to-One, (650) 261-5940,
   www.broadvision.com
Commerce Exchange, (212) 301-2500,
   www.interworld.com
The Kana Platform, (650) 298-9282, www.kana.com
NetCommerce Family, (800) 772-2227, www.ibm.com
Spectra and ColdFusion, (888) 939-2545,
   www.altaire.com
Sun-Netscape Alliance, (650) 254-1900,
   www.netscape.com
GoLive from Adobe, (800) 833-6687, www.adobe.com
Homesite, (888) 939-2545, www.allaire.com
FrontPage 2000, (800) 426-9400, www.microsoft.com
WebLogic, (800) 817-4BEA, www.beasys.com
Oberon E-Enterprise, (800) 654-1215, www.oberon.com
Enfinity, (800) 736-5197, www.intershop.com
Infranet, (408) 343-4400, www.portal.com
Quickbooks Internet Gateway, (650) 944-6000,
   www.quicken.com
e-BIZ, (888) 4LUXENT, www.e-bixinabox.com

Have Others Do It

As with any other new endeavor, you will find people in every city who specialize in Web page strategy and design. Many of these are recent college grads who focused their training in this specialty. Others are employees of major advertising companies who have the advantage of the ad firm's years of experience and adapt it to the Web technology of modern communications.

Domain Name

A domain name is what people type into search engines to find your Web site. Most companies use several domain names and aliases such as "yourcompany.com" and even "international business"—a generic label that people might type into a search engine to find your specialty or industry.

   The trick is to get your domain name to the top of the search engine list.

GETTING OUT THERE

It is one thing to have a Web site; it's another to ensure that customers know it exists and how to find it. First of all, put your Web site and e-mail addresses on your brochures, flyers, trucks, ships, billboards, ads, stationery, and business cards. Next get your Web site address listed in an Internet business directory such as www.directory.net. There are many such directories and many do not charge listees to be included. Another approach is to join a virtual mall—a group of Internet businesses using the metaphor of a shopping mall. Last but not least, be certain to get your address on as many search engines as possible.

Search Engines

Search engines compile lists for consumers who surf for a product. The trick is to get your address as high on the search engine list as possible. Because engines use different criteria, there are several strategies. First in importance is your domain name. For instance the name "international business" will bring domain names such as internationalbusiness.com, international-business.com, and internationalbusiness.org to the top of the list. If your business domain name just uses the initials of your company, you will find yourself near the bottom of the list. The right strategy is to use several domain names. The second trick is to use descriptive words in the title of your Web pages. A title such as "ABCD company discount sunglasses" will come up closer to the top than just the company name. The same applies to the HTML document. Sunglass.html will get you closer to the top than 1234.doc or abbreviated names.

TOP SEARCH ENGINES

37.com searches 37 search engines at once.
altavista.com
infoseek.com
excite.com
aol.com/netfind
hotbot.com
google.com
lycos.com
webscrawler.com
yahoo.com

Finding Foreign Markets

There are more than 200 million on-line users worldwide—over half are in the United States and Canada. Yet the potential market is phenomenal because everyone who has a computer or television set is getting on the Net.

Finding foreign buyers continues to be a market research problem. As always, start with the country or region. But where to look? Try the following databases.

STAT-USA/Internet.   A service of the U.S. Department of Commerce, and the site for the U.S. business, economic, and trade community, STAT-USA provides authoritative information from the federal government and includes access to the National Trade Data Bank (NTDB) for country and market research.   http://www.stat-usa.gov/

Strategis.   A Canadian government trade assistance site, Strategis has international trade information and statistics that can be turned into a graphic presentation of the top 10 markets for most products. Follow the international and trade links.   http://www.strategis.ic.gc.ca/eng-doc/main.html

Central Intelligence Agency.   The CIA Fact Book is one of the best sources of basic information on any country. http://www.odci.gov/cia/ciahome.html

The SBA Office for International Trade.   The SBA provides   extensive   links   and   training   resources. http://www.sbaonline.sba.gov/OIT/info/Iinks.html

Michigan State University, Center for International Business   and   Education   Research   (CIBER)— International   Business   Resources   on   the   WWW. CIBER has one of the best and most extensive sites for international markets, including trade leads and hotlinks on all aspects of global markets.   http://ciber.bus.msu.edu/busres.htm

Tradeport.   One of the most extensive international trade resources on the Internet, Tradeport is a free site with market information, guidance, and resource listings as well as trade   leads   and   international   events   in   the   Southern California area.   http://www.tradeport.org

Finding Foreign Buyers

Of course, there are over 400 trade lead sites; the United Nations   (www.un.org)   and   the   World   Trade   Centers

Association (www.wtca.org) have lead services. To reach more than 2 million traders, try these resources.

NEOS—National Export Offer Service. NEOS is a comprehensive site for links and access to foreign buyers, directions, and guidance resources.   http://www.exportservices.com/

Europages.   With information on 500,000 companies in 30 countries, Europages is an excellent place to search for companies to contact, by product or service search as a buyer or for market research.   http://www.europages.com/

Clear Freight.   Follow the trade lead links section for an extensive set of contacts and go back to the main page for freight forwarder information.   http://.clearfreight.com/clear_internet_trc/trade.htm

Global Electronic Commerce Korea.   This is a great site with links to many other countries with company directories. Try EC Links for an extensive list of other areas and trade lead sites.   http://commerce.ktnet.co.kr/

Import Export Bulletin Board (IEBB).   Sponsored by the *Journal of Commerce,* IEBB is an extensive buy/sell listing and information site with access to STAT-USA (trade research) and UN data. It is fee based for full access. http://www.iebb.com

Beaucoup.   This search engine directory lists country-specific searches of many nations and several directories in each country.   http://www.beaucoup.com/

Europeonline.   A central access site to all countries in Europe in local languages and English, for business, financial, and general information, Europeonline also provides access to European Union information and Europages. http://www.europeonline.com/

Trade Show Central.   This free Internet service provides information on more than 50,000 trade shows, conferences, and seminars as well as 5000 service providers and 8000 venues and facilities around the world.   http://www.tscentral.com/

Government Procurement

Ever since the World Trade Organization formalized opportunities for bidding, government procurement competition has become worldwide. Here are a few valuable addresses.

www.wto.org/wto/govt/memobs.htm
www.arnet.gov.far
www.ld.com/cgd.html
www.texas-one.org/market/newposts.html
www.financenet.gov/financenet/sales/saleint.html
www.setro.go.jp.cgi-bin/gov/govinte.cgi
www.govcon.com
www.sbaonline.sba.gov

PRICING AND MARKETING YOUR PRODUCT

Gone are the days of arbitrary pricing. Because the Internet offers worldwide openness, pricing without substance is gone forever. You must continually check the market and competition, and provide additional services and features as necessary to maintain your price. Places to search are www.price.com and mysimon.com.

Marketing Techniques

The Internet is a place where creativity reigns. Here are some techniques that have evolved as the Web grows from childhood to adolescence.

- Set up a chat area.
- Sell advertising on your page.
- Create contests for your customers.
- Build customer lists.
- Offer a free catalog.
- Offer coupons.
- Provide information.
- Publish a newsletter.
- Sell access to your products or services.
- Upload your annual report.

Communications

If you don't have an e-mail address, you may as well pack up and move to the South Pole—in today's business world it is a must.

E-mail is currently being used 10 to 1 over postal services, and the rate of change is growing. Business contracts are being negotiated between nations routinely. The author recently negotiated book contracts with a London publisher by e-mail.

Getting Paid

Yes, you can ask for cash, you can take checks, and you should accept credit cards, but the world's standard method of payment for big sales is still the documentary letter of credit (see Chapter 6 for a complete discussion). The Internet is able to combine technology with standard business systems to continue to use the letter of credit as an easy, trustworthy payment method.

Internet technologies available include document management software, document imaging, electronic mail, interactive forms within Web browsers, and password security protocols. One source of good information about this subject is www.AVGTSG.com, a company that specializes in payment solutions, including methods for the Internet.

Keeping in Touch

Things are changing so fast in international trade that businesspeople must read and digest enormous amounts of material to keep up. However, here are several publications that manage to keep pace with the trends:

www.tradeport.com
www.aaatrading.com
www.exporter.com
www.worldtrademag.com
www.exporttoday.com
www.AVGTSG.com
www.pangaea.net
www.tradecompass.com
www.euromktg.com
www.fedex.com
www.dhl.com
www.bankamerica.com
www.worldbank.com
www.vivid.com/ground/gulch/gulch.html
www.merklerweb.com/imall/imall/htm

FURTHER READING

How to Grow Your Business on the Internet (3d ed.), by Vince Emery, published by Coriolis Group Books. A most comprehensive discussion of the best Internet business strategies, marketing strategies, and many aspects of on-line business, based on actual experience and several years of active participation in the field. Also has an active Web site.

Webonomics: Nine Essential Principles for Growing Your Business on the World Wide Web, by Evan Schwartz, published by Broadway Books. An excellent analysis about what works on-line and does not work. Contains fundamental insights into Internet business, global or otherwise.

How to Build a Successful International Web Site, by Mark Bishop, published by Coriolis Group Books. An excellent, detailed instruction manual for creating an international Web site, including software for language editing and information on international search engines.

Marketing Online for Dummies, by Bud Smith and Frank Catalano, published by IDG Books Worldwide. A comprehensive guide to marketing strategies on-line that includes a software package with many tools.

Selling Online for Dummies, by Leslie Heeter Lundquist, published by IDG Books Worldwide. A basic instruction manual for setting up business on-line, developing a Web site, and using the tools needed to enhance business results. Also comes with a package of software tools and tips.

Striking It Rich.com—Profiles of 23 Incredibly Successful Websites You've Probably Never Heard Of, by Jaclyn Easton, published by Commercenet Press. A very exciting account of a wide variety of Web sites and how they achieved success. This book contains the mistakes, ideas, and insights of different on-line businesses and provides a great understanding of what it takes for an emerging site to achieve success. Easton's active Web site contains updates on the subject and keeps the book from being outdated.

Doing Business on the Internet, by Mary Cronin, published by Van Nostrand. This is the handbook for all those serious about making the most of what the Internet has to offer their business. It provides a step-by-step framework for exploiting the business opportunities available on the Web.

The next chapter expands the concepts related to both import and export, developing the fundamentals needed to "complete the transaction"—namely, financing, avoiding risk, shipping, and documentation.

5

Completing a Successful Transaction

NOW YOU ARE READY FOR THE STEPS NEEDED TO COMPLETE AN import or export transaction. In Chapter 2 you learned the basics of start-up. Chapter 3 led you through the concepts of planning and negotiating a transaction. Chapter 4 explained how to compete in the Internet marketplace. This chapter covers the four remaining commonalities, which encompass paying for the goods and physically moving them from one country to another.

1. Finance your import/export transaction.
2. Avoid risk.
3. Pack and ship your product (physical distribution).
4. Supply all documentation.

FINANCING

Why do you need financing in the import/export business?

To start, expand, or take advantage of opportunities, all businesses need new money sooner or later. New money means money that you have not yet earned, but that can become the engine for growth.

For the importer, financing offers the ability to pay for the overseas manufacture and shipment of foreign goods destined for the domestic market. For the exporter, financing means working capital to pay for international travel and the marketing effort. New money can also be loans to foreign buyers to enable them to purchase an exporter's goods.

If you have done the homework phase well and have purchase orders for your product(s) in hand, there is plenty of currency available—banks or factors are waiting to assist you.

The Bank

Commercial banking is the primary industry that supports the financing of importing and exporting. Selection of a banking partner is an essential part of the teamwork required for international trade success. When shopping for a bank, look for the following:

1. A strong international department.
2. Speed in handling transactions. (Does the bank want to make money on your money—called the float?)
3. Relationship with overseas banks. (Does the bank have corresponding relationships with banks in the countries in which you wish to do business?)
4. Credit policy.

HOT TIP: In the import/export industry there is a saying: "Walk on two legs." This means choose carefully, then work closely with a good international bank and a customs broker or freight forwarder

Forms of Bank Financing

Loans for international trade fall into two categories: secured and unsecured.

Secured Financing

Banks are not high risk takers. To reduce their exposure to loss, they often ask for collateral. Financing against collateral is called *secured financing* and is the most common method of raising new money. Banks will advance funds against payment obligations, shipment documents, or storage documents. The most common method is advancement of funds against payment obligations or documentary title. In this case, the trader pledges the goods for export or import as collateral for a loan to finance them. The bank maintains a secure position by accepting as collateral documents that convey title, such as negotiable bills of lading, warehouse receipts, or trust receipts.

How a Banker's Acceptance Works

Another popular method of obtaining secured financing is the *banker's acceptance* (B/A). This is a time draft presented to a bank by an exporter. (It differs from a *trade acceptance* between buyer and seller, in which a bank is not involved.) The bank stamps and signs the draft "accepted" on behalf of its client, the importer. By accepting the draft, the bank undertakes and recognizes the obligation to pay the draft at maturity, and has placed its creditworthiness between the exporter (*drawer*) and the importer (*drawee*). Banker's acceptances are negotiable instruments that can be sold in the money market. The B/A rate is a discount rate generally 2 to 3 points below the prime rate. With the full creditworthiness of the bank behind the draft, eligible B/As attract the very best of market interest rates. There are specific criteria for eligibility.

1. The B/A must be created within 30 days of the shipment of the goods.
2. The maximum tenor is 180 days after shipment.
3. The B/A must be self-liquidating.
4. The B/A cannot be used for working capital purposes.
5. The credit recipient must attest to no duplication.

Shipping documents: Commercial invoices, bills of lading, insurance certificates, consular invoices, and related documents. *Draft:* The same as a "bill of exchange." A written order for a certain sum of money to be transferred on a certain date from the person who owes the money or agrees to make the payment (the drawee) to the creditor to whom the money is owed (the drawer of the draft).

Unsecured Financing

In truth, *unsecured financing* is only for those who have a sound credit standing with their bank or have had long-term trading experience. It usually amounts to expanding already existing lines of working credit. For the small import/export business, unsecured financing will probably be limited to a personal line of credit.

Factors

A *factor* is an agent who will, at a discount (usually 5 to 8 percent of the gross), buy receivables. Banks do 95 percent of factoring; the remainder is done by private specialists. The factor makes a profit on the collection and provides a source of cash flow for the seller, albeit less than if the business had held out to make the collection itself.

For example, suppose you had a receivable of $1000. A factor might offer you a $750 advance on the invoice and charge you 5 percent on the gross of $1000 per month until collection. If the collection is made within the first month, the factor would keep only $50 and return $200. If it takes two months, the factor would keep $100 and return only $150.

The importer benefits from having the cash to reorder products from overseas. For a manufacturer, the benefit can be cash flow available for increased or new production.

Other Private Sources of Financing

The United States has several major private trade financing institutions, all in competition to support your export programs.

PEFCO.   The Private Export Funding Corporation (PE-FCO) was established in 1970 and is owned by about 60 banks, 7 industrial corporations, and an investment banking firm. PEFCO operates with its own capital stock, an extensive line of credit from the U.S. government's EXIMBank (see below), and the proceeds of its secured and unsecured debt obligations. It provides medium- and long-term loans, subject to EXIMBank approval, to foreign buyers of U.S. goods and services. PEFCO generally deals in sales of capital goods with a minimum commitment of about $1 million—there is no maximum. Contact: PEFCO, 280 Park Avenue (4-West),

New York, NY 10017; phone: (212) 916-0300; fax: (212) 286-0304; Web: www.pefco.com.

OPIC. The Overseas Private Investment Corporation (OPIC) is a private, self-sustaining institution whose purpose is to promote economic growth in developing countries. OPIC's programs include insurance, finance, missions, contractors' and exporters' insurance, small contractor guarantees, and investor information services. For more information, contact: OPIC, 1615 M Street, NW, Washington, DC 20527; phone: (202) 336-8400; fax: (202) 408-9859; Web: www.opic.gov.

Government Sources

Many nations are short on foreign exchange, and what they have is earmarked for priority national imports or large international credit commitments. Nevertheless, there are probably more sources of competitive financing available today to support exporting than at any other time in history. The major complaint is that not enough firms are taking advantage of the programs.

Small Business Administration (SBA). All nations support the growth of small business. For example, the U.S. government's Small Business Administration (SBA) guarantees eight-year working capital loans for about 2.25 percent over prime to small companies that can show reasonable ability to pay. The maximum maturity may be up to 25 years, depending on the use of the loan proceeds. The SBA's export revolving-line-of-credit guarantee program provides pre-export financing to aid in the manufacture or purchase of goods for sale to foreign markets and to help a small business penetrate or develop a foreign market. The maximum maturity for this financing is 18 months. The SBA, in cooperation with EXIMBank, participates in loans between $200,000 and $1 million.

EXIMBank. When U.S. exporters find buyers who cannot obtain financing in their own country, the Export-Import Bank of the United States (EXIMBank) may provide credit support in the form of loans, guarantees, and insurance for small businesses. EXIMBank is a federal agency to help finance the export of U.S. goods and services. Rates vary but are available for a 5- to 10-year maturity period.

Programs include medium- and long-term loans and guarantees that cover up to 85 percent of a transaction's export value, with repayment terms of a year or longer. Long-term loans and guarantees are provided for over 7 years but not usually more than 10 years. The Medium-Term Credit Program has more than $300 million available for small businesses facing subsidized foreign competition. The Small Business Credit Program also has funds available, with direct credit for exporting medium-term goods; competition is not necessary. The EXIM Working Capital Program guarantees the lender's repayment on capital loans for exports.

Agency for International Development (AID). A subordinate division of the U.S. State Department, AID provides loans and grants to nations for both developmental and foreign policy reasons. Under the AID Development Assistance Program funds are available at rates of 2 percent and 3 percent over 40 years. The AID Economic Development Fund has funds at similar interest rates. Generally, these funds are available through invitations to bid placed in the *Commerce Daily Bulletin,* a publication available from the Government Printing Office, Washington, DC 20402.

International Development Cooperation Agency (IDCA). The IDCA Trade and Development Program loans funds on an annual basis to enable friendly countries to procure foreign goods and services for major development projects. Often, these funds support smaller firms in subcontract positions.

AVOIDING RISK

Doing business always involves some risk, so you should expect across-border business to be no different. A certain amount of uncertainty is always present in doing business across international borders, but much of it can be hedged, managed, and controlled. All major exporting countries have arrangements to protect exporters and the bankers who provide their funding support. Avoiding and/or controlling risks in global trade is an everyday occurrence for importers and exporters. Understanding the instruments available for avoiding risk is not difficult but is vital. There are essentially four kinds of risks:

Commercial	Not being paid; nondelivery of goods; insolvency or protracted default by buyer; competition; disputes over product or warranty
Foreign Exchange	Foreign exchange fluctuations
Political	War, coup d'état, or revolution; expropriation; expulsion; foreign exchange controls; cancellation of import/export licenses
Shipping	Risk of damage and/or loss at sea or via other transportation

Most risks allow for a method of avoidance. Of course, there is no insurance against a dispute over quality or loss of market as a result of competition, but there are management instruments for three aspects of risk: not being paid, transport loss or damage, and foreign exchange exposure.

Avoidance of Commercial Risk

The *seller* wants to be certain that the buyer will pay on time once the goods have been shipped. The goal is at least to minimize risk of nonpayment. On the other hand, the *buyer* wants to be certain that the seller will deliver on time and that the goods are exactly what the buyer ordered.

These concerns are most often heard from anyone beginning an import/export business. Mistrust across international borders is natural; after all, there is a certain amount of mistrust even in our own culture. One key to risk avoidance is a well-written sales contract. In Chapter 3 you learned that an early step in the process of international trade is to gain contract agreement between yourself and your overseas business associate. The terms should include method of payment.

Getting Paid

Ensuring prompt payment often worries exporters more than any other commercial risk. The truth is that the likelihood of a bad debt from an international customer is very low. In the experience of most international businesses, overseas bad debts seldom exceed 0.5 percent of sales. The reason is that in overseas markets, credit is still something to be earned as a result of having a record of prompt payment. Use common sense in extending credit to overseas customers, but don't use tougher rules than you apply to domestic clients.

The methods of payment, in order of decreasing risk to the seller and increasing risk to the importer, are open account, consignment, time draft, sight draft, authority to purchase, letter of credit, and cash in advance. Table 5-1 summarizes the various methods of payment.

Open Account.   The *open account* is a trade arrangement in which goods are shipped to a foreign buyer without guarantee of payment. Though the riskiest, this method is used by many firms that have a long-standing business relationship with the same overseas buyer. Needless to say, the key is to know your buyer and your buyer's country. You should use an open account when the buyer has a continuing need for the seller's product or service. Some experienced exporters say that

Table 5-1. Comparison of Various Methods of Payment

(In order of decreasing risk to exporter and increasing risk to importer)

Method	Goods available to buyers	Usual time of payment	Exporter risk	Importer risk
Open account	Before payment	As agreed	Most: relies on importer to pay account	Least
Consignment	Before payment	After sold	Maximum: exporter retains title	Minor inventory cost
Time draft	Before payment	On maturity of draft	High: relies on importer to pay draft	Minimal check of quantity/ quality
Sight draft	After payment	On presenting draft to importer	If unpaid, goods are returned/ disposed	Little if inspection report required
Authority to purchase	After payment	On presenting draft	Be careful of recourse	Little if inspection report required
Letter of credit	After payment	When documents are available after shipment	None	None if inspection report required
Cash	After payment	Before shipment	Least	Most

they deal only in open accounts. But they always preface that statement by saying that they have close relationships and have been doing business with their overseas clients for many years. An open account can be risky unless the buyer is of unquestioned integrity and has withstood a thorough credit investigation. The advantage of this method is its ease and convenience, but with open-account sales, you bear the burden of financing the shipment. Standard practice in many countries is to defer payment until the merchandise is sold, sometimes even longer. Therefore, among the forms of payment, open-account sales require the greatest amount of working capital. In addition, you bear the exchange risk if the sales are quoted in foreign currency. Nevertheless, competitive pressures may force the use of this method.

> **HOT TIP:** Relationships between buyer and seller make the difference by reducing mistrust. Make an effort to meet and get to know your trading partner.

Consignment.   In a *consignment* arrangement, the *consignor* (seller) retains title to the goods during shipment and storage of the product in the warehouse or retail store. The *consignee* acts as an agent, selling the goods and remitting the net proceeds to the consignor. Like open-account sales, consignment sales can be risky and lend themselves only to certain kinds of merchandise. Great care should be taken in working out this contractual arrangement. Be sure it is covered with adequate risk insurance.

Bank Drafts.   Payment for many sales is arranged using one of many time-tested banking methods. *Bank drafts* (bills of exchange) are written orders that activate payment either at sight or at "tenor," a future time or date. Each is useful under certain circumstances.

A bank draft is a check, drawn by a bank on another bank, used primarily when it is necessary for the customer to provide funds payable at a bank in some distant location. The exporter who undertakes this payment method can offer a range of payment options to the overseas customer.

Time (Date) Draft.   The time draft is an acceptance order drawn by the exporter on the importer (customer), payable a certain number of days after "sight" (presentation) or days from date to the holder. Think of it as nothing more than an IOU, or promise to pay in the future.

Documents such as negotiable bills of lading, insurance certificates, and commercial invoices accompany the draft and are submitted through the exporter's bank for collection. When the draft is presented to the importer's bank, the importer acknowledges that the documents are acceptable and commits to pay by writing "accepted" on the draft and signing it. The importer normally has 30 to 180 days, depending on the draft's term, to make payments to the bank for transmittal.

Sight Draft. The sight draft is similar to the time draft except that the importer's bank holds the documents until the importer releases the funds. Sight drafts are the most common method employed by exporters throughout the world. They are nothing more than written orders in standardized bank format requesting money from the overseas buyer. Although this method costs less than the letter of credit (defined below), it has greater risk because the importer can refuse to honor the draft.

Bill of lading: A document that provides the terms of the contract between the shipper and the transportation company to move freight between stated points at a specified charge. *Commercial or customs invoice:* A bill for the goods from the seller to the buyer. It is one method used by governments to determine the value of the goods for customs valuation purposes. *At sight:* A term indicating that a negotiable instrument is to be paid upon presentation or demand.

Authority to Purchase. Authority to purchase is occasionally used in the Far East. It specifies a bank where the exporter can draw a documentary draft on the importer's bank. The problem with this method is that if the importer fails to pay the draft, the bank has "recourse" to the exporter for settlement. Therefore, before consenting to an authority to purchase, the exporter may wish to specify "without recourse" and so state on drafts.

The major risk with the time, sight, and authority to purchase methods is that the buyer can refuse to pay or to pick up the goods. The method of avoidance is to require cash or a sight draft against documents. Unfortunately, banks are slow in transferring funds because they want to use the time float (short-term investment of bank money) to earn interest. Using a wire transfer can get around the delay.

Letter of Credit (L/C). Ideally an exporter deals only in cash, but in reality few businesses are initially able or willing to operate under those terms. Because of the risk of non-payment due to insolvency, bankruptcy, or other severe deterioration, procedures and documents have been developed to help ensure that foreign buyers honor their agreements.

The most common form of collection is payment against a *letter of credit* (L/C). The L/C is the time-tested method whereby an importer's bank guarantees payment to the exporter if all documents are presented in exact conformity with the terms of the L/C. The procedure is not difficult to understand, and most cities have bank personnel familiar with the mechanics of L/Cs.

This method is well understood by traders around the world, is simple, and is as good as your bank. Internationally the term *documentary credit* is synonymous with letter of credit. L/Cs involve thousands of transactions and billions of dollars every day in every part of the world. They are almost always operated in accordance with the Uniform Customs and Practice for Documentary Credits of the International Chamber of Commerce, a code of practice that is recognized by banking communities in 156 countries. A *Guide to Documentary Operations,* which includes all the standard forms, is available from: ICC Publishing Corporation, Inc., 156 Fifth Avenue, Suite 302, New York, NY 10010; phone: (212) 206-1150; fax (212) 633-6025; Web: www.iccbooks.com.

An L/C is a document issued by a bank at the importer's or buyer's request in favor of the seller. It promises to pay a specified amount of money upon receipt by the bank of certain documents within a specified time or at intervals corresponding with shipments of goods. It is a universally used method of achieving a commercially acceptable compromise. Think of a letter of credit as a loan against collateral wherein the funds are placed in an escrow account. The amount in the account depends on the relationship between the buyer and the buyer's bank.

Standby L/Cs. Sometimes when dealing in an open account, the exporter requires a *standby L/C.* This means just what the name implies—the L/C is executed only if payment is not made within the specified period, usually 30 to 60 days. Bank handling charges for standby letters of credit are usually higher than for commercial (import) L/Cs.

Typically, if you don't already have an account, the bank will require 100 percent collateral. With an account, the bank will establish a line of credit against that account.

Commercial letter of credit charges are competitive, so you should shop around. Typical charges are shown in Table 5-2.

Table 5-2. Typical L/C Charges

Type of credit	Typical charges
Import and domestic	$1/8$ of 1 percent of transaction with a minimum of $75 to $100. Amendments: $1/8$ of 1 percent flat, minimum $70. Payment fee: $1/4$ of 1 percent flat, minimum $90 per draft. Acceptance fee: per annum (360-day) basis, minimum $75 for each draft accepted. Discrepancy fee: $40.
Export	Advising: $60. Confirmation: subject to country risk conditions, minimum $75. Amendments: $55. Assignment of proceeds/transfers: $1/8$ of 1 percent of transaction, minimum $75. Discrepancy fee: $45. Payment/negotiation: $1/10$ of 1 percent, minimum $85 to $95.
Standby	Issuance fee: An annual percentage (360-day basis) based on credit risk considerations, minimum $250. Amendment: risk-related fee, minimum $250. Payment fee: $1/4$ of 1 percent flat, minimum $90 per draft.
Collections— documentary	Incoming: sight, $75; time, $95. Outgoing: sight, $75; time, $95.

Issuing, Confirming, and Advising Banks.   As noted, letters of credit are payable either at sight or on a time draft basis. Under a sight L/C, the *issuing* (buyer's) bank pays, with or without a draft, when satisfied that the presented documents conform with the forms. An *advising* bank (most often the *confirming* or seller's bank) informs the seller or beneficiary that an L/C has been issued. *Confirmation* means that a local bank guarantees payment by the issuing bank. Under a time (acceptance) L/C, once the associated draft is presented and found to be in exact conformity, the draft is stamped "accepted" and can then be negotiated as a banker's acceptance by the exporter, at a discount to reflect the cost of money advanced against the draft.

Once the buyer and the seller agree to use an L/C for payment, and have worked out the conditions, the buyer or importer applies for the L/C at his or her international bank. Figure 5-1 is an example of a letter of credit application.

Types of L/Cs.   There are two types of letters of credit: revocable and irrevocable. *Revocable credit* means that the document can be amended or canceled at any time without prior warning or notification of the seller. *Irrevocable credit* means that the terms of the document can be amended or canceled only with the agreement of all parties thereto.

Using the application as its guide, the bank issues a document of credit incorporating the terms agreed to by the parties. Figure 5-2 exemplifies an L/C.

Figure 5-3 shows the three phases of documentary credit in their simplest form. In Phase I, the buyer's (issuing) bank notifies the seller through an advising bank or the seller's (confirming) bank that a credit has been issued. In Phase II, the seller then ships the goods and presents the documents to the bank, at which time the seller is paid. In Phase III, the "settlement" phase, the documents are transferred to the buyer's bank, whereupon the buyer pays the bank any remaining moneys in exchange for the documents. Thus, on arrival of the goods, the buyer or importer has the proper documents for entry.

Special Middleman Uses of the Letter of Credit. There are three special uses of commercial letters of credit for the import/export middleman: transferable, assignment of proceeds, and back-to-back L/Cs. Figure 5-4 compares the risks involved with each method.

To: Importer's international bank
_____

Request to open documentary
credit (commercial letter of
credit and security agreement)

Date _____

Please open for my/our account a documentary credit (letter of credit)
in accordance with the undermentioned particulars.

We agree that, except so far as otherwise expressly stated, this credit
will be subject to the Uniform Customs and Practice for Documentary
Credits, ICC Publication #290.

We undertake to execute the Bank's usual form of indemnity.

Type of Credit: Irrevocable, i.e., cannot be canceled without benefi-
                            ciary's agreement.
                Revocable, i.e., subject to cancellation.
Method of Advice: [ ]   Airmail   [ ]   Cable, short
details   [ ]   Cable, full details.
Beneficiary's blank: _____

In favor of beneficiary: Company name and address.

Amount or sum of:

Availability: Valid until_____in_____for negotiation/date
                                              place acceptance/payment.

This credit is available by drafts drawn at ____ sight/
accompanied by the required documents.

Documents   Invoice in three copies
required: Full set "clean on board" bills of lading to order of
                 shipper, blank endorsed. In case movement of goods
                 involves more than one mode, a "Combined
                 Transport Document" should be called for.

                 Negotiable Marine and War risk insurance for %
                 (usually 110%) of invoice value covering all risks.

Fig. 5-1. Request to open a letter of credit

                    Certificate of Inspection

Other
Documents: Certificate of origin issued by Chamber of Commerce
              in three copies.

                              Packing List

Quantity &
Description
of Goods

Price per unit:

Terms &
relative port
or place: CIF/C&F/FOB/FAS/_____
Place _____

Dispatch/
Shipment   From _____ to _____

Special
Instructions
(if any):

Fig. 5-1. Request to open a letter of credit (*Continued*)

Transferable L/C.   Figure 5-5 shows how the *transferable* L/C works. The buyer opens the L/C, which states clearly that it is transferable on behalf of the middleman as the original beneficiary, who in turn transfers all or part of the L/C to the supplier. The transfer must be made under the same terms and conditions as the original L/C with the following exceptions: amount, unit price, expiration date, and shipping date. In this instance the buyer and supplier are usually disclosed to each other.

Assignment of Proceeds.   Figure 5-6 illustrates the *assignment of proceeds* method, and Figure 5-7 shows a typical letter of assignment. It should be noted that the proceeds of all letters of credit may be assigned. In this instance the buyer opens the L/C as the beneficiary and relies on the middleman to comply so that he can be paid. Any discrepancy in middleman documents

Name of Issuing Bank	Documentary Credit No._____
_____	_____
Place and date of issue	Place and date of expiration
Applicant	Amount
	Credit available with
	[ ] Payment [ ] Acceptance
	[ ] Negotiation
Shipment from _____	Against presentation of
Shipment to _____	documents detailed herein
	[ ] Drawn on _____
	Bank

Invoice in three copies

Full set "clean on board" bills of lading to order of shipper, blank endorsed. In case movement of goods involves more than one made, a "Combined Transport Document" should be called for.

Negotiable Marine and War risk insurance for _____%
(usually 110%) of invoice value covering all risks.

Certificate of Inspection

Certificate of origin issued by Chamber of Commerce in three copies.

Packing List

Documents to be presented within _____ days after date of issuance of
the shipping document(s) but within the validity of the credit.

We hereby issue this Documentary Credit in your favor.

Issuing Bank

Fig. 5-2. Sample letter of credit

will prevent payment under the L/C. The middleman instructs
the advising bank to effect payment to the supplier when the
documents are negotiated. In this way, buyers and sellers are
not disclosed to each other.

Back-to-Back L/C.   When using the *back-to-back* method,
shown in Figure 5-8, the middleman must have a line of credit.

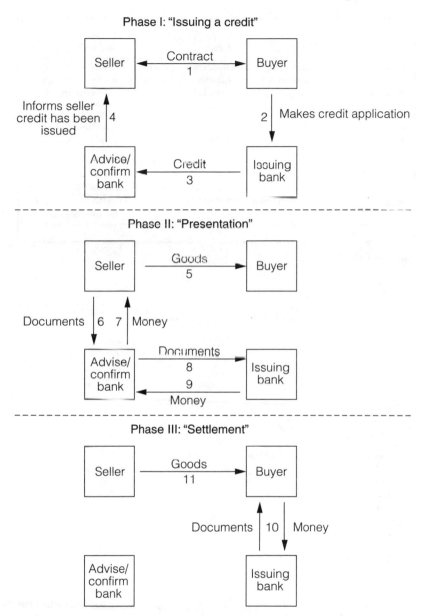

Fig. 5-3. The three phases of a letter of credit

	Assignment of Proceeds	*Transferable L/C*	*Back-to-Back L/C*
Risk to middleman	Supplier relies on middleman to comply with L/C	Middleman relies on supplier to comply with L/C	Supplier's performance must satisfy both L/Cs
Risk to middleman's bank	None	Minimal	Supplier does not comply with master L/C
Disclosure	Buyer and seller are not disclosed	Buyer and seller are disclosed	Buyer and seller are not disclosed (with third-party documents)

Fig. 5-4. Comparison of L/C risks

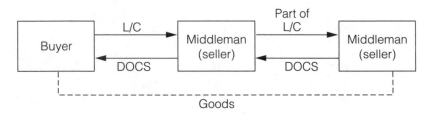

- L/C must state that it is transferable
- Original beneficiary transfers all or part of L/C to supplier(s)
- Transfer must be made under the same terms and conditions with the following exceptions:
  Amount
  Unit price
  Expiration date
  Shipping date
- Buyer and supplier are usually disclosed to each other

Fig. 5-5. Transferable letter of credit

The reason is that the middleman is responsible for paying the second (backing) L/C regardless of receipt of payment under the first (master) L/C. Great care should be exercised when using this method because discrepancies on the first L/C will result in nonpayment, and the middleman's ability to pay could be a substantial credit risk. Back-to-back L/Cs should be issued on

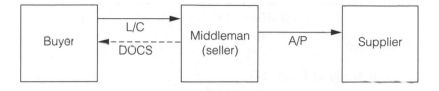

- Supplier relies on middleman to comply with L/C so that he or she can be paid. Discrepancy in middleman's documents will prevent payment under L/C
- Middleman instructs advising bank to effect payment to supplier when documents are negotiated
- Buyer and seller are not disclosed to each other
- Proceeds of all letters of credit can be assigned

Fig. 5-6. Assignment of proceeds

nearly identical terms and must allow for third-party documents.

Cash in Advance.   Cash in advance is the most desirable method of getting paid, but the foreign buyer usually objects to tying up his or her capital. On the grounds that seeing the merchandise is the best insurance, most foreign buyers try not to pay until they actually receive the goods. Furthermore, a buyer may resent the implication that he or she is not creditworthy.

Avoiding Bad Credit

Pick your customer carefully. Bad debts are more easily avoided than rectified. If there are payment problems, keep communicating and working with the firm until the matter is settled. Even the most valued customers have financial problems from time to time. If nothing else works, request your department of industry or commerce or the International Chamber of Commerce to begin negotiations on your behalf.

Information that is current and accurate is the backbone of good financing decisions. Basically there are two types of international credit information: (1) the ability and willingness of importing firms to make payment, and (2) the ability and willingness of foreign countries to allow payment in a convertible currency.

ASSIGNMENT OF PROCEEDS

Gentlemen:

Here is Letter of Credit No. _____ issued by _____ in favor of _____ _____ for an amount in excess of $ _____ expiring _____.

Our drafts and documents in terms of this credit will be presented by us to your office. We authorize and direct you to pay to _____ the sum of $ _____ from the proceeds of these drafts, in consideration of value received.

These instructions are irrevocable and shall continue under any extension of this Letter of Credit. Please acknowledge receipt of these instructions directly to _____ by forwarding them a copy of this letter.

Sincerely yours,

_____

Signature verified:

_____
    Name of Bank

_____
    Authorized Signature

The above assignment has been duly noted on our records.

_____
    The Bank of San Diego International Banking Department
    Authorized Signature

Fig. 5-7. Typical letter of assignment

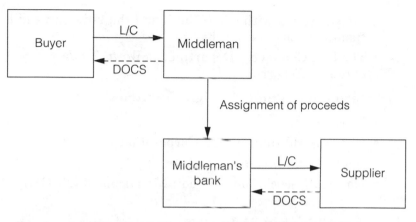

- Requires credit line for middleman
- Middleman is responsible for paying the second (backing) L/C regardless of receipt of payment under first (master) L/C
- Substantial credit risk in that discrepancies on the first L/C will result in non-payment
- L/Cs are issued on nearly identical terms
- Middleman's ability to pay is a key consideration
- L/C must allow third-party documents

Fig. 5-8. Back-to-back letter of credit

There are several sources of credit information on companies and their countries.

Information About Domestic Firms

- Commercial banks
- Commercial credit services, such as Dun & Bradstreet
- Trade associations

Information About Foreign Firms

- National Association of Credit Management (NACM)
- Foreign credit specialists in the credit departments of large exporting companies
- Commercial banks, which check buyer credit through their foreign branches and correspondents
- Commercial credit reporting services, such as Dun & Bradstreet

- Consultations with EXIMBank and the Foreign Credit Insurance Association (FCIA)
- The U.S. Commerce Department's *World Trade Directory Reports*

Information About Foreign Countries

- World Bank
- Chase World Information Corporation
- *Institutional Investor* magazine
- National Association of Credit Management (NACM)

Avoiding Shipping Risks

Marine cargo insurance is an essential business tool for import/export. Generally, coverage is sold on a warehouse-to-warehouse basis (i.e., from the sender's factory to the receiver's platform). Coverage usually ceases a specific number of days after the shipment is unloaded. Policies are purchased on a per shipment or "blanket" basis. Freight forwarders usually have a blanket policy to cover clients who do not have their own policy. Most insurance companies base cargo insurance on the value of all charges of the shipment (freight handling, etc.) plus 10 percent to cover unseen contingencies. Rates vary according to product, client's track record, destination, and shipping method.

Ocean cargo insurance costs about $0.50 to $1.50 per $100 of invoice value. Air cargo is usually about 25 to 30 percent less.

Avoiding Political Risk

No two national export credit systems are identical. However, there are similarities, the greatest of which is the universal involvement of government through the export credit agency concerned and of the commercial banking sector through the workings of the system.

Most countries have export-import banks. In the United States, EXIMBank provides credit support in the form of loans, guarantees, and insurance. All EXIM branches cooperate with commercial banks in providing a number of arrangements to help exporters offer credit guarantees to commercial banks that finance export sales. The Overseas

Private Investment Corporation (OPIC) and the Foreign Credit Insurance Association (FCIA) also provide insurance to exporters, enabling them to extend credit terms to their overseas buyers. Private insurers cover the normal commercial credit risks; EXIMBank assumes all liability for political risk.

For more information on FCIA, contact: FCIA, Marketing Department–11th Floor, 40 Rector Street, New York, NY 10006; phone: (212) 306-5000; fax: (212) 306-5218.

The programs available through OPIC and FCIA are well advertised and easily available. Commercial banks are essentially intermediaries to EXIMBank for export guarantees on loans (beginning at loans up to 1 year and ending at loans of 10 to 15 years). FCIA offers insurance in two basic maturities: (1) a short-term policy of up to 180 days, and (2) a medium-term policy from 181 days up to 5 years. You may also obtain a combination policy of those maturities. In addition, FCIA has a master policy offering *blanket protection* (one policy designed to provide coverage for all the exporter's sales to overseas buyers).

Avoiding Foreign Exchange Risk

When the dollar is strong—as strong as it was in the early 1980s—traders prefer to deal in the dollar. When the opposite is true, traders begin to deal in other currencies. Of course, the dollar is as good as gold because it is a politically stable currency that is traded internationally. Because of its stability, it has become the vehicle currency for most international transactions.

So long as exporters deal only in their own currency, there is no foreign exchange risk. However, the strength and popularity of currencies are cyclical, and the dollar is not always the leader. Often, an exporter is faced with the prospect of pricing products or services in currencies other than dollars. Importers must buy foreign currency to pay for products and services from risk-avoiding foreign suppliers that demand payment in their own currency. In the current era of floating exchange rates, there are risks of exposure whenever cash flows are denominated in foreign currencies.

Exposure: The effect on a firm or an individual of a change in exchange rates.

Forward or future exchange rate: The rate (agreed-on price) that is contracted today for the delivery of a currency at a specified date in the future.

Hedging (covering): Use of the forward foreign exchange market to avoid foreign currency risk.

Successfully managing currency risk is imperative. No longer can an importer or exporter speculate by doing nothing, then pass foreign exchange losses on to customers in the form of higher prices. The best decision for an import/export business is to hedge or cover in the forward market when there is risk of exposure. To do otherwise is to be a speculator, not a businessperson. Use the forward rate for the date on which payment is required. This avoids all foreign exchange risk, is simple, and is reasonably inexpensive. The cost of a forward contract is small—the difference between the cost of the spot market (today's cost of money) and the cost of the forward market. Major international banks and brokerage houses can help you arrange a foreign exchange forward contract. Spot and forward markets are quoted daily in the *Journal of Commerce* and the *Wall Street Journal*.

Agency/Distributor Agreements

Chapter 3 explored your relationship with overseas distributors. A manufacturer or import/export business will seldom agree to all a distributor's conditions. Most terms are negotiable, and a firm that is not internationally known may have to grant more demands than one that enjoys a more favorable position. The following tips may help you avoid risk in doing business with distributors:

1. *Put the agency agreement in writing.*   The rights and obligations resulting from a written agreement require no extraneous proof and are all that is necessary to record or prove the terms of a contract in most countries.

2. *Set forth the benefit to both parties.*   Well-balanced agreements should not place an excess of profitless burden on one of the parties. Performance of the agreement may be im-

possible to enforce against a party that has no apparent benefit from it.

3. *Give clear definition and meaning to all contract terms.*
Many English terms that are spelled similarly in other languages have entirely different meanings. Require that the
English version prevail when there is doubt. To avoid conflict,
use INCOTERMS (see Chapter 2).

4. *Expressly state the rights and obligations of the parties.*
The agency contract should contain a description of the rights
and duties of each party, the nature and duration of the relationship, and the reasons for which the agreement may be
terminated.

5. *Specify a jurisdictional clause.* If local laws allow it,
specify a jurisdiction to handle any legal disputes that may
arise. When possible, use arbitration. Basic arbitration rules
and principles are universal. Clauses in the contract should
identify the arbitration body or forum. Model arbitration
clauses may be obtained from the American Arbitration
Association, 140 West 51st Street, New York, NY 10020;
phone (212) 484-4000, fax: (212) 765-4874; or from the U.S.
Council for International Business, 1212 Avenue of the
Americas, New York, NY 10036; phone: (212) 354-4480; fax:
(212) 575-0327; Web: www.uscib.org.

PHYSICAL DISTRIBUTION (SHIPPING AND PACKING)

Physical distribution, often referred to as logistics, is the
means by which goods are moved from the manufacturer in
one country to the customer in another. This section discusses
two vital aspects for which the importer/exporter should have
an appreciation: shipping and packing.

Shipping

The import/export business can directly arrange its own land,
ocean, and air shipping of international cargo. Inland transportation is handled in much the same way as a domestic
transaction, except that certain export marks must be added
to the standard information shown on a domestic bill of lading. Also, the inland carrier must be instructed to notify the
ocean or air carrier.

Water Transportation

There are three types of ocean service: conference lines, independent lines, and tramp vessels. *Conference lines* are associations of ocean carriers that have joined together to establish common rates and shipping conditions. Conferences have two rates: the regular tariff and a lower, contract rate. You can obtain the lower rate if you sign a contract to use conference vessels exclusively during the contract period. *Independent lines* accept bookings from all shippers contingent on the availability of space, and are often less expensive than conference lines. An independent usually quotes rates about 10 percent lower than a conference carrier in situations where the two are in competition. *Tramp vessels* usually carry only bulk cargoes and do not follow an established schedule; rather, they operate on charters.

Regardless of the type of carrier you use, the carrier will issue a booking contract, which reserves space on a specific ship. Unless you cancel in advance, you may be required to pay even if your cargo doesn't make the sailing. You must be insured with ocean marine insurance. An insurance broker or your freight forwarder can arrange the coverage for you.

Marine insurance: Insurance that compensates the owner of goods transported overseas (by ship or air) in the event of loss that would not be legally recovered from the carrier.

Air Transportation

Air freight continues to grow as a popular and competitive method for shipping international cargoes. The growth has been facilitated by innovation in the cargo industry. Air carriers have excellent capacity, use very efficient loading and unloading equipment, and handle standardized containers. The advantages are (1) the speed of delivery, which gets perishable cargoes to the place of destination in prime condition, (2) the ability to respond to unpredictable product demands, and (3) the rapid movement of repair parts.

Air freight moves under a general cargo rate or a commodity rate. A special unit load rate is available when approved air shipping containers are used.

Land Transportation

Transportation over land has become less regulated and, therefore, more competitive and efficient. The largest import/export market (NAFTA) can be served directly by road and rail. Importers and exporters look primarily to land transportation to move their goods to the nearest port of departure or as one leg of a sea/land/air combination often referred to as *intermodalism*.

Intermodalism

The movement of international shipments via container using sequential transportation methods is the system of the future. The concept makes use of the most efficient and cost-effective methods to move goods.

Load Centers. The load center concept stimulated the sophistication of today's intermodal world. As ships grew to hold more containers, they became more expensive to operate. One way to reduce costs was to hold down the number of port calls. In order to fill the ships at fewer ports, the cargo had to be funneled into load centers. The simplification and organization of movements of cargo have become the "fair-haired child" of transportation specialists. An entirely new set of terms has developed around the concept.

Land Bridges. A *microbridge* routes a container to or from any port in a given country. A *minibridge* moves a container that originates or terminates in a domestic port other than the one where it enters or leaves the country. A *land bridge* off-loads a container at any domestic port, ships it cross-country by rail, then reloads it aboard a vessel for final movement to a foreign destination. The *RO/RO* (roll on/roll off) capability of containerized cargo is the foundation of intermodalism.

An example of intermodalism is a container of goods originating in Europe but destined for Japan. The cargo could be rolled off a European ship by truck then onto a train in Newport News, Virginia (RO/RO), where it would be joined by another container trucked in from Florida (minibridge), also destined for Japan. The containers would be moved by train across the United States (land bridge) and then rolled onto a ship in Long Beach, California, to complete the movement to Tokyo. Figure 5-9 illustrates the intermodal concept.

HOT TIP: If the details of transportation and all the "new-fangled" ideas are not for you, then see your nearest freight forwarder, as explained in Chapter 7.

Packaging and Marking for Overseas Shipment

Whether importing or exporting, you must ship your product thousands of miles in an undamaged condition. Your package must protect against breakage, dampness, careless storage, rough handling, thieves, and weather. Insurance might cover the loss, but lost time and the ill will of your overseas trading partner are a high price to pay. It has been estimated that as much as 70 percent of all cargo loss could be prevented by proper packaging and marking.

An excellent source on all aspects of packing and packaging is the *Modern Packaging Encyclopedia,* published annually by McGraw-Hill.

Breakage.   Ocean cargo is often loaded roughly onto ships by stevedores using forklifts, slings, nets, and conveyors. During the voyage, rough water and storms can cause loads to shift and sometimes crash into other containers. Even small packages sent through the mails can be squeezed, thrown, or crushed.

Assume the worst when packaging for overseas delivery. Use stronger and heavier materials than you do for domestic shipments. On the other hand, don't overpack—you pay by

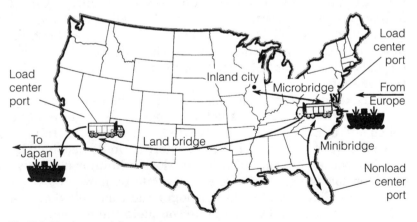

Fig. 5-9. The intermodal concept

weight and volume. For large ocean shipments, consider standardized containers that can be transferred from truck or rail car without opening.

Pilferage (Theft).   Use strapping and seals, and avoid trademarks or content descriptions.

Moisture and Weather.   The heat and humidity of the tropics as well as rainstorms and rough weather at sea can cause moisture to seep into the holds of a ship. From that moisture comes fungal growths, sweat, and rust. Waterproofing your shipment is essential for most ocean shipments. Consider plastic shrink-wrap or waterproof inner liners and coat any exposed metal parts with grease or other rust inhibitors.

Marking (Labeling).   Foreign customers have their needs, shippers have theirs, and terminal operators have theirs. Each will specify certain marks (port, customer identification code, package numbers, and number of packages) to appear on shipments. Other markings such as weight, dimensions, and regulations that facilitate clearing through customs can be specified. Figure 5-10 is a sample of markings.

Checklist for Shipping

- Write your customer's name and address or shipping code on the package.
- Use black waterproof ink for the stencils.
- Include port of exit and port of entry on your label.
- Don't forget package and case number.
- Include dimensions (inches and metric units).
- Mark exports "Made in U.S.A." to get through customs in most foreign countries.
- Express gross and net weight in pounds and/or kilograms.
- Don't forget cautionary markings such as "This side up" and "Handle with care" in *both* languages.
- Don't use brand names or advertising slogans on packages.
- Make sure that shipments of explosives or volatile liquids conform to local law and international agreements.

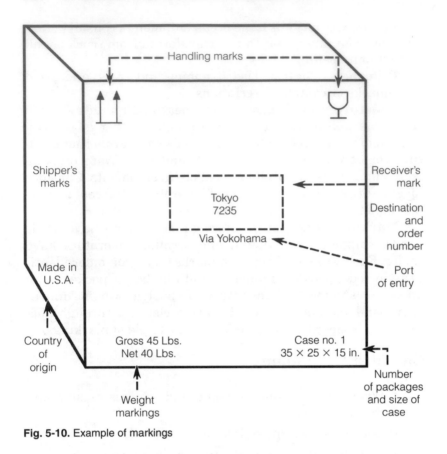

Fig. 5-10. Example of markings

DOCUMENTATION

"Attention to detail" is the byword when preparing documentation. The naive pass off paperwork as a by-product of the transaction, but the experienced trader knows that shipments can be detained on the pier for weeks because of inattention. As ex-Yankee catcher Yogi Berra once said, "It ain't over till it's over," and that's the way it is in international trade. The exporter doesn't get his or her money and the importer doesn't get his or her goods unless the paperwork is complete and accurate. Therefore, be attentive to detail.

Basically, documentation falls into two categories: *shipping* and *collection.*

Shipping Documents

Shipping documents permit an export cargo to be moved through customs, loaded aboard a carrier, and shipped to its foreign destination. These documents include:

- Export licenses
- Packing lists
- Bills of lading
- Export declarations

Collection Documents

Collection documents are those needed for submission to the importer (in the case of a draft) or to the importer's bank (in the case of an L/C) in order to receive payment. These documents include:

- Commercial invoices
- Consular invoices
- Certificates of origin
- Inspection certificates
- Bills of lading

When a negotiable bill of lading is endorsed by the shipper, you can use it as a sight draft or for L/C shipments. Other documents sometimes required for collection are manufacturing and insurance certificates and dock or warehouse receipts. Keep in mind that customs house brokers and freight forwarders are specialists in documentation as well as physical distribution.

> *Collection:* The procedure whereby a bank collects money for a seller against a draft drawn on a buyer abroad, usually through a correspondent bank.

The Documents

This section describes the various documents in detail and provides samples of each.

Certificate of Origin.   The *certificate of origin* certifies to the buyer the country in which the goods were produced. A recognized officer of the manufacturing corporation usually signs the certificate of origin of merchandise. Some countries require a separate certificate, sometimes countersigned by a chamber of commerce and possibly even visaed by the resident consul at the port of export. These statements are required to indicate preferential rates of import duties such as "most favored nation." Often, as little as 35 percent of a nation's materials and/or labor can qualify it for favorable duties. Some nations require special forms, while others accept a certification on the shipper's own letterhead. Figure 5-11 is an example of a certificate of origin.

Checklist for Certificates of Origin

- The letter or form should originate from the address of the manufacturer of the product.
- A responsible and knowledgeable person within the manufacturing company (an *officer* of the corporation) must sign the letter.
- The letter or form will not be accepted if it is from an outside sales office or distributor. It cannot be signed by a salesperson.
- The letter should clearly state where the product in question was manufactured.

Commercial Invoice.   The *commercial invoice* is a bill that conforms in all respects to the agreement between importer and exporter. It may have the exact terms of the pro forma invoice first offered in response to a quotation, or it may differ in those terms that were the result of final negotiations. In any case, there should be no surprises for the importer. The commercial invoice should (1) itemize the merchandise by price per unit and any charges paid by the buyer, and (2) specify the terms of payment and any marks or numbers on the packages. Figure 5-12 shows a commercial invoice.

Consular Invoice.   A *consular invoice* (not required by all countries) is obtained from the commercial attaché or through the consular office of that country in the port of export. When required, it is in addition to a commercial invoice and must conform in every respect to that document as well as

Our Company, Inc.

Home Town, Wherever

Date _____

Your Company

Home Town, Wherever

Point of Origin Declaration

For the purpose of positively identifying certain components as

being manufactured in _____ and therefore qualifying for
(Country)

entry under _____.
(Tariff code identification)

Component(s) description: _____

_____

Part number: _____

_____

The manufacturer _____ warrants and repre-

sents that the articles supplied to _____

_____
(Company)

and described above are articles of _____.
(Country)

The articles were manufactured at _____

(Address of location of plant)
_____

Authorized signature and date

_____

Title

Fig. 5-11. Certificate of origin

XYZ Foreign Co.
2A1 Moon River
Yokohama, Japan

Purchase Order:
Invoice Number:
00012
Invoice Date:

Sold To: Our Company, Inc.   Ship To: Our Company, Inc.
         Hometown, U.S.A.   Hometown, U.S.A.

Forwarding Agent:

Via: Country of Origin: Japan

Quantiy	Part No.	Description	Price Each	Total Price
10	A2Z	Machines	$100.00	$1,000.00

Inland freight, export packing & forwarding fees $ 100.00

  Free alongside (FAS) Yokohama $1,100.00
  Estimated ocean freight $ 100.00
  Estimated marine insurance $ 50.00

Packed in 10 crates, 100 cubic feet   _____
Gross weight 1000 lbs.
Net weight   900 lbs.
Payment terms: Confirmed irrevocable letter of credit confirmed by a
U.S. bank. Shipment to be made two (2) weeks after receipt of firm order.
Additional conditions of sale: XYZ Foreign Co. to provide:
Certificate of Origin
Consular Invoice
Certificate of Manufacture
Insurance Certificate
Inspection Certificate

Fig. 5-12. Commercial invoice

to the bill of lading and any insurance documents. Its purpose is to allow clearance of a shipment into the country that requires it. Figure 5-13 presents an example.

Commercial attaché: The commercial expert on the diplomatic staff of an embassy or large consulate in a foreign country.

Certificate of Manufacture. The *certificate of manufacture* certifies that the goods ordered by the importer have been produced and are ready for shipment. It may be used in cases when the manufacturer has moved ahead in production with only a down payment, thus allowing the importer to avoid allocation of the full amount too far in advance. Generally, invoices and packing lists are forwarded to the importer along with the certificate. Figure 5-14 shows a certificate of manufacture.

Export Licenses. Export licensing procedures are described in detail in Chapter 7 as one of the six topics unique to exporting. They apply to products that a government wants to control closely for either strategic or economic reasons. Certain weapons, technologies, and high-tech products are often set forth on a commodity control list (CCL). Export Administration regulations detail all licensing requirements for commodities under the jurisdiction of the Bureau of Export Administration (BXA), International Trade Administration. Once it has been determined that a license is needed, the "Application for Export License" must be prepared and submitted to the OEA. (See Figure 7-1 in Chapter 7.)

Insurance Certificates. *Insurance certificates* provide evidence of coverage and may be a stipulation of a contract, purchase order, or commercial invoice in order to receive payment. The certificate indicates the type and amount of coverage and identifies the merchandise in terms of packages and markings. You should make certain that the information on the certificate agrees exactly with invoices and bills of lading. A sample certificate is given in Figure 5-15.

Inspection Certificates. *Inspection certificates* protect the importer against fraud, error, or poor quality performance. The inspection is most often conducted by an independent firm, but it is sometimes performed by the shipper. An

FACTURA COMERCIAL

No. de la Factura............
(Commercial Invoice #)

Lugar (Ciudad)............
Place (City)

Fecha: Día........ Mes........ Año........
Date: Day   Mo.   Year

INTERVIENEN	Nombre de la Cía. o del Agente autorizado	DOMICILIO (Address)			
		Número (No.)	Calle (Street)	Ciudad (City)	Tel. (Phone)
Vendedor o remitente (Seller or shipper)					
Comprador (Buyer)					
Consig. a Destinatario (Consigned to)					
Agente o Gestor Agent-Broker					

Lugar y Puerto de Embarque Port of Loading	Lugar y Puerto de Destino Port of Unloading	Fecha de Embarque Date of Shipment	Nombre del Buque o Cía. Aérea Transp. Vessel/Airline Name

SEGURO (Insurance) : ....

CONDICIONES DE VENTA: FOB - CIF

Cantidad y Número de Bultos	PESO		Detalle descriptivo de la mercadería, indicando marca, lugar de fabricación, clase o tipo del producto, series, números, etc. y cualquier otra información adicional relacionada. (Denomination and details of each article: quantity, quality, measure, merch. origin, etc.)	Precio de la Mercadería (Merchandise Price)
	Kilogramos	Libras		

116

El agente autorizado que firma la presente, declara bajo juramento que todos los datos declarados en la presente factura, son exactos y verdaderos y que los precios pagados o por pagarse, son los reales y convenidos, que no existe convenio o arreglo alguno que permita la alteración o modificación de éstos, ni tampoco de su cantidad o calidad.

Firma del Agente, Vendedor o
Despachante autorizado. Fecha..

FACTURA COMERCIAL No.

Certifico que la firma que aparece en este

documento y dice ....

....

es auténtica y pertenece al funcionario des-

cripto.

Los Angeles, Calif. ....

Número de orden ....

No. del arancel ....

Der. percib. U$S. ....

Depositado en el Banco

Importe mercad. ...U$S	
Merch. Price	
Transporte ....U$S	
Otros (other) ....U$S	
SUB-TOTAL........U$S	
Tasa Consular, Fee U$S	
IMPORTE TOTAL U$S	

The.............

A recognized Chamber of Commerce under the laws of the State of California has examined the manufacturer's invoice or shipper affidavit concerning the origin of the merchandise and according to the best of its knowledge and belief, finds that the products named originated in the United States of North America.

Authorized Officer................................ Date..............

Espacio para Certificacion Consular

Fig. 5-13. Consular invoice

117

DATE:

REFERENCE: ACCOUNT NAME & ADDRESS
              PURCHASE ORDER NO. AND/OR
              CONTRACT NO.

BANK NAME AND LETTER OR CREDIT NO:

MERCHANDISE DESCRIPTION:

        CERTIFICATE OF RECENT MANUFACTURE

WE HEREBY CERTIFY THAT THE HEREIN DESCRIBED MER-
CHANDISE IS OF RECENT MANUFACTURE, IN THIS CASE
NOT OLDER THAN _____ YEAR(S) FROM THIS DATE.

NAME AND ADDRESS OF MANUFACTURER:

            BY: _____
                    (Original signature)

Fig. 5-14. Certificate of manufacture

affidavit that certifies the inspection is often required under terms of a letter of credit. For example, a Taiwanese firm wanted to import used diesel generators from the United States. That company insisted that an independent engineer certify satisfactory operation of each generator, at specifications, prior to shipment. Figure 5-16 shows a sample.

Packing Lists. A *packing list* accompanies the shipment and describes the cargo in detail. It includes the shipper, the consignee, measurements, serial numbers, weights, and any other data peculiar to the shipment. The completed list is placed in a waterproof bag or envelop and attached with the words "Packing list enclosed." Figure 5-17 shows a packing list.

Shipper's Export Declaration. In the United States the shipper's export declaration (SED) is prepared by the exporter or freight forwarder for the federal government. It is a

CERTIFICATE OF MARINE INSURANCE

No. 573951

🌐 International Cargo & Surety Insurance Company

*$ _____
(sum insured)

This is to Certify, That on the _____ day of _____ 19 ___ , this Company

insured under Policy No. _____ made for

for the sum of _____ Dollars,

on

(Amounts in excess of $1,000,000.00 cannot be insured under this Certificate)

Valued at sum insured. Shipped on board the S/S or M/S _____ and/or following steamer or steamers

at and from _____
(Initial Point of Shipment)

_____ , via _____
(Port of Shipment)

to _____
(Port of Places of Destination)

is payable to the order of _____ and it is understood and agreed, that in case of loss, the same

conveys the right of collecting any, such loss as fully as if the property were covered by a special policy direct to the holder hereof, and free from any liability for unpaid premiums. This certificate is issued subject to the standard International Cargo & Surety Insurance Company open cargo policy, which is incorporated herein by reference. To the extent that any terms or conditions in this certificate are inconsistent with the standard policy, the standard policy shall govern the rights and duties of all parties subject to the contract of insurance. Copies of the standard policy are available, upon request, from International Cargo & Surety Insurance Company, 1501 Woodfield Road, Schaumburg, Illinois 60173.

SPECIAL CONDITIONS

Merchandise shipped with an UNDER DECK bill of lading insured—
Against all risks of physical loss or damage from any external cause, irrespective of percentage, excepting those excluded by the F.C & S and S.R & C.C. Warranties, arising during transportation between the points of shipment and of destination named herein

SAMPLE

ON DECK SHIPMENTS (with an ON DECK bill of lading) and/or shipments of used merchandise insured:
Warranted free of particular average unless caused by the vessel being stranded, sunk, burnt, on fire or in collision but including risk of jettison and/or washing overboard, irrespective of percentage

MARKS & NUMBERS

SCHEDULE B CODE (commodity)	SCHEDULE C-E CODE (country)

TERMS AND CONDITIONS—SEE ALSO BACK HEREOF

WAREHOUSE TO WAREHOUSE This insurance attaches from the time the goods leave the Warehouse and/or Store at the place named in the Policy for the commencement of the transit and continues during the ordinary course of transit, including customary transhipment if any, until the goods are discharged overside from the overseas vessel at the final port. Thereafter the insurance continues whilst the goods are in transit and/or awaiting transit until delivered to final warehouse at the destination named in the Policy or until the expiry of 15 days (or 30 days if the destination to which the goods are insured is outside the limits of the port) whichever shall first occur. The time limits referred to above to be reckoned from midnight of the day on which the discharge overside of the goods hereby insured from the overseas vessel is completed. Held covered at a premium to be arranged in the event of transhipment, if any, other than as above and/or in the event of delay in excess of the above time limits arising from circumstances beyond the control of the Assured.

Fig. 5-15. Certificate of marine insurance

119

NOTE – IT IS NECESSARY FOR THE ASSURED TO GIVE PROMPT NOTICE TO THESE ASSURERS WHEN THEY BECOME AWARE OF AN EVENT FOR WHICH THEY ARE 'HELD COVERED' UNDER THIS POLICY AND THE RIGHT TO SUCH COVER IS DEPENDENT ON COMPLIANCE WITH THIS OBLIGATION.

PERILS CLAUSE: Touching the adventures and perils which this Company is contented to bear, and takes upon itself, they are of the seas, fires, assailing thieves, jettisons, barratry of the master and mariners, and all other like perils, losses and misfortunes (illicit or contraband trade excepted in all cases), that have or shall come to the hurt, detriment or damage of the said goods and merchandise, or any part thereof.

SHORE CLAUSE: Where this insurance by its terms covers while on docks, wharves or elsewhere on shore, and/or during land transportation, it shall include the risks of collision, derailment, overturning or other accident to the conveyance, fire, lightning, sprinkler leakage, cyclones, hurricanes, earthquakes, floods (meaning the rising of navigable waters), and/or collapse or subsidence of docks or wharves, even though the insurance be otherwise F.P.A.

BOTH TO BLAME CLAUSE: Where goods are shipped under a Bill of Lading containing the so-called "Both to Blame Collision" Clause, these Assurers agree as to all losses covered by this insurance, to indemnify the Assured for the Policy's proportion of any amount (not exceeding the amount insured) which the Assured may be legally bound to pay to the shipowners under such clause. In the event that such liability is asserted the Assured agree to notify these Assurers who shall have the right at their own cost and expense to defend the Assured against such claim.

MACHINERY CLAUSE: When the property insured under this Policy includes a machine consisting when complete for sale or use of several parts, then in case of loss or damage covered by this insurance to any part of such machine, these Assurers shall be liable only for the proportion of the insured value of the part lost or damaged, or at the Assured's option, for the cost and expense, including labor and forwarding charges, of replacing or repairing the lost or damaged part but in no event shall these Assurers be liable for more than the insured value of the complete machine.

LABELS CLAUSE: In case of damage affecting labels, capsules or wrappers, these Assurers, if liable therefor under the terms of this policy, shall not be liable for more than an amount sufficient to pay the cost of new labels, capsules or wrappers, and the cost of reconditioning the goods, but in no event shall these Assurers be liable for more than the insured value of the damaged merchandise.

DELAY CLAUSE: Warranted free of claim for loss of market or for loss, damage or deterioration arising from delay, whether caused by a peril insured against or otherwise, unless expressly assumed in writing hereon.

AMERICAN INSTITUTE CLAUSES: This insurance, in addition to the foregoing, is also subject to the following American Institute Cargo Clauses, current forms:

1. CRAFT, ETC.
2. DEVIATION
3. WAREHOUSING & FORWARDING CHARGES.
   PACKAGES TOTALLY LOST LOADING, ETC.
4. GENERAL AVERAGE
5. EXPLOSION
6. BILL OF LADING, ETC.
7. MARINE EXTENSION CLAUSES
8. INCHMAREE
9. CONSTRUCTIVE TOTAL LOSS
10. CARRIER
11. S.R & C.C. ENDORSEMENT
12. WAR RISK INSURANCE
13. SOUTH AMERICA 60 DAY CLAUSE

PARAMOUNT WARRANTIES: THE FOLLOWING WARRANTIES SHALL BE PARAMOUNT AND SHALL NOT BE MODIFIED OR SUPERSEDED BY ANY OTHER PROVISION INCLUDED HEREIN OR STAMPED OR ENDORSED HEREON UNLESS SUCH OTHER PROVISION REFERS SPECIFICALLY TO THE RISKS EXCLUDED BY THESE WARRANTIES AND EXPRESSLY ASSUMES THE SAID RISKS:

F.C. & S. (a) Notwithstanding anything herein contained to the contrary, this insurance is warranted free from capture, seizure, arrest, restraint, detainment, confiscation, preemption, requisition or nationalization, and the consequences thereof or any attempt thereat, whether in time of peace or war and whether lawful or otherwise; also warranted free, whether in time of peace or war, from all loss, damage or expense caused by any weapon of war employing atomic or nuclear fission and/or fusion or other reaction or radioactive force or matter or by any mine or torpedo, also warranted free from all consequences of hostilities or warlike operations (whether there be a declaration of war or not), but this warranty shall not exclude collision or contact with aircraft, rockets or similar missiles or with any fixed or floating object (other than a mine or torpedo), stranding, heavy weather, fire or explosion unless caused directly (and independently of the nature of the voyage or service which the vessel concerned or, in the case of a collision, any other vessel involved therein, is performing) by a hostile act by or against a belligerent power; and for the purposes of this warranty 'power' includes any authority maintaining naval, military or air forces in association with a power

Further warranted free from the consequences of civil war, revolution, rebellion, insurrection, or civil strife arising therefrom, or piracy

S. R & C. C. (b) Warranted free of loss or damage caused by or resulting from strikes, lockouts, labor disturbances, riots, civil commotions or the acts of any person or persons taking part in any such occurrence or disorder.

This Certificate is issued in Original and Duplicate, one of which being accomplished the other to stand null and void. To support a claim local Revenue Laws may require this certificate to be stamped.

Not transferable unless countersigned

Countersigned _____

ADDITIONAL CONDITIONS AND
INSTRUCTIONS TO CLAIMANTS ON REVERSE SIDE
OM18

President

Secretary

SAMPLE ORIGINAL

Fig. 5-15. Certificate of marine insurance (*Continued*)

```
DATE:

REFERENCE:    ACCOUNT NAME & ADDRESS
              PURCHASE ORDER NO. AND/OR
              CONTRACT NO.

BANK NAME AND LETTER OR CREDIT NO.

MERCHANDISE DESCRIPTION:


              INSPECTION CERTIFICATE

WE HEREBY CERTIFY THAT THE HEREIN DESCRIBED MER-
CHANDISE HAS BEEN INSPECTED AND FOUND TO BE OF
HIGHEST QUALITY AND IN GOOD WORKING ORDER.


              PORTER INTERNATIONAL INC.

              BY: _____
                       (Original signature)
```

Fig. 5-16. Inspection certificate

data collection document required on all exports in excess of $2500. The declaration is prepared to provide statistical information to the Bureau of the Census and to indicate the proper authorization to export. It is the basis for measuring the volume and types of exports leaving the country. The document requires complete information about the shipment, including description, value, net and gross weights, and relevant license information, thus closing the licensing information loop back to the BXA. Figure 5-18 shows a completed SED.

Bills of Lading. A *bill of lading* is a contract between the owner of the goods (exporter) and the carrier. It is both evidence that the shipment has been made and a receipt for the goods that have been shipped. Figure 5-19 is an air waybill, or bill of lading for an air carrier. Figure 5-20 is an ocean bill of lading. While e-commerce has not yet reached the bill of lading, it is getting close. Several shipping lines have automated

To: Your Company   Date: _____
    2A1 Moon River
    Yokohama, Japan

Gentlemen:

Under your order No. <u>123</u> the material listed below was shipped <u>1/1/18</u> via <u>Truck and vessel</u>

To <u>Yokohama</u>

Via:

Shipment Consists of: Marks:

___ Cases ___ Packages   Your Company, Ltd.
                          2A1 Moon River
___ Crates ___ Cartons   Yokohama, Japan

___ Bbls ___ Drums   Made in U.S.A.

___ Reels   #7235

Package Number	Weights (Lbs or Kilos)		Dimensions			Quality	Contents
	Gross	Legal Net	Ht.	Wth.	Lth.		
7235	45	40	35	25	15		Toys

Fig. 5-17. Packing list

U.S. DEPARTMENT OF COMMERCE — BUREAU OF THE CENSUS — INTERNATIONAL TRADE ADMINISTRATION

SHIPPER'S EXPORT DECLARATION

FORM **7525-V** (3-19-85)

OMB No. 0607-0018

1a. EXPORTER *(Name and address including ZIP code)*

ZIP CODE

2. DATE OF EXPORTATION

3. BILL OF LADING/AIR WAYBILL NO.

b. EXPORTER EIN NO.

c. PARTIES TO TRANSACTION

☐ Related ☐ Non-related

4a. ULTIMATE CONSIGNEE

b. INTERMEDIATE CONSIGNEE

NONE

5. FORWARDING AGENT

Porter International, Inc.
P.O. Box 41-A
San Ysidro, California 92173

6. POINT (STATE) OF ORIGIN OR FTZ NO.

7. COUNTRY OF ULTIMATE DESTINATION

MEXICO

8. LOADING PIER/TERMINAL

9. MODE OF TRANSPORT *(Specify)*

TRUCK

10. EXPORTING CARRIER

Truck Lic.:

11. PORT OF EXPORT

San Diego, (S.Y.), California

12. FOREIGN PORT OF UNLOADING

13. CONTAINERIZED *(Vessel only)*

☐ Yes ☐ No

Fig. 5-18. Shipper's export declaration

123

14. SCHEDULE B DESCRIPTION OF COMMODITIES. *(Use columns 15—19)*

MARKS, NOS., AND KINDS OF PKGS. (15)	D/F (16)	SCHEDULE B NUMBER (17)	QUANTITY — SCHEDULE B UNIT(S) (18)	SHIPPING WEIGHT *(Pounds)* (19)	VALUE (U.S. dollars, omit cents) *(Selling price or cost if not sold)* (20)

21. VALIDATED LICENSE NO./GENERAL LICENSE SYMBOL

22. ECCN *(When required)*

23. Duly authorized officer or employee — The exporter authorizes the forwarder named above to act as forwarding agent for export control and customs purposes.

24. I certify that all statements made and all information contained herein are true and correct and that I have read and understand the instructions for preparation of this document, set forth in the **"Correct Way to Fill Out the Shipper's Export Declaration."** I understand that civil and criminal penalties, including forfeiture and sale, may be imposed for making false or fraudulent statements herein, failing to provide the requested information or for violation of U.S. laws on exportation (13 U.S.C. Sec. 305; 22 U.S.C. Sec. 401; 18 U.S.C. Sec. 1001; 50 U.S.C. App. 2410).

Signature

Title   **EXPORT CLERK**

Date

Confidential - For use solely for official purposes authorized by the Secretary of Commerce (13 U.S.C. 301 (g)).

Export shipments are subject to inspection by U.S. Customs Service and/or Office of Export Enforcement.

25. AUTHENTICATION *(When required)*

THESE COMMODITIES LICENSED BY U.S. FOR ULTIMATE DESTINATION — MEXICO — DIVERSION CONTRARY TO U.S. LAW PROHIBITED.

Fig. 5-18. Shipper's export declaration *(Continued)*

124

Not negotiable

Air Waybill
(Air Consignment note)

Issued by

Shipper's Name and Address

Shipper's Account Number

Copies 1, 2 and 3 of this Air Waybill are originals and have the same validity

Consignee's Name and Address

It is agreed that the goods described herein are accepted in apparent good order and condition (except as noted) for carriage SUBJECT TO THE CONDITIONS OF CONTRACT ON THE REVERSE HEREOF. THE SHIPPER'S ATTENTION IS DRAWN TO THE NOTICE CONCERNING CARRIERS' LIMITATION OF LIABILITY. Shipper may increase such limitation of liability by declaring a higher value for carriage and paying a supplemental charge if required.

To expedite movement, shipment may be diverted to motor or other carrier unless shipper gives other instructions hereon.

Issuing Carrier's Agent Name and City

Accounting Information

SEE WARSAW NOTICE AND CONDITIONS OF CONTRACT ON REVERSE SIDE.

Agent's IATA Code

Account No.

Airport of Departure (Addr. of first Carrier) and requested Routing

By first Carrier	Routing and Destination	For Carrier Use only	Flight/Date				Currency	WT/VAL		Other		Declared Value for Carriage	Declared Value for Customs
								PPD	COLL	PPD	COLL		

Airport of Destination

Flight/Date

Amount of Insurance

INSURANCE - If Carrier offers insurance, and such insurance is requested in accordance with conditions on reverse hereof, indicate amount to be insured in figures in box marked amount of insurance.

Handling Information

These commodities licensed by the United States for ultimate destination . . . . Diversion contrary to United States law prohibited.

Fig. 5-19. Air waybill (bill of lading)

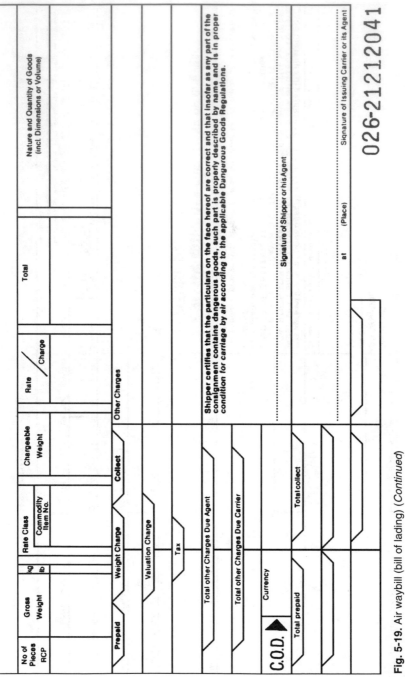

Fig. 5-19. Air waybill (bill of lading) (*Continued*)

Shipper	B/L No.
	M132-11156

Consignee

BILL OF LADING

COPY
NON - NEGOTIABLE

ALL TERMS, CONDITIONS AND EXCEPTIONS
AS PER ORIGINAL BILL OF LADING

"SUBJECT TO ALL THE TERMS AND
CONDITIONS OF THE APPLICABLE
TARIFF"

Notify party

Pre-carriage by	Place of receipt KAOHSIUNG CY

Ocean vessel	Voy. No.	Port of loading
AMERICA MARU	55227B	KAOHSIUNG

Port of discharge LOS ANGELES	Place of delivery TIJUANA CY	Final destination for the Merchant's reference

Container No. Seal No. Marks and Numbers	No. of Containers or pkgs.	Kind of packages; description of goods	Gross weight	Measurement
''SHIPPER'S LOAD & COUNT''				
	3 CONTAINERS (677 CTNS)		9,014 KGS	120.32 M3
TIJUANA B.C. MEXICO VIA LOS ANGELES CA. MODEL: H260 C/NO. 1-235 MADE IN TAIWAN REPUBLIC OF CHINA -DO-BUT H667 C/NO.1		MODEL: H260,H670,H667 MODEL: JOB NO. & CODE NO. MODEL: JOB NO. CODE NO.		
	MODEL: C/NO. 1-441 MADE IN TAIWAN REPUBLIC OF CHINA	MODEL: JOB NO. & CODE NO. ''FREIGHT COLLECT''		
	GSTU-8135538	C/S-480409 HS-41019 (192 C/T)		
	GSTU-8135939	C/S-480410 HS-41014 (192 C/T)		
	MOLU-2021646	C/S-480411 HS-41015 (293 C/T)		

*Total number of Containers or other packages or units received by the Carrier (in words)   THREE CONTAINERS ONLY

Freight and charges	Revenue tons	Rate	per	Prepaid	Collect
BOX RATE		(40'x3)	US $2,100.00/VAN (INCLUDING D.D.C.)		US$6,300.00
+ CY RECEIVING CHARGE			NT$900.00/VAN	NT$2,700.00	

Exchange rate	Prepaid at	Payable at TIJUANA	Place and date of issue TAIPEI TAIWAN JUL 30 1987
	Total prepaid in national currency	No.of original BI s/L THREE/3	

LADEN ON BOARD THE VESSEL   by

Date   JUL 30 1987   Signature

Fig. 5-20. Ocean bill of lading

part of the process, and there are indications that a system to replace paper bills of lading with electronic communications will soon be marketed.

The *straight bill of lading* is a nonnegotiable instrument that consigns the goods to an importer or other party named on the document. Once the transaction is consummated, the seller and/or the seller's bank loses title control because the goods will be delivered to anyone who can be identified as the consignee.

The *order bill of lading* is a negotiable instrument. Unlike the straight bill, it represents the title to the goods in transit and the original copy must be endorsed before it is presented to the bank for collection. In other words, the order bill can be used as collateral in financing—as documentation to discount or sell a draft. L/C transactions specify to whom the endorsement is to be made. Typically, order bills are made "in blank," or to the order of a third party such as a bank or broker. Air bills of lading are usually straight (i.e., nonnegotiable). Ocean bills of lading can be straight or "to order."

To verify shipping performance, the carrier indicates the condition of the goods upon acceptance. A bill of lading marked *clean on board* means that the carrier accepted the cargo and loaded it on board the vessel without exception.

A *foul bill* indicates an exception—the carrier noted some damage on the bill of lading. Discuss the problem with your carrier or freight forwarder to make sure you have an opportunity to exchange any damaged goods and obtain a "clean" bill.

The next chapter explains, from A to Z, how to set up and build your import/export company. It discusses how to decide on a name, how to go about obtaining start-up funds, and, most important, how to think through and write a business plan.

6

How to Set Up Your Own Import/Export Business

"HOW DO I START MY OWN IMPORT/EXPORT BUSINESS?"

That question is universal. The language might be different, but in any country in the world you will hear the same words.

The answer depends on these questions: Have you done your homework? What is your product? Do you have contacts? Who will buy your product? Is it profitable? Do you have a marketing plan?

By incorporating what you've learned about the fundamentals of import/export in Chapters 2 through 5 with the methods explained in this chapter, you should be ready to start your own import/export business.

The first part of this chapter describes the mechanics of start-up. The second part shows you how to develop a business plan so that you can raise capital and grow.

THE MECHANICS OF START-UP

The process for starting a small business is the same in any country in the world. You need capital, know-how, and management skills, but you do not need a fancy college degree. Any good manager can operate a business.

Start-Up Capital

In the initial stages of starting your own import/export business, the funds needed to support expenses will most likely come from your own pocket. It is possible to begin an import/export business with as little as $1000 a year.

Sources of Financial Capital

When your personal finances will not sustain the expenses of start-up until you reach breakeven and begin to show a profit, you must look for outside financial assistance. Unfortunately, banks are seldom the source of start-up capital. Why? Banks do not take risks. They generally expect a track record and collateral. Catch-22? Where, then, can you go for financing? Most often, the best sources are relatives and/or friends—people who know you and believe in you. Even they may want a description of your intended business, so from the beginning you should develop a written business plan. You may want to skip to the second part of this chapter immediately to learn how to write that plan. You can return to this section when you complete your business plan.

Business Name/Logo

Think of a name for your business. The company's name should reflect what your business does and be easily advertised by letter, by fax, or over the Internet. For example, you can easily visualize the nature of a business called "Southeast U.S.A. Furniture Import." It gives a more accurate picture of that company than would "Kim Yee and Son." If the name you choose does not contain the owner's surname, you will probably need to file a request to use a fictitious name or DBA (doing business as). If the name of your business includes your last name, you may not be required to file for approval. The cost of registering your fictitious name is about $20 in most countries. There is also a requirement to publish that name in a newspaper for several days. That cost is usually $30 to $40.

The Business Organization

Next, decide how your business will be organized. The three common legal forms are sole proprietorship, partnership, or corporation. Most start-up import/export businesses begin as proprietorships or partnerships. They find little need to take on the extra paperwork and reporting requirements of a corporation in the beginning. Select the appropriate form according to the intent, complexity, tax implications, and liability requirements of the business. If in doubt, consult a lawyer. Partnership agreements and incorporation papers can be expensive, ranging from a few hundred dollars to several thousand.

Business License

Some countries require licenses to do international trade. In the United States, however, there is no regulatory body that requires you to show special qualifications in order to hold yourself out as an importer or exporter. However, as with any other business, you will have to meet local and state business licensing requirements. It is possible that the foreign country you are doing business in will require a license as well (see Chapter 7).

Seller's Permit

Most nations and states have a sales tax. In order to ensure collection, these jurisdictions often require a seller's permit. Permits are usually state controlled, so as you begin your own import/export business you should investigate your local laws.

Financial Records

Open a separate bank account in the name of your business. Keep accurate records, and pass all business income and expenses through your business account. Do not pay personal expenses from this account or otherwise mix personal income and expenses with business income and expenses. You may list personal "capital contributions" and "capital withdrawals," but keep these infrequent and in reasonably large sums—don't take out money in dribbles and drops.

Accounting

From the beginning, learn to keep a simple set of books to feed into your Internal Revenue Service (IRS) forms at tax time. Keep a careful record (receipts) of all business expenses, and invoice all work on your letterhead paper. At a minimum, you will need a general ledger organized into four sections: expenses, income, receivables (sales invoiced), and payables (bills received). For example, your expenses, like the cost of your trip to Hong Kong or Paris, should be listed chronologically, by month, down the left margin of the expense section. Across the page, the categories should correspond to the tax categories. Check current IRS publications.

What kinds of expenses should you expect in your own import/export business? Here are the most common.

- Stationery and business cards
- Telephone, answering machine, adding machine, copier, typewriter, facsimile, telex machine
- Rent, utilities, office furniture
- Inventory
- Business checking account
- Salaries and other staff expenses
- Travel

Table 6-1 shows an example of the categories listed in the expense section of your general ledger. The other sections of your ledger should be set up similarly.

The Office

You can set up an office in your home or elsewhere. The location and outfitting will be determined by the volume and complexity of your firm. In the beginning, you may do business by letter and telex, and hire part-time employees occasionally. However, as your import/export business grows, you may need

Table 6-1. Categories of Expenses

Date	Utilities	Telephone/ Fax	Travel Air	Travel Auto	Office Expense
January					
February					
March					

warehouse space for inventory and a larger office for a growing staff.

Employees

As your office and trading staff grows, the complexity of paperwork and record keeping will also grow. Prior to hiring anyone, you must obtain an employer ID number from the IRS, and consider worker's compensation and benefits insurance.

Business Insurance

Other business insurance that you should consider on a case-by-case basis are liability, disability, an FCIA umbrella policy, and a customs bond.

Support Team

Early in the establishment of your import/export business, you should develop a relationship with your international support team. After a brief period of shopping around, settle on a long-term relationship with an international banker, a freight forwarder, a customs house broker, an international accountant, and an international attorney. Also, consider contacting the Small Business Administration (SBA) if you run into problems. Members of the SBA's Service Corps of Retired Executives (SCORE) are often available to provide free advice.

THE 10 COMMANDMENTS OF STARTING AN OVERSEAS BUSINESS

1. Limit the primary participants to people who not only can agree and contribute directly but also are experienced in some form of international business.
2. Define your import/export market in terms of what is to be bought, precisely by whom, and why.
3. Concentrate all available resources on two or three products or objectives within a given time period.
4. Obtain the best information through your own industry.
5. Write down your business plan and work from it.
6. "Walk on two legs." Pick a good freight forwarder or customs house broker to walk alongside your banker.

7. Translate your literature into the language of each country in which you will do business.

8. Use the services of the Departments of Commerce and Treasury.

9. Limit the effects of your inevitable mistakes by starting slowly.

10. Communicate frequently and well with your international contacts, and visit the overseas markets and manufacturers.

THE BUSINESS PLAN

In the beginning you may have only a notion of your plan tucked away in your head. As the concept of your business grows, it will be necessary to formalize your plan and stick to it. Putting out brushfires in order to maintain marginal survival is hardly a wise use of your time.

The underlying concept of a business plan is to write out your thoughts. By raising, then systematically answering, basic operational questions, you force self-criticism. Once the plan is on paper, others can read it and you can invite their opinions. Don't let your ego get in your way. Ask for constructive criticism from the most experienced people you can find. Often it is better to seek out strangers, because friends and relatives tend to shield you from hurt. Explain to your readers that you want to hear both the bad news and the good news. The more eyes that see the plan, the more likely you will (1) identify hazards while you still can act or avoid them, and (2) spot opportunities while you can easily act to maximize them.

"The plan is nothing; planning is everything."
—President (General) Dwight Eisenhower

A business plan can be as brief as 10 pages and as long as 50. The average plan runs about 20 pages. Table 6-2 suggests an outline format for your business plan.

Table 6-2. Business Plan Outline

Cover Sheet: Name, principals, address, etc.

International Costumes, Inc.
Business Plan
Fiscal Year 20XX

Statement of Purpose:

Table of Contents: (corresponds to each exhibit)

   A. Executive summary
   B. Description of the business
   C. Product-line plan
   D. Sales and marketing plan
   E. Operations plan
   F. Organization plan
   G. Financial plan
   H. Supporting documents
   I. Summary

Exhibits:
Exhibit A   Executive Summary
   1. Written last, summarizes in global terms the entire plan;
      succinct expression of long- and short-term goals

Exhibit B   Description of the Business
   1. Long- and short-term goals
      Financial
      Nonfinancial

   2. Strategies
      Product line
      Sales and marketing
      Product development
      Operations
      Organizational
      Financial

   3. Location
      Reasons

Exhibit C   Product-Line Plan
   1. Product line and products
      Description

(*Continued*)

Price
Costs
Historical volume
Future expectations

2. Competition's product line and product position
Pricing
Advertising and promotion

Exhibit D   Sales and Marketing Plan
1. Person(s) responsible for generating product line and product sales
2. Competition's approach to sales and marketing

Exhibit E   Operations Plan
1. Production and operations function
Production scheduling
Inventory (product line and product)

2. Capital expenditures (if required)

Exhibit F   Organization Plan
1. Organization's structure
Organization chart
Résumés of key personnel
Managerial style

Exhibit G   Financial Plan
1. Summary of operating and financial schedules
2. Schedules *
Capital equipment
Balance sheet
Cash flow (breakeven analysis)
Income projections
Pro forma cash flow
Historical financial reports for existing business
(Balance sheets for past three years; income statements for past three years; tax returns)

Exhibit H   Supporting Documents
1. Personal résumés
2. Cost of living budget
3. Letters of reference
4. Copies of leases
5. Anything else of relevance to the plan
Exhibit I   Summary

*See Figures 6-1 to 6-4.

How to Begin the Business Plan

Stop everything and begin writing. The first draft of your plan will contain about 80 percent of the final version and can be finished in less than two days. One measure of the success of the process is the amount of pain it causes you. By looking at your business as an onlooker would, you may find that some of your vision—a pet project, for instance—may have to be abandoned. The process involves eight major steps:

1. Define long-term objectives.
2. State short term goals.
3. Set marketing strategies.
4. Analyze available resources (personnel, material, etc.).
5. Assemble financial data.
6. Review for realism.
7. Rewrite.
8. Implement.

Defining Long-Term Objectives.   Start with the objectives of your import/export business. Think ahead. What do you want the business to be like in 3 years? 5 years? 20 years? How big a business do you want?

Stating Short-Term Goals.   Define your import/export business in terms of sales volume and assets. Be precise; state goals in measurable units of time and dollars.

Setting Marketing Strategies.   If you have done the homework tasks outlined in Chapter 2 and applied the marketing concepts offered in Chapter 3, this part of the business plan should be simple.

If not, go back and review the marketing section of Chapter 3, because nothing will happen with your business until you make a sale. If sales aren't made, projections and other plans fall apart. Profitable sales support the business, so be prepared to spend 75 percent of your planning time on marketing efforts. Ultimately, the best marketing information comes through your own industry, here or overseas. Talk to those with experience. Talk to manufacturers as well as other importers and exporters. Don't overlook the data that can be found in libraries and over the Internet.

Make your market plan precise. Describe your competitive advantage. Outline your geographical and product-line priorities. Write down your sales goals. List your alternatives for market penetration. Will you sell direct or through agents? What is your advertising budget? Travel in an import/export business is a must. What is your travel budget? How much will it cost to expand your markets? What will be the cost of communications? Don't minimize your cost projections. It is not unusual to underestimate expenses. They are often three times more than you think.

Analyzing Available Resources.   Now for the pain. You must ask yourself whether you have the resources to make the plan work. Take a management inventory. Do you have the skills to market your products? Do you need administrative or accounting skills? Will you need warehouse space? Will you need translators? How much cash will you need?

Assembling Financial Data.   After all the dreaming and reality testing of the first four steps, you must now express the plan in terms of cash flow, profit and loss projections, and balance sheets. Figure 6-1 (pages 140–141) is a pro forma sales projection, Figure 6-2 (pages 142–143) is a pro forma income (profit/loss) statement, Figure 6-3 (pages 144–145) is a pro forma balance sheet, and Figure 6-4 (pages 146–147) is a pro forma cash flow statement. (All are three-year summaries, with detail by month for the first year and detail by quarter for the second and third years.) *Pro forma* here means estimating information in advance in a prescribed form.

The cash flow and the profit and loss projections serve double duty. They quantify the sales and operating goals, including use of personnel and other resources expressed in dollars and time. As a guide to the future, they can serve as control documents and as a measure of progress toward goals. The balance sheet shows what your business owns, what it owes, and how those assets and liabilities are distributed.

Reviewing for Realism.   Your plan must not set contradictory goals. You cannot expand the introduction of goose liver from China at the same time that you are getting out of animal products and into irrigation machinery. Look at your plan and ask, "Does this make good business sense?"

Rewriting.   Now that the first draft is complete, let at least 10 experienced people look at it. Ask them to be critical and to tell you the truth. Let them know up front that you have a lot of ego in this project, but that because you want to be a success, you need their criticism, no matter how much it hurts.

Implementation.   Your business plan provides a road map, but the acid test is whether it will work. At times you may have to detour to get where you are going, so don't put the map on the shelf and forget about it. Use it as an operating document. Review it and revise it as experience dictates.

Now you're ready to go. You've done your homework and written your business plan. If you've gotten this far, you have the style and determination to make it work.

By now, you have written your first letter and made your first contact. As an importer you've asked for literature and samples, or as an exporter you've sent them. You want early orders, and if you have done your homework they should start rolling in, but be patient. Everything takes a little longer in international business.

As you have learned in the previous four chapters, most of the fundamentals of international trade are common to both importing and exporting, but some major elements are specific to one or the other. Part 2 of the book explains those things that are unique to exporting or to importing, such as government support systems, information systems, tax considerations, tariffs, and private sector support organizations.

Pro Forma Sales (Shipments) Projections
Fiscal Year 20xx

Product Line(s) / Product(s)	Jan	Feb	March	April	May	June	July	Aug	Sept	Oct	Nov	Dec	Year
A. Product Line A													
1. Product 1													
Shipments (Units)													
× Ave. Price/Unit													
Gross Sales	$	$	$	$	$	$	$	$	$	$	$	$	$
2. Product 2													
3. Product 3													
— — —													
n. Product N													
Product Line A— Gross Sales	$	$	$	$	$	$	$	$	$	$	$	$	$
B. Product Line B													

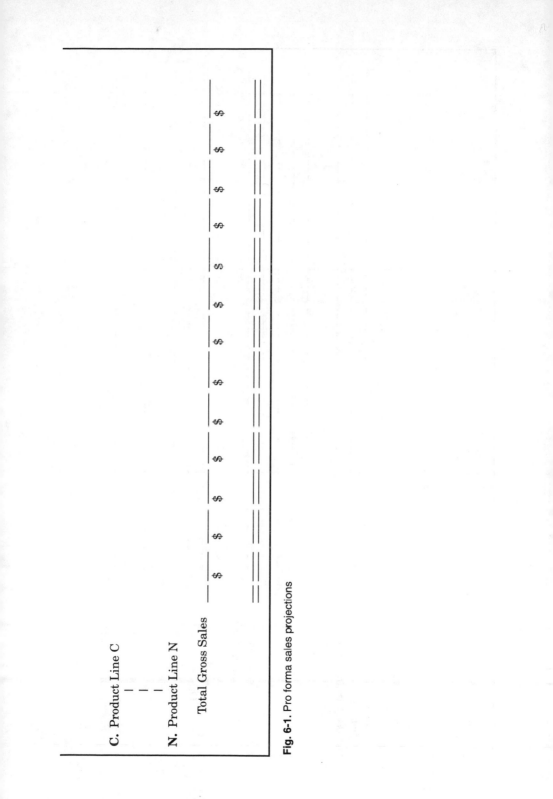

Fig. 6-1. Pro forma sales projections

Pro Forma Income Statement
Fiscal Year 20xx

	Jan	Feb	March	April	May	June	July	Aug	Sept	Oct	Nov	Dec	Year
Gross Sales													
less: Discounts, allowances, etc.	—	—	—	—	—	—	—	—	—	—	—	—	—
Net Sales	—	—	—	—	—	—	—	—	—	—	—	—	—
less: Variable costs	—	—	—	—	—	—	—	—	—	—	—	—	—
Manufacturing:													
Material	—	—	—	—	—	—	—	—	—	—	—	—	—
Labor	—	—	—	—	—	—	—	—	—	—	—	—	—
Variable overhead	—	—	—	—	—	—	—	—	—	—	—	—	—
Other	—	—	—	—	—	—	—	—	—	—	—	—	—
Variable costs (manufacturing)	—	—	—	—	—	—	—	—	—	—	—	—	—
Operating:													
Commissions	—	—	—	—	—	—	—	—	—	—	—	—	—
Other	—	—	—	—	—	—	—	—	—	—	—	—	—
Variable costs (operating)	—	—	—	—	—	—	—	—	—	—	—	—	—
Variable costs (total)	—	—	—	—	—	—	—	—	—	—	—	—	—
Contribution													
Percent of net sales	(%)												

less: Fixed costs
Manufacturing
Engineering
Selling
General and
Administrative
Financial
Fixed costs (total)
Profit before taxes
less: Taxes
Net income

Fig. 6-2. Pro forma income (profit/loss) statement

Pro Forma Balance Sheet
Fiscal Year 20xx

A. *Assets Employed*

1. *Current Assets*

	Actual Dec	Jan	Feb	March	April	May	June	July	Aug	Sept	Oct	Nov	Dec
Cash	—	—	—	—	—	—	—	—	—	—	—	—	—
Accounts receivable (net)	—	—	—	—	—	—	—	—	—	—	—	—	—
Inventory	—	—	—	—	—	—	—	—	—	—	—	—	—
Prepaids	—	—	—	—	—	—	—	—	—	—	—	—	—
Other	—	—	—	—	—	—	—	—	—	—	—	—	—
Subtotal	—	—	—	—	—	—	—	—	—	—	—	—	—

2. *Current Liabilities*
    (excluding debt)

	Actual Dec	Jan	Feb	March	April	May	June	July	Aug	Sept	Oct	Nov	Dec
Accounts payable	—	—	—	—	—	—	—	—	—	—	—	—	—
Accrued liabilities	—	—	—	—	—	—	—	—	—	—	—	—	—
Taxes payable	—	—	—	—	—	—	—	—	—	—	—	—	—
Other	—	—	—	—	—	—	—	—	—	—	—	—	—
Subtotal	—	—	—	—	—	—	—	—	—	—	—	—	—
Working capital (1–2)	—	—	—	—	—	—	—	—	—	—	—	—	—

3. *Property, Plant and*
    Equipment

	Actual Dec	Jan	Feb	March	April	May	June	July	Aug	Sept	Oct	Nov	Dec
Land	—	—	—	—	—	—	—	—	—	—	—	—	—
Building	—	—	—	—	—	—	—	—	—	—	—	—	—

Equipment
Less: Accumulated
            depreciation

        Subtotal

4. *Other Assets*
Investments
Other

        Subtotal

Assets Employed

B. *Capital Structure*
    1. *Debt*

        Short-term Notes
        Long-term (current
            portion)
        Long-term Debt
        Other

        Subtotal

    2. *Deferred Taxes*

    3. *Shareholders Equity*
        Paid-in Capital
        Retained Earnings

        Subtotal

    Capital Structure

Fig. 6-3. Pro forma balance sheet

145

Pro Forma Cash Flow Statement (Operational)
Fiscal Year 20xx

	Jan	Feb	March	April	May	June	July	Aug	Sept	Oct	Nov	Dec	Year
Cash Receipts													
Collection of accounts receivable													
Sale of assets													
Borrowings													
Equity financing													
Other													
Cash receipts													
Cash Expenditures													
Material													
Freight													
Wages and salaries													
Commissions													
Fringe benefits													
Manufacturing expenses													
Selling expenses													
General and administrative expenses													
Financial expenses													
Subtotal													

Capital expenditures	—	—	—	—	—	—	—
Debt repayment	—	—	—	—	—	—	—
Dividends	—	—	—	—	—	—	—
Other	—	—	—	—	—	—	—
Cash expenditures	—	—	—	—	—	—	—
Cash flows	—	—	—	—	—	—	—
Cumulative cash flows	—	—	—	—	—	—	—

Fig. 6-4. Pro forma cash flow statement

2
The Differences

7

Exporting from the United States

PART 1 OF THIS BOOK EXPLAINED THE COMMONALITIES OF IMPORT/ export; this part describes the differences—those aspects of the international trade transaction that are not the same. For example, government controls (except for import quotas) apply to exporting, whereas tariffs are a characteristic of importing. What is important to remember is that exporting and importing are mirror-image functions, and to be successful you must understand your trading partner's problems.

This chapter explores the basics of the transaction that are unique to exporting from the United States. Among other things, you will learn which public and private organizations support the export function and where to go for export information. The topics specific to export are:

- Government export counseling
- Information sources
- Freight forwarding
- Export controls
- "Made in U.S.A."
- Tax incentives for exporting
- Relief from unfair import practices

GOVERNMENT EXPORT COUNSELING

All governments promote exporting because it brings needed foreign exchange and stimulates job expansion. Therefore, every nation and many state and provincial governments provide a wide range of export counseling and assistance programs.

International Trade Administration (ITA)

Most countries have an organization similar to the U.S. International Trade Administration (ITA), which is a division of the U.S. Department of Commerce. Its importance to the nation is emphasized by the fact that it gets a dominant share of that department's budget. The ITA is organized basically into three arms: overseas, headquarters, and domestic (covering the territorial boundaries of the United States).

Overseas Offices.   The *overseas* function of the ITA is the Foreign Commercial Service (FCS). The FCS maintains offices in more than 100 major foreign cities in the 70 countries that are principal trading partners with the United States. To help U.S. firms compete, these offices provide a full range of business services, trade leads, and financial counseling. Services include political and credit risk analysis, advice on market entry strategy, sources of financing, and major project identification, tracking, and assistance. Commercial Service officers identify and evaluate importers, buyers, agents, distributors, and joint-venture partners. Through their network of Commercial Service Centers they can introduce you to local business and government leaders, and assist in trade disputes. These services are available to U.S. companies that either produce or have the export rights to a product or service that is 51 percent or more U.S. content. For information, call or write your local Export Assistance Center (see below) within the U.S. Department of Commerce or check the list of offices found at www.ita.doc.gov.

The senior Commercial Service officer in each country is a principal adviser to the U.S. Ambassador. Commercial Service staff members gather data on specific export opportunities, country trends affecting trade and investment, and prospects for specific industries. They also monitor and analyze local laws and practices that affect business conditions.

Headquarters Offices (Washington, D.C.). At its headquarters in Washington, D.C., the International Trade Administration of the U.S. Department of Commerce has approximately 165 country and regional desk officers whose job is to be experts in assigned countries, from Afghanistan through Zimbabwe. These desk officers are specialists who can look at the needs of an individual firm wishing to sell in a particular country in the full context of that country's economy, trade policies, and political situation. They provide specific information about the country's laws and products to American business personnel.

Desk officers are organized into two groups: market access and commercial policy, and trade information/trade development. Trade officers are industry specialists who work with manufacturing and service industry associations and firms to identify trade opportunities and obstacles by product or service, industry sector, and market.

Exporters who are planning to visit Washington and would like to schedule appointments with either desk officers or program specialists within the Commerce Department (and/or other agencies involved in international marketing) should contact the nearest Export Assistance Center or call (800) USA-TRADE.

Domestic Offices.   Domestically the ITA offers a broad range of trade-related information as well as one-on-one counseling by experienced trade specialists located in more than 50 Export Assistance Centers (EACs) in industrial and commercial centers throughout the United States. These are customer-focused offices designed to streamline export marketing and trade finance assistance by integrating in a single location the counselors and services of the Commercial Service, EXIMBank, the Small Business Administration, and in some cities the U.S. Agency for International Development. To contact an EAC, call (800) USA-TRADE or check the local Commercial Service addresses listed at www.ita.doc.gov.

The EACs can help exporters and other prospective businesses with:

- Market research
- Trade and investment opportunities abroad
- Foreign markets for U.S. products and services

- Grant opportunities
- Insurance
- Tax advantages of exporting
- International trade exhibitions
- Export documentation requirements
- Economic facts on foreign countries
- Export licensing requirements
- Promotion of products and services
- Export prospects

District Export Councils

District Export Councils (DECs) are organizations of leaders from the local business community, appointed by successive Secretaries of Commerce, whose knowledge of international business provides a source of professional advice for local firms.

In order to help small businesses succeed in the world economy, DECs volunteer their time to sponsor and participate in numerous trade promotion activities, as well as to supply specialized expertise and mentoring programs to small and medium-size businesses that are interested in exporting. They create seminars on export basics and trade finance, host international buyer delegations, design breakthrough guides to help firms export, and put exporters on the Internet to help build export assistance partnerships to strengthen the support given to local businesses in exporting.

Export Assistance Centers work closely with these experienced regional and international business leaders through 55 DECs nationwide. The 1700 volunteer DEC members are available to:

- Counsel prospective exporters on the how-to's of international trade.
- Cosponsor seminars and workshops with Export Assistance Centers.
- Address business groups on international business opportunities.

- Promote awareness of the trade assistance programs of the Department of Commerce.

Small Business Development Centers (SBDCs)

SBDCs provide a full range of export assistance services to small businesses, particularly those new to export, and offer counseling, training, and managerial and trade finance assistance. Contact (800) U-ASK-SBA, (202) 606-4000, or www.sba.gov.

SCORE

The Service Corps of Retired Executives (SCORE), usually colocated with a local SBA office, provides one-on-one counseling and training seminars. For the office nearest you, call (800) 634-0245 or (202) 205-6762, fax (202) 205-7636, or visit www.score.org.

Office of Export Trading Company Affairs

The Office of Export Trading Company Affairs (OETCA), a part of the ITA's Trade Development Group, was established to promote the team concept of exporting through the formation and use of export trading companies (ETCs), export management companies (EMCs), and, in general, the intermediary industry. OETCA administers the Export Trade Certificate of Review Program, which permits an antitrust "insurance policy" under the Export Trading Company Act (ETCA). This law, passed on October 8, 1982, allows bankers' banks and holding companies to invest in ETCs, reduces the restrictions on export financing provided by financial institutions, and modifies the application of the antitrust laws to certain export trade.

Export joint ventures offer firms the opportunity to reduce economies of scale and spread the risks. Specific areas in which gains can be obtained are:

- Market research
- Market development
- Overseas bidding

- Nontariff barriers
- Transportation and shipping
- Joint bidding and selling arrangements
- Pricing policies
- Service and promotional activities

For information, call (202) 482-5131, fax (202) 482-1790, or go to www.ita.doc.gov/oetca/teamup.htm.

INFORMATION SOURCES

Information needed for exporting is easier to obtain than for domestic sales. Why? Because most governments subsidize the gathering and analysis of international trade data. A wealth of information, both on paper and computerized, exists to promote exporting. More information is available than the user could digest in a lifetime, and the U.S. Department of Commerce has made it easy to acquire. For example, the Trade Opportunities Program (TOP) and the Export Contact List Service files are available in both printed form and up-to-the-minute computer-resident databases.

Export Assistance

Your nearest Export Assistance Center offers the following information services to U.S. exporters.

Trade Information Center (TIC). The TIC is a one-stop, comprehensive resource for information on all government export assistance programs. The center's staff advises exporters on how to locate and use government programs, guides exporters through the export process, supplies general market information, and provides basic export counseling. Call (800) USA-TRADE or (202) 482-0543, fax (202) 482-4473, or go to www.tradeinfo.doc.gov. A special line is available for those using a TDD machine: (800) TDD-TRADE. Ask for a free copy of the excellent pamphlet *Export Programs: A Business Directory of U.S. Government Services.*

National Trade Data Bank (NTDB). The NTDB is a one-stop source for export promotion and international trade data collected by 17 U.S. government agencies. Updated each month and released on two CD-ROMs (for Windows-based

PCs), the NTDB provides access to over 100,000 trade-related documents. Contact (800) STAT-USA or www.stat-usa.gov or tradeport.org.

The Economic Bulletin Board (EBB). The EBB, a PC-based electronic bulletin board, is an on-line source for trade leads as well as for the latest statistical releases from the Bureau of the Census, the Bureau of Economic Analysis, the Bureau of Labor Statistics, the Federal Reserve Board, and other federal agencies. Contact (800) STAT-USA or (202) 482-3870 or 482-1986. You may use your fax machine to receive trade leads and the latest trade and economic information from the federal government. For access, dial (900) RUN-A-FAX. You can also call the EBB/FAX help line at (202) 482-1986 or fax (202) 482-2164.

Industry Sector Analysis (ISA). ISA market research reports are produced on location in leading overseas markets. They cover market size and outlook, characteristics, and competitive and end-user analyses for a selected industry sector in a particular country. Selected analyses are available on the National Trade Data Bank (NTDB).

International Market Insights (IMI). Market insights are short profiles of specific foreign market condition or opportunities prepared in overseas markets and at multilateral development banks. These nonformatted reports include information and updates on dynamic sectors of a particular country and could profile new major projects or trade events. These are also available on the NTDB.

Export Prospects

Most governments have programs to help exporters make cross-border contacts. The U.S. government is no exception. As a matter of fact, it has a full range of programs you should take advantage of.

Agent Distributor Service (ADS). ADS performs a custom overseas "search" for interested and qualified foreign representatives on behalf of a U.S. client. Foreign Commercial Service staff conduct the search and prepare a report identifying up to six foreign prospects that have personally examined the U.S. firm's product literature and have expressed interest in representing the firm. ADS charges a fee per market or specific area. Contact your local EAC or call (800) USA-TRADE or go to www.ita.doc.gov/uses/useshelp.html.

Trade Opportunities Program (TOP). Commercial specialists around the world collect TOP leads at trade shows, through conversation, and through market research. Individual sales lead messages are then sent directly to subscribers and the EACs nationwide. They can be sent via computer, facsimile, or printed hard copy. Each message contains detailed information regarding a current foreign trade lead, typically including the specifications, quantities, end use, and delivery and bid deadlines for the product or service desired by the foreign customer. A fee is required to set up the subscriber's interest file and for each block of 50 leads up to five blocks. Call (800) STAT-USA or (202) 482-1986 or go to www.stat-usa.gov.

> **HOT TIP:** The Trade Opportunities Program matches product interests of foreign buyers with those of U.S. subscribers.

International Company Profile (ICP). Information provided in an ICP includes type of organization, year established, size, general reputation, territory covered, sales, product lines, principal owners, financial information, and trade references, with recommendations from on-site commercial officers as to the firm's suitability as a trading partner.

Commercial Service International Contacts (CSIC). CSIC provides the name and contact information for directories of importers, agents, trade associations, government agencies, and other contacts on a country-by-country basis. It is available on the NTDB.

Overseas Promotion

The ITA, Department of State offices within U.S. embassies, and consulates worldwide collaborate to assist in the promotion of your products and services.

Commercial News USA. This export marketing magazine promotes U.S. products and services worldwide. It is disseminated in print to screened agents, distributors, buyers, and end users and on-line to electronic bulletin board subscribers. Selected portions of *Commercial News*

USA are reprinted in business newsletters in several countries. You can access it at www.cnewsusa.com and http://e-expousa.doc.gov.

Gold Key Service.   Gold Key is a custom-tailored service that combines orientation briefings, market research, appointments with potential partners, interpreter service for meetings, and assistance in developing follow-up strategies. It is offered by the Commercial Service in export markets around the world. Prices and conditions vary by country.

Matchmaker Trade Delegations.   These delegations match U.S. firms with prospective agents, distributors, and joint venture or licensing partners abroad. For each "matchmaker," the Commercial Service staff evaluates U.S. firms' product/service marketing potential, finds and screens contacts, and handles all event logistics. U.S. firms visit the designated countries with the delegation and, in each country, receive a schedule of business meetings and-in-depth market and finance briefings.

International Buyer Program (IBP).   IBP supports selected leading U.S. trade shows in industries with high export potential. Department of Commerce offices abroad recruit delegations of foreign buyers and distributors to attend the U.S. shows while program staff help exhibiting firms make contact with international visitors at the show. The International Buyer Program achieves direct export sales and international representation for interested U.S. exhibitors.

Multistate/Catalog Exhibitions.   These exhibitions showcase U.S. company product literature in fast-growing markets within a geographic region. During Multistate/Catalog Exhibitions, U.S. Department of Commerce staff and representatives from state development agencies present product literature to hundreds of interested business prospects abroad and send the trade leads directly to participants.

Trade Fair Certification.   Trade fair certification supports major international industry trade shows that provide high-profile promotion of U.S. products. Certification encourages private organizers to recruit new-to-market, new-to-export U.S. exhibitors to maintain Commerce Department standards for events and to provide services ranging from advance promotion to on-site assistance for U.S. exhibitors.

Overseas Trade Promotions Calendar. Revised quarterly, this calendar provides a 12-month schedule of U.S. trade center exhibitions and international trade fairs in which U.S. participation is planned. It also includes other overseas promotional activities organized by the U.S. Department of Commerce.

How to Get the Most from Overseas Exhibitions. This booklet contains helpful planning tips and details the steps to be taken to participate in an overseas exhibition. It is available free of charge from the Office of Export Development, International Trade Administration, U.S. Department of Commerce, Washington, DC 20230.

Export Statistics Profiles. This service provides a variety of export statistics by product and arrays the data in ways that make market analysis easy. It provides multiyear coverage, percentage of market shares, and top markets for products in rank order. Go to www.ita.doc.gov.

Customs Service Statistics. This statistical service provides customs statistics in four export and/or import tables:

1. For up to 10 selected products showing trade to 9 major world market areas.
2. For up to 10 selected products showing trade to every country worldwide in rank order.
3. For up to 10 selected countries showing trade in individually specified products in rank order.
4. For the top 30 countries showing trade in up to 10 individually specified products in rank order.

They are available from www.ita.doc.gov.

Understanding United States Foreign Trade Data. This guide explains the different foreign trade classifications and valuation systems and other factors that complicate the understanding of U.S. foreign trade data. It is available for $7.50 from the Superintendent of Documents, U.S. Government Printing Office, Washington, DC 20402; phone: (202) 783-3238.

United States Government Information: Publications, Periodicals, and Electronic Products. This catalog annotating almost 1000 popular government publications is organized into subject areas. It can be ordered at no charge from any of the 24 bookstores operated by the government Printing Office (GPO) all around the United States (see Appendix B). Call (202) 512-0000 for a catalog or order online at www.access.gpo.gov/su_docs.

A Basic Guide to Exporting.   This booklet is designed to show step by step how to expand an existing manufacturing business into the international marketplace. It is also an excellent resource for the small importer or exporter. Cost is about $16. Published by the U.S. Department of Commerce, the guide can be obtained by writing the Superintendent of Documents, U.S. Government Printing Office, Washington, DC 20402; phone: (202) 512-0000. It is also available on-line on NTDB's "International Trade Library."

The EMC—Your Export Department.   This booklet describes the services provided to exporters by export management companies as well as how to go about selecting a suitable EMC. It is available from the Office of Export Development, International Trade Administration, U.S. Department of Commerce, Washington, DC 20230.

Exporter Yellow Pages.   This compendium, published by a public/private partnership, features over 20,000 providers, trading companies, and manufacturers that have registered their export interest with EACs. It can be found at www.myexports.com.

The U.S. Export Management Companies (EMCs) Directory.   This directory emphasizes the marketing capability of EMCs. It can be ordered from the Directory of Publishers, Inc., P.O. Box 9449, Baltimore, MD 21228.

Exporter's Encyclopaedia (**Annual**).   This valuable publication for the serious trader's library is chock full of fingertip information. Found in most libraries, it can also be ordered from Dun & Bradstreet International, 99 Church Street, New York, NY 10007; phone: (800) 526-0651 or (800) 624-0324 in New Jersey. The cost is about $450. Go to www.dnb.com/prods_svcs/allprods.htm.

An Introduction to the Overseas Private Investment Corporation (OPIC).   This introduction reviews how OPIC can assist firms interested in investing in developing nations. It is available free of charge from the Overseas Private Investment Corporation, 1129 20th Street NW, Washington, DC 20527.

Export-Import Bank of the United States.   This free guide explains U.S. export financing programs and can be ordered from the Export-Import Bank of the United States, 811 Vermont Avenue NW, Washington, DC 20571; Web: www.exim.gov.

Carnet.   This booklet explains what a carnet is and how it can benefit exporters, with application forms for applying for a carnet. It can be ordered free of charge from the U.S. Council for International Business, 1212 Avenue of the Americas, New York, NY 10036; phone: (212) 354-4480; Web: www.uscib.org.

FREIGHT FORWARDING

A *freight forwarder* is a private service company licensed to support shippers and the movement of their goods. This specialist in international physical distribution acts as an agent for the exporter (shipper) in moving cargo to an overseas destination. Freight forwarders are familiar with:

- The import rules and regulations of foreign countries
- Methods of shipping
- U.S. government export regulations
- The documents connected with foreign trade

From the beginning, freight forwarders can assist with the order by advising on freight costs, consular fees, and insurance costs. They can recommend the degree of packing, arrange for an inland carrier, find the right airline, and even arrange for the containerization of the cargo. They quote shipping rates, provide information, and book cargo space. These firms are invaluable because they can handle everything from the factory to the final destination, including all documentation, storage, and shipping insurance, and will route your cargo at the lowest customs charges.

Shipper

Any person whose primary business is the sale of merchandise may, without a license, dispatch and perform freight forwarding services on behalf of his or her own shipments or on behalf of shipments or consolidated shipments of a parent, subsidiary, affiliate, or associated company. The shipper may not, however, receive compensation from the common carrier.

A large manufacturer usually has a shipping department that serves as its own freight forwarder, but smaller manufacturing firms and small import/export businesses seldom have either the staff or the time to make their own arrangements. Often freight forwarders are called upon to help an exporter put together the final price quotation to a distributor. For example, when quoting CIF (cost, insurance, and freight), in addition to the manufacturer's price and the commission, the forwarder can provide information on dock and cartage fees, forwarder's fees, marine insurance, ocean freight costs, duty charges, consular invoice fees, and packing charges. It's not unusual (and may be quite prudent) to review a price quotation with the freight forwarder before putting it on the fax.

How to Become a Freight Forwarder

There are two types of freight forwarders—ocean and air—but most freight forwarding businesses can do both.

An *ocean freight forwarder* must be licensed by the Federal Maritime Commission (FMC). The criteria to become eligible for a freight forwarding license are:

- Three years' experience in ocean freight forwarding duties
- Necessary character to render forwarding services
- Possession of a valid surety bond

For more information on how to submit an application, contact the Office of Freight Forwarders, Bureau of Tariffs, Federal Maritime Commission, Washington, DC 20573.

Air cargo agents are administered by the International Air Transportation Association (IATA), headquartered in Montreal, Quebec, Canada. This organization, through its subsidiary Cargo Network Services, Inc., administers the qualifications and certification of agents in the United States. Additional information can be obtained by writing CNS, 300 Garden City Plaza, Suite 400, Garden City, NY 11530.

HOT TIP: You can become a licensed freight forwarder, but you do not have to be one to arrange movement of goods on behalf of your own shipments. Caution: Don't act as a forwarder for someone else before being issued a license.

EXPORT CONTROLS

Another area in which exporting differs from importing is the licensing required to control exports. The history of export controls in the United States is based on the presumption that all exported goods and technical documentation are subject to regulation by the government. This presumption is fundamentally different from that of most nations, which presume the freedom to export unless there is an explicit statement of a need to control.

The exercise of controls by the United States varies from minimal restriction (as in the case of Canada) to embargo (as in the case of North Korea and Cuba). Several departments have legal authority to control exports. Arms, ammunition, implements of war, technical data relating thereto, and certain classified information are licensed by the Department of State. Narcotics and dangerous drugs are licensed by the Department of Justice. Nuclear material is licensed by the Nuclear Regulatory Commission. There are other exceptions, but in general, the Department of Commerce's control system, administered through the Bureau of Export Administration (BXA), affects most exporters. Export Administration Regulations (EAR), Section 15 of Federal Regulations 730-774 published in 1996, as amended, are designed to promote the foreign policy of the United States, protect the national security, and protect the domestic economy from the excessive drain of scarce materials.

An *export license* is a grant of authority from the government issued to a particular exporter to export a designated item to a specific destination. An export license is granted on a case-by-case basis either for a single transaction or for several transactions within a specified period of time. If an export license from BXA is required, the exporter must prepare Form BXA-748P (Multipurpose Application Form) and submit it to BXA. The applicant must be certain to follow the instructions on the form carefully. In some instances, technical manuals and support documentation must also be included. BXA also gives the applicant the option to file for a license electronically.

If the application is approved, an export license is mailed to the applicant. The license contains an export authorization number and expiration date that must be placed on the shipper's export declaration (SED). The SED is used as an indication of the type of export authorization for U.S. customs, and as an export control document for BXA. The SED is also used by the Department of Commerce's Bureau of the Census to compile statistics on U.S. trade.

Export controls are organized on the Commerce Department's Commodity Control List (CCL) according to country or by item. Some, however, have a more general focus, such as controls that advance the human rights cause or controls that prohibit doing business with entities that boycott for ethnic or political reasons.

With few exceptions, an exporter must complete a shipper's export declaration (SED) (Commerce Form 7525-V) or its electronic equivalent and deposit it with the exporting carrier regardless of whether a shipment is exported under an export license or a "license exception."

The vast majority of exports *do not* need a validated export license and require instead only the appropriate "license exception" notation on the SED. The symbol NLR (no license required) is used in specific instances where (1) an item is subject to the EAR but is not listed on the CCL under a specific Export Commodity Control Number (ECCN) or (2) an item is listed on the CCL but does not require a license to the destination in question. Virtually all shipments to Canada and the majority of shipments to other destinations are exported from the United States under NLR. Currently, less than 4 percent of U.S.-manufactured exports require an export license.

Exporter Obligations

There are five questions that you need to ask to determine your obligations under the EAR:

1. What is being exported? You need to determine the item's classification according to the CCL.

2. Where is it going? The country of ultimate destination is a factor in determining export licensing requirements using the country chart.

3. Who will receive it? There are restrictions on certain end users, such as persons denied export privileges.

4. What will they do with it? The ultimate end use of your item will affect the licensing requirements related to the proliferation of nuclear, chemical, or biological weapons, and missile delivery systems.

5. What else is involved in your transaction? You may be restricted from engaging in a transaction—including contracting, financing, and freight forwarding—in support of a proliferation project.

Once you determine that you need a validated license for a specific export, you should submit an application to the Bureau of Export Administration (BXA), P.O. Box 273, Washington, DC 20044. An application consists of a completed Form BXA-748P (Multipurpose Application Form) and required supporting information. Figure 7-1 shows the application form for an export license.

Within 10 days after the date BXA receives the application, the office will issue the license, deny it, send the application to the next step in the license process, or, if the application is improperly completed or additional information is required, return the application without action. Once the approved license is received, the exporter keeps the validated license on file. Only the SED is submitted; however, all information on the SED must conform with that found in the validated license.

To avoid export control violations and shipping delays, you should seek assistance from your ITA district office or the Exporter's Service Staff, Bureau of Export Administration (BXA), International Trade Administration, P.O. Box 273, Washington, DC 20044; phone: (202) 482-4811.

B	U.S. DEPARTMENT OF COMMERCE Bureau of Export Administration	DATE RECEIVED (Leave Blank)	**X**
FORM BXA-748P FORM APPROVED OMB NO. 0694-0088, 0694-0089	**MULTIPURPOSE APPLICATION**		

1. CONTACT PERSON	Information furnished herewith is subject to the provisions of Section 12(c) of the Export Administration Act of 1979, as amended, 50 U.S.C. app. 2411(c), and its unauthorized disclosure is prohibited by law.
2. TELEPHONE	APPLICATION CONTROL NUMBER **This is NOT an export license number**
3. FACSIMILE	**Z181053**

3. DATE OF APPLICATION

5. TYPE OF APPLICATION	6. DOCUMENTS SUBMITTED WITH APPLICATION		7. DOCUMENTS ON FILE WITH APPLICANT	8. SPECIAL COMPREHENSIVE LICENSE
☐ EXPORT	☐ BXA-748P-A	☐ LETTER OF EXPLANATION	☐ BXA-711	☐ BXA-752 OR BXA-752-A
☐ REEXPORT	☐ BXA-748P-B	☐ FOREIGN AVAILABILITY	☐ LETTER OF ASSURANCE	☐ INTERNAL CONTROL PROGRAM
☐ CLASSIFICATION REQUEST	☐ BXA-711	☐ OTHER	☐ IMPORT/END-USER CERTIFICATE	☐ COMPREHENSIVE NARRATIVE
☐ SPECIAL COMPREHENSIVE LICENSE	☐ IMPORT/END-USER CERTIFICATE		☐ NUCLEAR CERTIFICATION	☐ CERTIFICATIONS
☐ OTHER	☐ TECH. SPECS		☐ OTHER	☐ OTHER

9. SPECIAL PURPOSE

10. RESUBMISSION APPLICATION CONTROL NUMBER	11. REPLACEMENT LICENSE NUMBER	12. FOR ITEM(S) PREVIOUSLY EXPORTED, PROVIDE LICENSE EXCEPTION SYMBOL OR LICENSE NUMBER

13. IMPORT/END-USER CERTIFICATE COUNTRY   **NUMBER:**

14. APPLICANT	15. OTHER PARTY AUTHORIZED TO RECEIVE LICENSE
ADDRESS LINE 1	ADDRESS LINE 1
ADDRESS LINE 2	ADDRESS LINE 2
CITY / POSTAL CODE	CITY / POSTAL CODE
STATE/COUNTRY / EMPLOYER IDENTIFICATION NUMBER	STATE/COUNTRY / TELEPHONE OR FAX

17. PURCHASER	17. INTERMEDIATE CONSIGNEE
ADDRESS LINE 1	ADDRESS LINE 1
ADDRESS LINE 2	ADDRESS LINE 2
CITY / POSTAL CODE	CITY / POSTAL CODE
COUNTRY / TELEPHONE OR FAX	COUNTRY / TELEPHONE OR FAX

24. ADDITIONAL INFORMATION

For all applications: I certify that to the best of my knowledge, all the information on this form is true and correct, and that it conforms to the instructions accompanying this form and the Export Administration Regulations. For license applications: I certify or agree as appropriate that (a) to the best of my knowledge all statements in this application, includin the description of the commodities, software or technology and their end-uses, and any documents submitted in support of this application are correct and complete and that they fully and accurately disclose all the terms of the order and other facts of the transaction. (b) I will retain records pertaining to this transaction and make them available as required by the Export Administration Regulations; (c) I will report promptly to the Bureau of Export Administration any material changes in the terms of the order or other facts or intentions of the transaction as reflected in this application and supporting documents, whether the application is still under consideration or a license has been granted; and (d) if the license is granted, I will be strictly accountable for its use in accordance with the Export Administration Regulations and all the terms and conditions of the license. A number of the parts of this form include certifications based on a person's knowledge. As defined in Part 772 of the Export Administration Regulations, "Knowledge" of a circumstance includes not only positive knowledge that the circumstance exists or is substantially certain to occur, but also an awareness of a high probability of its existance or future occurrence. Such awareness is inferred from evidence of the conscious disregard of facts known to a person and is also inferred from a persons willful avoidance of facts.

25. SIGNATURE (of person authorized to execute this application)	NAME OF SIGNER	TITLE OF SIGNER

This license application and any license issued pursuant thereto are expressly subject to all rules and regulations of the Bureau of Export Administration. Making any false statement or concealing any material fact in connection with this application or altering in any way the license issued is punishable by imprisonment or fine, or both, and by denial of export privileges under the Export Administration Act of 1979, as amended, and any other applicable Federal statutes. No license will be issued unless this form is completed and submitted in accordance with Export Administration Regulation.

X	**X**	**B**

USCOMM-DC 96-24024

Fig. 7-1. Export license application form

HOT TIPS: How to Avoid Export Control Violations

* Determine whether an export license is required. When in doubt, contact the Export License Application and Information Network for assistance.
* Fully describe commodities or technical data on export shipping documents.
* Use the applicable destination control statement on commercial invoices, air waybills, and bills of lading, as required by Section 386.6 of the Export Administration Regulations (EAR).
* Avoid overshipments by maintaining an accurate account of the quantity and value of goods shipped against an export license.
* Be mindful of the expiration date on export licenses to avoid shipments after the applicable license has expired.
* Enter the applicable export license number or license exception symbol on the shipper's export declaration (SED).
* Make certain that shipping documents clearly identify the exporter, intermediate consignee, and ultimate consignee.
* Mail completed Form BXA-748P.

Where to Get Assistance

In addition to obtaining the applicable export license, U.S. exporters should be careful to meet all other international trade regulations established by specific legislation, regulation, or other authority of the U.S. government. The import laws and regulations of foreign countries must also be taken into account. The exporter should keep in mind that even if banks, freight forwarders, or consultants provide help with the license and documentation, the exporter remains responsible for ensuring that all statements are true and accurate.

To avoid confusion, the exporter is strongly advised to seek assistance in determining the proper licensing requirements. The best source is the Bureau of Export Administration's

Office of Exporter Services. Telephone or write to the Exporter Counseling Division, Room 1099C, U.S. Department of Commerce, Washington, DC 20230; phone: (202) 482-4811. You may also contact one of the Western regional office locations, 3300 Irvine Avenue, Suite 345, Newport Beach, CA 92660; phone: (949) 660-0144; or 101 Park Center Plaza, Suite 1001, San Jose, CA 95113; phone: (408) 998-7402.

BXA also has a Web site (www.bxa.doc.gov) from which you can access a variety of information related to exports, such as seminars, up-to-date regulations, policy issues, and lists of countries, government agencies, companies, and individuals for whom specific controls apply. Whenever there is any doubt about how to comply with BXA's regulations, Department of Commerce officials should be contacted for guidance.

"MADE IN U.S.A."

Buyers have the right to know the true origin of the product they are purchasing. The coveted label "Made in U.S.A." or "Made in America" cannot be randomly used—there are rules and the rules are more and more important in an international marketplace where U.S. manufacturers scour the globe for the right components at the best price, using inputs made in foreign countries.

The Federal Trade Commission (FTC) has a voluntary requirement that "all or virtually all" of a product be made in the United States and it has issued a guidebook, *Complying with the Made in the U.S.A. Standard,* that spells out the requirements. The three essential rules are noted below:

- Origin of the product's significant parts (must be U.S.A.)
- Dominant value (must be in US$)
- Final assembly location (must be U.S.A.)

When in doubt, check the FTC guidebook, which can be ordered by calling (877) FTC-HELP (382-4357) or accessing www.ftc.gov.

TAX INCENTIVES FOR EXPORTING

A prominent tax attorney once said, "Business in America? It's all about taxes." International business is no exception.

Taxes on income derived from international trade are in accordance with current laws for other income except that tax incentives for exporting are substantial. There are no tax incentives for importing.

Tax incentives for exporters amount to an exclusion of approximately 15 percent of the combined taxable income earned on international sales. The tax law provides for a system of tax deferrals for domestic international sales corporations (DISCs) and foreign sales corporations (FSCs). *Note:* The validity of these two premises has been questioned by the WTO.

Prior to December 31, 1984, the DISC was the only medium for distributing export earnings. DISCs do not require a foreign presence and, in fact, are legal entities established only on paper. The DISC incentive was created by the Revenue Act of 1971 and provides for deferral of federal income tax on 50 percent of the export earnings allocated to the DISC, with the balance treated as dividends to the parent company. Following its enactment, the DISC became the subject of an ongoing dispute between the United States and certain other signatories of the General Agreement on Tariffs and Trade (GATT). Other nations contended that the DISC amounted to an illegal export subsidy because it allowed indefinite deferral of direct taxes on income from exports earned in the United States.

Under new rules put into effect on January 1, 1985, to receive a tax benefit that is designed to equal the tax deferral provided by the DISC, exporters must establish an office abroad. The office must also be a foreign sales corporation (FSC), maintain a summary of its permanent books of account at the foreign office, and have at least one director resident outside the United States.

Meeting the new regulations isn't difficult for big U.S.-based multinationals with overseas offices and ample resources, but thousands of small businesses involved in international commerce are concerned about administrative costs and other overhead. Actually small exporters have several options for their foreign sales operations. They may continue to export through a DISC, paying an interest charge on the deferred income, or they may join together with other exporters to own an FSC. Up to 25 exporters may jointly own an

FSC and through the use of several classes of common stock divide the profits of the FSC among the several shareholders.

Another alternative is that individual exporters may take advantage of relaxed rules for small FSCs, which need not meet all the tests required of large FSCs. A small FSC, one with up to $5 million of gross receipts during the taxable year, is excepted from the foreign management and foreign economic process requirements.

The mechanics of setting up a DISC or FSC are somewhat complex but within the capability of most accountants. Some 23 foreign countries, those that have an agreement to exchange tax information with the United States, along with U.S. possessions like the Virgin Islands, Guam, and Saipan, have established offices that are capable of providing direct assistance in setting up an FSC.

Exporters with up to $10 million of annual exports may continue to operate through DISCs, generally under the present rules. But they must pay an annual interest charge on the amount of tax that would be due if the post-1984 accumulated DISC income were included in the shareholder's income. This interest is imposed on the shareholder and paid to the Treasury of the United States.

RELIEF FROM UNFAIR IMPORT PRACTICES

Remaining competitive in world markets is an internal management problem. The underlying elements are quantity, quality, and price. Nevertheless, government intervention is sometimes necessary when foreign firms fail to compete on what has become known as a "level playing ground."

The Department of Commerce's Import Administration (IA) participates with the U.S. Trade Representative in monitoring and negotiating fair and transparent international rules. IA enforces laws and agreements to prevent unfairly traded imports and to safeguard jobs and the competitive strength of American industry.

The *Rules of Practice and Procedure* of the U.S. International Trade Commission (ITC) set forth the procedures for the filing and conduct of investigations. Copies are available from the Docket Section, U.S. International Trade Commission, 500 E Street SW, Washington, DC 20436; phone: (202) 205-1802.

The IA, ITC, Congress, and/or U.S. Trade Representative can investigate the following allegations:

- Countervailing duties imposed by a foreign country.
- Antidumping.
- General investigations of trade and tariff matters.
- Investigations of costs of production.
- Alleged unfair practices in import trade.
- Investigations of injury from increased imports.
- Worker's adjustment assistance.
- Firm's adjustment assistance.
- Enforcement of U.S. rights under trade agreements and response to certain foreign trade practices.
- U.S. response to foreign trade practices that restrict or discriminate against U.S. commerce.
- Investigations of market disruptions by imports from Communist countries.

The main point of contact for instituting investigations is:

Import Administration (IA)
International Trade Administration
U.S. Department of Commerce
Washington, DC 20230
(202) 482-5497
www.ita.doc.gov/import_admin/records/aboutus.htm

The next chapter explains those elements of international trade that are unique to importing, such as customs, tariffs, and quotas.

8

How to Import into the United States

IMPORTING IS SIMPLY THE FLIP SIDE OF EXPORTING. A person or business in one country buys the goods and services of an exporter in another to sell for profit. Some aspects of importing don't apply to exporting. For example, the tariff schedule applies only to importing, and the U.S. Customs Service is concerned only with goods coming into a country.

The following basics, unique to importing, are discussed in this chapter:

- Government support
- Import information sources
- Customs house brokers
- Getting through the customs maze
- The Harmonized Tariff System
- Import quotas
- Special import regulations
- Free trade zones
- Customs bonded warehouses

GOVERNMENT SUPPORT

The U.S. Customs Service, a division of the Department of the Treasury, cannot be thought of as promoting importing in the way that the Department of Commerce encourages exporting. Nevertheless, it is responsible for enforcement of the relevant trade.

The Customs Service is one of the nation's oldest public institutions. Provision for the service was probably the next thing Congress did after forming the new nation. Created in 1789, it provided most of the federal government's revenue for almost 130 years. After the income tax became the federal government's primary revenue source, the major responsibility of the Customs Service shifted to the administration of the Tariff Act of 1930, as amended. These duties include (1) enforcing laws against smuggling, and (2) collecting all duties, taxes, and fees due on the volumes of goods moved through the nation's more than 300 ports of entry. A Customs Court, consisting of nine judges appointed by the U.S. President, reviews and settles disputes between importers and exporters and those that collect customs duties. To make contact, call (202) 927-0370 or visit www.customs.gov.

Like the Department of Commerce, the U.S. Customs Service is organized with a domestic as well as an overseas arm.

Domestic Offices

Domestic offices are organized into 5 strategic trade centers (STCs), 20 customs management centers (CMCs), and 300-plus port of entry offices.

The 20 CMCs are responsible for oversight of operations within their area of jurisdiction and exercise line authority over the ports. They provide technical assistance and participate with the ports in addressing operational problems. They oversee the execution of the core business processes—trade compliance, passenger operations, and outbound operations. They also coordinate with counterpart special agent-in-charge (SAIC) offices in executing antismuggling/K-9 and other enforcement strategies. CMCs are the point of contact for the answers to the following questions:

- Release, classification, and valuation of imported merchandise
- Processing and entry of passengers into the United States

- Exported merchandise
- Fines, penalties, and forfeitures
- Seized properties
- Other activities engaging the trade and travel communities

Ports of entry address all daily operational aspects of the Customs Service. They are responsible for maintaining a focus on trade compliance (imports/cargo), passenger operations, outbound operations (exports), and antismuggling/K-9 strategies. Figure 8-1 illustrates the Customs Service organization.

Overseas Offices

The U.S. Customs Service overseas arm, although not as extensive as the Commerce Department's Foreign Commercial Service

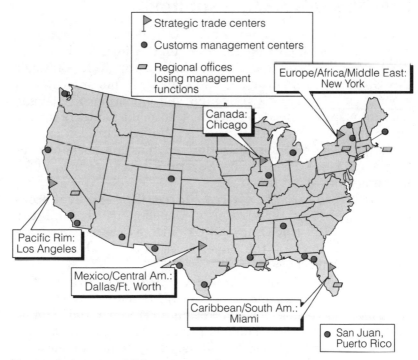

Fig. 8-1. Organization of U.S. customs service

(FCS), consists of customs attachés attached to embassies or missions in the countries listed below:

Bangkok, Thailand	Monterrey, Mexico
Beijing, China	Montevideo, Uruguay
Berlin, Germany	Moscow, Russia
Bogotá, Colombia	Ottowa, Canada
Bonn, Germany	Panama City, Panama
Brussels, Belgium	Paris, France
Caracas, Venezuela	Pretoria, South Africa
Central America (Miami)	Rome, Italy
Frankfurt, Germany	Seoul, Korea
Hermisillo, Mexico	Singapore
Hong Kong	Tijuana, Mexico
Interpol, Lyon, France	Tokyo, Japan
London, England	Vienna, Austria
Mexico City, Mexico	

IMPORT INFORMATION SOURCES

The Customs Service does provide considerable information related to the importing function in the form of booklets, newsletters, and seminars, all available through the CMCs or the Government Printing Office. Most of this information amounts to extractions from and simplification of customs regulations. Information about how to make contacts and/or perform the import function must be obtained through private sector publishers and organizations such as chambers of commerce and trade associations. Several sources are helpful for learning more about importing.

Importing into the United States. This excellent booklet, published by the Treasury Department through the Government Printing Office (GPO), outlines the requirements that must be met by the importer to enter goods. Contact: www.access.gpo.gov/su_docs.

Thomas Register of American Manufacturers. This compilation of names and locations of U.S. manufacturers is a valuable sourcebook for marketing in the United States. Published through the Thomas Publishing Company, 1 Penn Plaza, New York, NY 10001. It is easily found in most libraries.

Directory of Manufacturers Agents. This excellent publication can be used to make contact with industrial distributors. Published by McGraw-Hill, 2 Penn Plaza, New York, NY 10121.

Market Guide of Mass Merchandisers. This list of contacts for sales representatives is published by Dun & Bradstreet., 1 World Trade Center, New York, NY 10048.

CUSTOMS HOUSE BROKERS

The *customs house broker* is a private, for-profit liaison between the U.S. Customs Service and the importing public. Such liaison will be needed as long as there are legal requirements and regulations pertaining to the movement of merchandise.

Like the freight forwarder for exporting, the customs house broker is a private service company licensed to assist importers in the movement of their goods.

Formal entries of foreign-made goods representing billions of dollars in duty collections are filed each year with the Customs Service, and virtually all of them are prepared by customs brokers on behalf of importers. Some brokers are sole proprietors with a single office at one port of entry; others are large corporations with branches in many ports throughout the country and in some cases throughout the world. All customs brokers are licensed and regulated by the U.S. Treasury Department.

The customs broker is employed as an agent of the importer and frequently is the importer's only point of contact with the Customs Service. It is not necessary for an importer to employ a broker to enter goods on its own behalf; however, a bond is required if the importer chooses to handle entry.

Most experienced importers will seek out the services of a broker because of the extras involved. These include the comfort of knowing that a professional is supporting your project and can answer many technical questions for you. Another good reason is that at some point, your time will become more valuable in managing your company and marketing your product(s) than it might be in handling the paperwork of an entry.

A broker's duties include advising on the technical requirements of importing, preparing and filing entry documents, obtaining the necessary bonds, depositing U.S. import duties, securing release of the product(s), arranging delivery to the importer's premises or warehouse, and obtaining "drawback" refunds (see below). The broker often consults with Customs officials to determine the proper rate of duty or bases of appraisement and on many occasions. If dissatisfied with either rate or value, the broker will pursue appropriate administrative remedies on behalf of the importer.

Consult the yellow pages of the local phone book for a listing of customs house brokers in your area.

Surety Bond

Importers must post a *surety bond* with the Customs Service to ensure payment of the proper amounts of duties, taxes, and other charges associated with entry. Bonds can be for single entry or continuous (term). The value of the bond is based on the value of the shipment. Often customs officials require a bond three times the value of the shipment. A surety company usually requires 100 percent collateral in the form of an irrevocable L/C, trust deed, or cashier's check. Bond premiums are about 2 percent of the value, with a minimum of about $100. The premium for a term bond is usually higher (5 percent). Collateral depends on the financial condition of the importer.

Drawback

Drawback is the refunding of duties paid on imported goods and their derivatives if they are subsequently exported. Suppose, for example, that you simply reexport goods that are originally imported; or you export items that contain imported merchandise; or you export items that contain whole imported components. For each of these you might claim a drawback of tariffs paid when imported. The key to drawback is good inventory tracking and record-keeping procedures. Make application for drawback with your local customs port of entry office.

Automated Brokerage Interface (ABI)

The Automated Brokerage Interface (ABI) is for those large-volume importers who file many simple entries and wish to avoid the cost of a broker. ABI permits importers (and brokers) to electronically file preliminary entry data in advance of the arrival of cargo.

How to Become a Customs Broker

You can become a customs broker by first studying the Customs Service regulations and learning the application of the tariff schedules, and then passing an examination given several times a year. This license is not necessary to act in your own behalf, but it is needed if you act as an agent for others. Details about the examination and costs involved can be obtained from any Customs Service office. Figure 8-2 shows the application form required to gain a license.

GETTING THROUGH THE CUSTOMS MAZE

A *tariff* is a schedule of duties. It is also the duty or tax imposed by a country and the duty or tax within the tariff schedule. As a tax, it is placed on goods as they cross the border between two countries.

At one time, tariffs were the U.S. government's primary means of raising revenue. However, in the early 1900s, when the income tax was introduced, tariffs took on less importance as a revenue source. Since then, tariffs have been dominantly used to protect home industries.

HISTORY NOTE: According to most sources, the word *tariff* comes from the Arabic *ta'rif,* meaning inventory. The French word *tarif,* as well as the Spanish word *tarifa,* means price list or rate book. An alternate version has it that the word originated sometime after 700 A.D. At that time, near Gibraltar, a small band of thieves lived in the village of Tarifa. They stopped every merchant ship and forced the captain to pay a handsome sum of money before the vessel could proceed through the strait. Seamen began calling the money they were forced to pay a tariff.

The Four-Step Entry Process

When a shipment of goods intended for commercial use reaches the United States, it may not be legally entered until

Form Approved: O.M.B. No. 1515-0076

DEPARTMENT OF THE TREASURY
UNITED STATES CUSTOMS SERVICE

**APPLICATION
FOR
CUSTOMHOUSE BROKER'S LICENSE**
19 U.S.C. 1641; 111.12 C.R.

Privacy Act
Statement
on Reverse
of Form

1. APPLICANT'S NAME AND ADDRESS *(Principal Office OR Home Address)*

INSTRUCTIONS: Applicants must be United States citizens. Submit application in duplicate to the District Director of the District named in Block 3. All additional continuation sheets, if required, and attachments should also be in duplicate.

2. TYPE OF LICENSE APPLIED FOR

☐ Individual   ☐ Corporation   ☐ Partnership   ☐ Association

3. CUSTOMS DISTRICT FOR WHICH LICENSE IS APPLIED

4. HAVE YOU EVER APPLIED FOR A CUSTOMHOUSE BROKER'S LICENSE?   ☐ NO   ☐ YES *(Explain in item 17)*

5. HAS THE APPLICANT *(OR ANY OFFICER OR MEMBER THEREOF)* EVER HAD A LICENSE SUSPENDED, REFUSED, REVOKED, OR CANCELED?   ☐ NO   ☐ YES *(Explain in item 17)*

6. IF APPLICANT HAS A CURRENT LICENSE, STATE WHEN AND FOR WHAT DISTRICT ISSUED.

7. IS THE APPLICANT *(OR ANY OFFICER OR MEMBER THEREOF)* AN OFFICER OR EMPLOYEE OF THE UNITED STATES?   ☐ NO   ☐ YES *(Explain in item 17)*

SECTION I — INDIVIDUALS ONLY

8. DATE OF BIRTH   9. BIRTHPLACE *(City & State)*   10. SOCIAL SECURITY NO.   11. HOME PHONE NO.   12. BUSINESS PHONE NO.

13. U.S. CITIZENSHIP   ☐ NATURAL-BORN   ☐ NATURALIZED- *Give Date & Place* →

14. HAVE YOU EVER BEEN A DEFENDANT IN A CRIMINAL PROSECUTION? *(You may exclude minor traffic violations where the fine was $50 or less.)*   ☐ NO   ☐ YES *(Explain in item 17)*

15. DO YOU PROPOSE TO ENGAGE IN THE BUSINESS OF A CUSTOMHOUSE BROKER:

(More than one may apply. Explain answer(s) in Item 17.)

(a) ☐ ON YOUR OWN INDIVIDUAL ACCOUNT? *(State name in which business is to be conducted; if trade name, state authority for use of the name and attach evidence of such authority.)*

(b) ☐ AS A MEMBER OF A PARTNERSHIP? *(State name of partnership and list names of all the partners.)*

(c) ☐ AS AN OFFICER OF AN ASSOCIATION? *(State name of the association, the title of the office you hold, and the general nature of your duties.)*

(d) ☐ AS AN OFFICER OF A CORPORATION? *(State name of the corporation, the title of the office you hold, and the general nature of your duties.)*

(e) ☐ AS AN EMPLOYEE? *(State name and address of your employer (if different than item 1)and the nature of your employment.)*

16. LIST THE NAMES AND ADDRESSES OF SIX REFERENCES.

SECTION III — CERTIFICATION *(ALL APPLICANTS)*

INDIVIDUAL	ASSOCIATION, CORPORATION, OR PARTNERSHIP
I, _____ certify that the statements contained in the foregoing application and supporting attachments thereto are true and correct to the best of my knowledge and belief. Written notice of any change in my mailing address, any business connection, or the name and style under which I conduct my business will be given to the Commissioner of Customs.	I, _____, certify that I am an officer or partner of the applicant that I am a licensed customhouse broker; and that the statements contained in the foregoing application and supporting attachments thereto are true and correct to the best of my knowledge and belief. The officers or partners who are licensed customhouse brokers are aware of the requirements for the exercise by them of responsible supervision and control of the transaction of the customs business of the applicant. Written notice of any change in the applicant's mailing address, name, licensed officers or partners, or the charter, certificate, articles, or other instrument of organization of the applicant will be given to the Commissioner of Customs.

23. SIGNATURE │   24. DATE

Customs Form 3124 (03-03-81)

Fig. 8-2. Application for customs broker license

after: (a) it enters the port of entry, (b) estimated duties have been paid or bonded, and (c) customs authorizes delivery of the merchandise. During this process only the owner (or an agent) is responsible for the entry—the U.S. Customs Service simply checks each step to ensure correctness. Table 8-1 compares the steps of the commercial entry process.

The process, in its simplest form, has four steps: entry, valuation, classification, and payment.

Step 1: Entry. Within five working days of arrival of a shipment at a U.S. port of entry, the owner/agent must de-

Table 8-1. Commercial Entry Process

Who is responsible?	What does customs do?
Owner; agent; purchaser	
Step	Step
1. Entry: Shipment arrives within port	1. Check and verify. Store in general warehouse?
a. Decide consumption or bonded warehouse/FTZ	
b. If consumption, file entry documents	
c. Documents required	Check
1. Entry manifest	
2. Right to make entry	
3. Invoices	
4. Packing lists	
5. Entry summary*	
6. Evidence of bond	Verify
2. Valuation	
3. Classify/appraise	
4. Estimate and pay tariff (check or cash)	2. Examine
	3. Validate
	a. Classification
	b. Appraisement
	4. Authorize entry
	5. Liquidate transaction

*Often allowed 10 working days after entry.
- If pay more than required tariff: refund (90 days)
- If pay less: billed to pay or protest (90 days)
- Protest: U.S. Court of International Trade (180 days)
- If reexport: Drawback

cide whether to *enter* the goods for consumption or place them into a bonded warehouse or free (foreign) trade zone (explained in detail later in the chapter). If the decision is made to enter for consumption, the following entry documents must be filed:

- Entry Manifest (Form 7533) or Application and Special Permit for Immediate Delivery (Form 3461).
- Evidence of right to make entry.
- Commercial invoice or pro forma invoice.
- Packing list(s) if appropriate.

- Entry Summary (Form 7501) and other documents necessary to determine merchandise admissibility.
- Evidence of bond.

The Application and Special Permit for Immediate Delivery (Form 3461) is an alternative procedure that provides for the immediate release of a shipment. Figure 8-3 shows the form for land shipments, and Figure 8-4 shows the form for ocean and air shipments. Application should be made before the arrival of the goods so that, if approved, the goods won't sit on the dock or in a warehouse. They can be released on arrival. You are allowed 10 working days to file a proper Entry Summary (Form 7501) and deposit estimated duties. Release under this provision is limited to:

- Merchandise arriving from Canada or Mexico.
- Fresh fruits and vegetables for human consumption arriving from Canada or Mexico.
- Articles for a trade fair.
- Tariff-rate quota merchandise and, under certain circumstances, merchandise subject to an absolute quota.
- Merchandise specifically authorized by customs because of perishability or inconvenience to the importer, carrier, or agent.

Step 2: Valuation. This step determines the *value* of the goods for purposes of applying any tariffs or duties. Generally, the customs value is the transaction value, or the price actually paid or payable for the merchandise when sold for exportation to the United States, plus amounts for the following items if not included in the price:

- The packing costs incurred by the buyer.
- Any selling commission paid by the buyer.
- The value of any assist (e.g., tools, dies, molds, engineering, artwork).
- Any royalty or license fee that is required from the buyer as a condition of the sale.
- The proceeds from the sale of the imported goods that accrue to the seller.

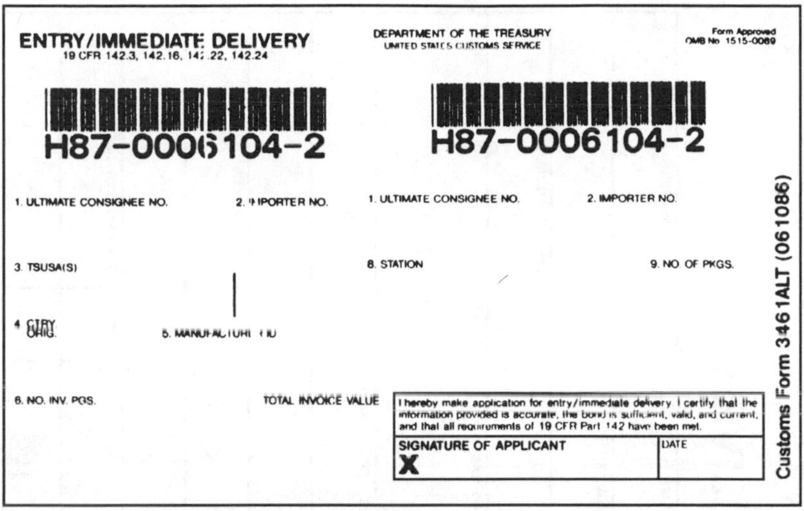

Fig. 8-3. Special immediate entry permit (land)

If the transaction value for the goods cannot be used, then secondary bases are used in the following order of precedence:

- Transaction value of identical merchandise
- Transaction value of similar merchandise
- Deductive value
- Computed value

Step 3: Classification. The responsibility for *classification* rests with the importer, customs house broker, or other person preparing the entry papers. The importance of this step cannot be overemphasized, because it determines the ad valorem (percentage) tariff rate that should be applied to the valuation of the goods. Familiarity with the Harmonized Tariff Schedule of the United States (HTSUS) facilitates the process (see page 187).

> **FIRST RULE OF IMPORTING:** *Always* get advance ruling from customs.

Step 4: Payment. *Payment* of duties is made by check or cash to the Treasurer of the United States.

DEPARTMENT OF THE TREASURY
UNITED STATES CUSTOMS SERVICE

ENTRY/IMMEDIATE DELIVERY

19 CFR 142.3, 142.16, 142.22, 142.24

1. ARRIVAL DATE	2. ELECTED ENTRY DATE	3. ENTRY TYPE CODE/NAME	4. ENTRY NUMBER
5. PORT	6. SINGLE TRANS. BOND	7. BROKER/IMPORTER FILE NUMBER	
	8. CONSIGNEE NUMBER		9. IMPORTER NUMBER
10. ULTIMATE CONSIGNEE NAME		11. IMPORTER OF RECORD NAME	
12. CARRIER CODE	13. VOYAGE/FLIGHT/TRIP	14. LOCATION OF GOODS—CODE(S)/NAME(S)	
15. VESSEL CODE/NAME			
16. U.S. PORT OF UNLADING	17. MANIFEST NUMBER	18. G.O. NUMBER	19. TOTAL VALUE
20. DESCRIPTION OF MERCHANDISE			

21. IT/BL/ AWB CODE	22. IT/BL/AWB NO.	23. MANIFEST QUANTITY	24. TSUSA NUMBER	25. COUNTRY OF ORIGIN	26. MANUFACTURER NO.

27. CERTIFICATION

I hereby make application for entry/immediate delivery. I certify that the above information is accurate, the bond is sufficient, valid, and current, and that all requirements of 19 CFR Part 142 have been met.

SIGNATURE OF APPLICANT

✗

PHONE NO.   DATE

29. BROKER OR OTHER GOVT. AGENCY USE

28. CUSTOMS USE ONLY

☐ OTHER AGENCY ACTION REQUIRED, NAMELY:

☐ CUSTOMS EXAMINATION REQUIRED.

☐ ENTRY REJECTED, BECAUSE:

DELIVERY AUTHORIZED: SIGNATURE   DATE

Paperwork Reduction Act Notice: This information is needed to determine the admissibility of imports into the United States and to provide the necessary information for the examination of the cargo and to establish the liability for payment of duties and taxes. Your response is necessary.

Customs Form 3461 (112085)

Fig. 8-4. Special immediate entry permit (ocean and air)

185

Customs Service Responsibilities

Involvement of the Customs Service in the entry process can be characterized by five steps: check and verify, examine, validate, authorize entry, and liquidate.

Step 1: Check and Verify. For this step customs officers *check* the entry documents and *verify* evidence of a bond. Of course, on arrival of the goods at the port of entry the owner or agent is responsible to immediately make arrangements for the shipment and storage of the goods. Any goods not claimed are stored in a general warehouse. Storage is billed to the owner when the goods are retrieved; unclaimed goods are sold at auction.

Step 2: Examine. This step, which is the customs officer's *examination* to determine the value of the goods and their suitability for entering, has five substeps:

- Valuing the goods for customs purposes and determining their dutiable status.

- Checking the proper markings of the goods with the country of origin.

- Determining whether the shipment contains prohibited items.

- Determining whether the goods are correctly invoiced.

- Taking inventory to determine whether there are excesses or shortages of the invoiced quantities.

Step 3: Validate. The *validation* step consists of checking the classification of the goods and appraising to ensure correct valuation.

Step 4: Authorize Entry. After the classification and valuation, as well as other required import information, have been reviewed for correctness, proper appraisement, and agreement of the submitted data, the merchandise may be *authorized* for actual import.

Step 5: Liquidate. If the goods are accepted without changes, they are *liquidated* "as entered." This step is finalized in the traditional way of posting a notice on the public bulletin board at the customs house. The bulletin board is now a computer printout. After the liquidation, an importer may pursue claims for adjustment or refund by filing, within 90 days, a protest on Customs Form 19. Time limits do not begin to run until the date of posting. If, after further review, the importer is still not satisfied, a summons may be filed with the U.S. Customs Court of International Trade.

THE HARMONIZED TARIFF SYSTEM

The Harmonized Tariff System is an international, multipurpose classification system designed to improve the collection of import and export statistics as well as to serve customs purposes. Intended as a core for national systems, it promotes a high degree of international uniformity in the presentation of customs tariffs and foreign trade statistics.

The U.S. Harmonized Tariff Schedule (HTS) is about the size of a major city's telephone book, and is available through the Government Printing Office in three-hole, looseleaf form for about $80. Or download it from the International Trade Commission's Web site at www.usitc.gov.

The HTS is a complete product classification system, organized in a framework that employs a numbering system. To assist the user, a section in the front of the book gives General Rules of Interpretation (GRI), which explain the use and interpretation of the schedule.

At the international level, about 5000 article descriptions are grouped into 21 sections and arranged into 97 chapters. The U.S. version has 22 sections and 99 chapters. Chapter 98 includes information from the "old" TSUSA Schedule 8 (Articles 806.20, 806.30, and 807) related to offshore assembly. Chapter 99 contains information transformed from the TSUSA Schedule 9. The 22 sections and their chapter headings are listed in a table of contents at the front.

HISTORY NOTE: For decades, the international trading community was confronted with problems caused by the number of differing classification systems covering the movement of goods in international trade. In 1970, representatives of the Customs Cooperation Council (CCC), formerly known as the Brussels Tariff Nomenclature (BTN), undertook a study of commodity description and coding with a view to developing a system capable of meeting the principal requirements of customs authorities, statisticians, carriers, and producers. The study concluded that the development of such a system was not only feasible but imperative. Some 13 years later the "Harmonized Commodity Description and Coding System" and a convention for its implementation were completed. Forty-eight countries and more than a dozen private and public organizations participated in its development.

HOT TIP: Reading the Harmonized Tariff Schedule

CHAPTER: FIRST TWO DIGITS Example: 44.

HEADING: FIRST FOUR DIGITS Example: 4409.

SUBHEADING: FIRST SIX DIGITS Example: 4409.10

ITEM: FIRST EIGHT DIGITS Example: 4409.10.10

Case Study—Guitars

Let's assume that you are an importer of "guitars valued at less than $100." Your order from Germany arrives. Assuming you wish to enter the guitars immediately into commerce, within five working days you must present the documents listed in step 1 of the entry process to customs.

Note: If the guitars were perishable or you had a special scheduling problem, you could have applied (in advance) for their immediate delivery using the Special Entry Permit (Form 3461).

In this case, let us assume there was no need for immediate entry, so you proceeded with a normal, formal entry.

Let's further assume that you used an L/C to make payment, so you can pick up your entry documents only after you square your account with your banker. The invoice shows 1000 guitars at $89 each, for a total of $8900. This is the transaction value for purposes of valuation. Because the value is over $2000, you must make a formal entry. Had the value been under $2000, the informal entry process would have been much simpler; you could very easily have done your own paperwork, and a bond would not have been required. Figure 8-5 shows the basic form used for both formal and informal entry. Table 8-2 lists the differences between a formal and an informal entry.

If the goods had been for your personal use and you had been out of the country for more than 48 hours, the first $400 ($800 when returning from a U.S. insular possession) would have been exempt, the next $1000 dutied at 10 percent, and the remainder dutied at the ad valorem rate from the TSUSA.

Beginners ask, "What if I entered the goods for personal use in small quantities and then sold them?" One customs agent told this author, "They may get away with it the first time, but we (the computers) remember, and sooner or later, we'll catch them. The penalty is at least a $5000 fine."

Full, complete, and honest disclosure is the responsibility of the importer. The penalties are severe. Make your money and pay your duties.

In this example, because the value is $2000 or greater ($8900), a formal entry is required. For the formal or informal entry process, you need to classify the product. Begin by scanning the HTS table of contents for the general category within which your product fits. In this case "Musical instruments" is in Section XVIII, Chapter 92.

Figure 8-6 reproduces page 92-2 from the Harmonized Tariff Schedule, covering articles related to our case study.

Table 8-2.   Formal vs. Informal Entry

	Informal	*Formal*
Value	Less than $2000*	$1250 or greater
Bond	No	Yes
Duties	Pay on entry	Pay within 10 days**
Liquidation	On the spot	Liquidation notice
Forms required	7501, invoice, B/L, check ($$$ duties), packing list	
	packing list	7501, entry invoice, B/L, packing list, check ($$$ duties), other agency, documents, bond

*For some articles, formal entry is specified regardless of value (check your local Customs Service office or customs house broker).
**An example of a good that might require immediate payment is an item under quota.

ENTRY SUMMARY

DEPARTMENT OF THE TREASURY
UNITED STATES CUSTOMS SERVICE

(1) Entry No.	(2) Entry Type Code	3. Entry Summary Date
4. Entry Date	(5) Port Code	
6. Bond No.	7. Bond Type Code	8. Broker/Importer File No.

9. Ultimate Consignee Name and Address

10. Consignee No.   (11) Importer of Record Name and Address   (12) Importer No.

State

(13) Exporting Country	14. Export Date
(15) Country of Origin	16. Missing Documents
(17) I.T. No.	(18) I.T. Date

(19) B L or AWB No.   20. Mode of Transportation   21. Manufacturer I.D.   22. Reference No.

(23) Importing Carrier   24. Foreign Port of Lading   25. Location of Goods/G.O. No.

26. U.S. Port of Unlading   (27) Import Date

Fig. 8-5. Sample entry summary

190

(28) Line No.	(29) Description of Merchandise			33. (A) Entered Value B. CHGS C. Relationship	34. (A) T.S.U.S.A. Rate B. ADA/CVD Rate (C) I.R.C. Rate D. Visa No.	(35) Duty and I.R. Tax	
	30. (A) T.S.U.S.A. No. B. ADA CVD Case No.	31. (A) Gross Weight B. Manifest Qty.	(32) Net Quantity in T.S.U.S.A. Units			Dollars	Cents

(36) Declaration of Importer of Record (Owner or Purchaser) or Authorized Agent

I declare that I am the

☐ importer of record and that the actual owner, purchaser, or consignee for customs purposes is as shown above. OR ☐ owner or purchaser or agent thereof.

I further declare that the merchandise

☐ was obtained pursuant to a purchase or agreement to purchase and that the prices set forth in the invoice are true. OR ☐ was not obtained pursuant to a purchase or agreement to purchase and the statements in the invoice as to value or price are true to the best of my knowledge and belief.

I also declare that the statements in the documents herein filed fully disclose to the best of my knowledge and belief the true prices, values, quantities, rebates, drawbacks, fees, commissions, and royalties and are true and correct, and that all goods or services provided to the seller of the merchandise either free or at reduced cost are fully disclosed. I will immediately furnish to the appropriate customs officer any information showing a different state of facts.

Notice required by Paperwork Reduction Act of 1980. This information is needed to ensure that importers/exporters are complying with U.S. Customs laws, to allow us to compute and collect the right amount of money, to enforce other agency requirements, and to collect accurate statistical information on imports. Your response is mandatory.

U.S. CUSTOMS USE		TOTALS	
A. Liq. Code	B. Ascertained Duty	(37) Duty	
	C. Ascertained Tax	(38) Tax	
	D. Ascertained Other	(39) Other	
	E. Ascertained Total	(40) Total	

(41) Signature of Declarant, Title, and Date

Customs Form 7501 (030984)

Fig. 8-5. Sample entry summary (*Continued*)

HARMONIZED TARIFF SCHEDULE of the United States (1993)
Annotated for Statistical Reporting Purposes

XVIII
92-2

Heading/ Subheading	Stat. Suf- fix	Article Description	Units of Quantity	Rates of Duty General 1	Special 1	2
9201		Pianos, including player pianos; harpsichords and other keyboard stringed instruments:				
9201.10.00	00	Upright pianos	No.	5.3%	Free (A, E, IL, J) 2.6% (CA)	40%
9201.20.00	00	Grand pianos	No.	5.3%	Free (A, E, IL, J) 2.6% (CA)	40%
9201.90.00	00	Other	No.	5.3%	Free (A, E, IL, J) 2.6% (CA)	40%
9202		Other string musical instruments (for example, guitars, violins, harps):				
9202.10.00	00	Played with a bow	No.	4.9%	Free (A, E, IL, J) 2.4% (CA)	37.5%
9202.90		Other: Guitars:				
9202.90.20	00	Valued not over $100 each, excluding the value of the case	No.	6.8%	Free (A, E, IL, J) 3.4% (CA)	40%
9202.90.40	00	Other	No.	13%	Free (A, E, IL, J) 6.5% (CA)	40%
9202.90.60	00	Other	No.	7%	Free (A, E, IL, J) 3.5% (CA)	40%
9203.00		Keyboard pipe organs; harmoniums and similar keyboard instruments with free metal reeds:				
9203.00.40	00	Keyboard pipe organs	No.	Free		35%
9203.00.80	00	Other	No.	5.3%	Free (A, CA, E, IL, J)	40%

Heading/Subheading	Stat. Suffix	Article Description	Unit	General	Special	2
9204		Accordions and similar instruments; mouth organs;				
		Accordions and similar instruments:				
9204.10		Piano accordions				
9204.10.40	00	Piano accordions	No.	4.7%	Free (A, CA, E, IL, J)	40%
9204.10.80	00	Other	No.	5.1%	Free (A, CA, E, IL, J)	40%
9240.20.00	00	Mouth organs	Doz.	4.7%	Free (A, E, IL, J) 2.3% (CA)	40%
9205		Other wind musical instruments (for example clarinets, trumpets, bagpipes):				
9205.10.00		Brass-wind instruments		5.8%	Free (A, E, IL, J) 2.9% (CA)	40%
	40	Valued not over $10 each	No.			
	80	Valued over $10 each	No.			
9205.90		Other:				
		Woodwind instruments:				
9205.90.20	00	Bagpipes	No.	Free	Free (A, E, IL, J)	40%
9205.90.40		Other		4.9%	Free (A, E, IL, J) 2.4% (CA) 1/	40%
	20	Clarinets	No.			
	40	Saxophones	No.			
	60	Flutes and piccolos (except bamboo)	No.			
9205.90.60	80	Other	No.	3.4%	Free (A, E, IL, J) 1.7% (CA)	40%
9206.00		Percussion musical instruments (for example, drums, xylophones, cymbals, castanets, maracas):				
9206.00.20	00	Drums	No.	4.8%	Free (A, CA, E, IL, J)	40%
9206.00.40	00	Cymbals	No.	Free		40%
9206.00.60	00	Sets of tuned bells known as chimes, peals or carillons	No.	2.5%	Free (A, CA, E, IL, J)	50%
9206.00.80	00	Other	No.	5.3%	Free (A, CA, E, IL, J)	40%

1/ See subheading 9905.92.10.

Fig. 8-6. Sample page from Harmonized Tariff Schedule

Run your finger down the page until you find "Guitars: valued not over $100." In this case, the classification of guitars is straightforward, but keep in mind that classifying a product is usually the most difficult part of using any tariff schedule. Determining the correct classification can save you money and heartache. Consult the Customs Service or your customs house broker if you have any doubts.

The heading for this product is 9202.90.20. The first two digits refer to the chapter number—in this case, Chapter 92. The next two refer to the heading, the next two to the international subdivision, then the U.S. subdivision, and finally the U.S. statistical subdivision.

Now, draw your finger across the page. Note that there are three vertical columns, each with an ad valorem duty rate. In column 1 "general," the rate is 6.8 percent. This is the rate for most favored nations (MFNs) such as the United Kingdom, France, and Germany. Thus, because your guitars came from Germany, you will pay 6.8 percent of $8900, or $605.20 ad valorem duty.

Note that the duty rate shown in column 1, "special," is *free* (pay no tariff) for country groups A, E, IL, and J, and only 3.4 percent for CA. The countries in these groups are listed in the "special" category programs in the front of the HTS under Headnotes. Table 8-3 lists these special programs.

The third column labeled 2, shows a rate of 40 percent for guitars valued under $100. This column shows the ad val-

Table 8-3. Special Tariff Treatment Programs

General System of Preferences	A or A*
Automotive Products Trade Act	B
Agreement on Trade in Civil Aircraft	C
North American Free Trade Agreement:	
Goods of Canada, under the terms of general note 12 of this schedule.	CA
Goods of Mexico, under the terms of general note 12 of this schedule.	MX
Caribbean Basin Economic Recovery Act	E or E*
United States–Israel Free Trade Area	IL
Andean Trade Preference Act	J or J*

*Extracted from the Harmonized Tariff Schedule of the United States.

orem duty rate for countries under "Communist domination or control," such as North Korea and Cuba. If the guitars had come from North Korea instead of Germany, the ad valorem duty paid to the U.S. Treasury would have been 40 percent of $8900, or $3560.

Having estimated your duties as $605.20, you now need to fill out the required entry documents and post surety in the form of cash or evidence of having a bond (minimum of $10,000). If a customs broker makes the entry for you, the broker may use its own bond. This is not automatic. In many cases brokers will assist you to obtain your own bond. There are three types of bonds:

- Term bonds cover only one port of entry.
- General bonds cover all U.S. ports.
- Continuous bonds can substitute for both.

After filling out the commercial customs invoice, the special (consular) customs invoice, the bill of lading, and the entry form, you may now pick up the goods from the carrier.

Remember that you or your agent (customs broker) originally classified and estimated the duties owed. Final liquidation of this transaction by the Customs Service could take as much as several months but must be finalized (with exceptions) within one year. You will receive notice of the date of liquidation and what amounts are due, if any.

General System of Preferences (GSP): General System of Preferences (GSP) countries are those designated by the United Nations as "developing." To assist in their economic growth, they are accorded special preference and therefore pay no tariff.

IMPORT QUOTAS

The importation of certain products is controlled by quantity. *Quotas* for this control are established by specific legislation, usually to protect infant industries or established industries under marketing pressure from foreign countries. Most textiles and apparel are subject to these quotas country by country, product by product. Most of the quotas have fixed ceilings for the amount that can imported in a calendar year. The status of quotas is maintained by a central Customs Service computer in Washington, D.C. Access to current quota status country by country can be obtained by calling (202) 927-5850, checking the "Quota Watch" column in the *Journal of Commerce,* or accessing www.customs.gov/impoexpo/impoexpo.htm.

U.S. import quotas are divided into two types: absolute and tariff-rate.

Absolute Quotas

Absolute quotas are *quantitative quotas*—that is, no more than the amount specified may be permitted during the quota period. Some are global, while others apply only to certain countries. When an absolute quota is filled, further entries are prohibited during the remainder of the quota period.

Tariff-Rate Quotas

Tariff-rate quotas provide for the entry of a specified quantity at a reduced rate of duty during a given period. Quantities entered in excess of the quota for the period are subject to higher duty rates.

SPECIAL IMPORT REGULATIONS

Many countries require a license to import, but the United States does not. Thousands of products are imported freely with no restrictions. Although the importation of goods does not require a license from the Customs Service, certain classes of merchandise may be prohibited or restricted by other agencies (1) to protect the economy and security of the country, (2) to safeguard health, or (3) to preserve domestic plant and animal life. The importer is wise to inquire (complete with samples and specifications) with the regulatory body involved, well before entering into any business arrangements. Many an importer has ended up with a warehouse full of products unfit for or prohibited from entering the United States. For more information, go to www.customs.gov/impoexpo/impoexpo.htm.

Agricultural Commodities

The U.S. Food and Drug Administration and the Department of Agriculture control or regulate the importation of most animals, animal foods, insects, plants, and poultry products.

Arms, Ammunition, and Radioactive Materials

The Bureau of Alcohol, Tobacco, and Firearms of the Department of the Treasury prohibits the importation of implements of war without a license. Even temporary importation, movement, and exportation are prohibited unless licensed by the Office of Munitions Control of the Department of State. Of course, the Nuclear Regulatory Commission controls all forms of radioactive materials and nuclear reactors. Call (202) 927-8320 or go to www.DOT.gov.

Consumer Products—Safety and Energy Conservation

Such consumer products as refrigerators, freezers, dishwashers, water heaters, television sets, and furnaces (and other energy-using products) are regulated by the Consumer Products Efficiency Branch of the Department of Energy. The Consumer Product Safety Commission (CPSC) oversees safety issues.

Electronic Products

Radiation-producing products, including sonic radiation (such as cathode-ray tubes), are regulated by the Food and Drug Administration's Center for Devices and Radiological Health and by the Federal Communications Commission.

Food, Drugs, Cosmetics, and Medical Devices

The federal Food, Drug, and Cosmetics Act governs the importation of food, beverages, drugs, devices, and cosmetics. This act is administered by the Food and Drug Administration of the Department of Health and Human Services.

Gold, Silver, Currency, and Stamps

Provisions of the National Stamping Act, enforced by the Department of Justice, regulate some aspects of importing silver and gold.

Pesticides and Toxic and Hazardous Substances

Three acts control the importation of these substances: the Insecticide, Fungicide, and Rodenticide Act of 1947, the Toxic Substances Control Act of 1977, and the Hazardous Substances Act.

Textile, Wool, and Fur Products

Textile fiber products must be stamped, tagged, and labeled as required by the Textile Fiber Products Identification Act. Similarly, wool products must be clearly marked in accordance with the Wool Products Labeling Act of 1939. Fur, not to be left out, must be labeled as required by the Fur Products Labeling Act. Regulations and pamphlets containing the text of these labeling acts may be obtained from the Federal Trade Commission.

Trademarks, Trade Names, and Copyrights

The Customs Reform and Simplification Act of 1979 strengthened the protection afforded trademark owners against the importation of articles bearing counterfeit marks. Articles bearing trademarks or marks that copy or simulate a registered trademark of a U.S. or foreign corporation are prohibited from importation. The Copyright Revision Act of 1976 provides that the importation into the United States of copies of a work acquired outside the United States without authorization of the copyright owner is an infringement of the copyright.

Wildlife and Pets

The U.S. Fish and Wildlife Service of the Department of the Interior controls the importation of (1) wild or game animals, birds, and other wildlife, or any part or product made therefrom, and (2) the eggs of wild or game birds. The importation of birds, cats, dogs, monkeys, and turtles is subject to the requirements of the U.S. Public Health Service, Centers for Disease Control and Prevention, Quarantine Division, located in Atlanta, Georgia.

FREE TRADE ZONES

Special zones for free trade, sometimes called in-bond regions, did not develop in any significant way until the nineteenth century. Some of the more notable zones worldwide are the port regions of Hamburg in Germany, Hong Kong in China, Koushieng in Taiwan, and Jurong Port in Singapore.

Inland free zones also exist, the most notable of which are the in-bond, free zones surrounding the Mexican Maquiladoras. Even Russia is establishing free zones to promote interchange of business with market economies.

Free zones, under legislation of the sovereign nation where they are located, are considered outside the customs territory of that country. The concept is an ancient one, dating back to Egyptian times. Goods entering the zone pay no tariff or other taxes, under a guarantee (bond) that such goods will not be entered into the domestic market. Should they enter the domestic market, all duties must be routinely paid. While in these free zones, goods can be altered, assembled, manufactured, and manipulated. Thus the zones become areas where barriers to free trade are circumvented.

U.S. Foreign Trade Zones (FTZs)

Everywhere else in the world they are called free zones. But in the United States they are called foreign trade zones (FTZ). As elsewhere, these zones are restricted areas considered outside the territory under the supervision of the U.S. Customs Service.

Typically an FTZ is a large warehouse—fenced and alarmed for security reasons—that tenants lease in order to bring in merchandise, foreign or domestic, to be stored, exhibited, assembled, manufactured, or processed in some way. Most FTZs are located in or near customs ports of entry, usually in industrial parks or in terminal warehouse facilities. The usual customs entry procedures and payment of duties are not required on foreign merchandise in the zone unless it enters the customs territory for domestic consumption. The importer has a choice of paying duties either on the original foreign material or on the finished product. Quota restrictions do not normally apply to foreign merchandise in a zone.

From the point of view of the local governments in the United States that build them, FTZs stimulate international trade and thus contribute to the economic growth of a region by creating jobs and income. But from the point of view of an importer or exporter, it's all about *profits*.

HISTORY NOTE: The success of free zones like the "free port" of Hamburg, which stimulated American interest, culminated in the passage of the Foreign Trade Zones Act of 1934 and its amendment in 1950. The early history of American foreign trade zones (FTZs) is not glamorous. Growth was slow and profits modest. Until the early 1970s, fewer than 25 FTZs were authorized and in operation in the United States, and that number had not changed appreciably since the enabling legislation was passed in 1934. However, since 1975 the number of FTZs has grown at an almost exponential rate. At last count the number of authorized general-purpose zones was more than 110, with 56 special subzones and 50 applications pending.

Advantages of Using an FTZ

Actually, perceived advantages of FTZs are limitless. Unfortunately, many firms that began operations in FTZs have lost money. Each operation in the zone must make business and profit sense and must be individually analyzed. Here is a list of the regulatory advantages:

- Customs procedural requirements are minimal.
- Merchandise may remain in a zone indefinitely, whether or not it is subject to duty.
- Customs security requirements provide protection against theft.
- Customs duty and internal revenue tax, if applicable, are paid when merchandise is transferred from a foreign trade zone to the customs territory for consumption.
- While in a zone, merchandise is not subject to U.S. duty or excise tax. Tangible personal property is generally exempt from state and local ad valorem taxes.
- Goods may be exported from a zone free of duty and tax.
- The zone user that plans to enter merchandise for consumption in the customs territory may elect to pay duty and taxes either on the foreign material placed in the zone or on the article transferred from the zone. The rate of duty and tax and the value of the merchandise

may change as a result of manipulation or manufacture in the zone. Therefore the importer may pay the lowest duty possible on the imported merchandise.

- Merchandise under bond may be transferred to a foreign trade zone from the customs territory for the purpose of satisfying a legal requirement to export or destroy the merchandise. For instance, merchandise may be taken into a zone in order to satisfy an exportation requirement of the Tariff Act of 1930, or an exportation requirement of any other federal law insofar as the agency charged with its enforcement deems it advisable. Exportation or destruction may also fulfill requirements of certain state laws.

The Role of the Customs Service

The director of the Customs Service district office is responsible for controlling the admission of merchandise into the FTZ, the handling and disposition of merchandise within the FTZ, and the removal of merchandise from it.

Operations That Might Be Performed in an FTZ

All businesses may not benefit from FTZ operations, and those contemplating leasing in a zone must analyze both the market potential and the economic potential. Some businesses that might benefit are:

- Automotive parts—repack, remark, and distribute.
- Clothing—cut and sew imported fabric for import and export.
- Foodstuffs—label, sample, and repack for shipment.
- Liquor—affix stamps, destroy broken bottles, and defer duty.
- Machinery—inspect, repair, clean, and paint.
- Office equipment—inspect and distribute.
- Televisions and other electronics—repackage for shipment.
- Sporting goods—sort and repackage for shipment.

Money-Saving Reasons to Use an FTZ

The uses of a foreign trade zone for money-saving reasons is limited only to the creativity of the user and the trade-off of the costs of leasing space in an FTZ versus storing goods in a commercial warehouse. Here are several standard reasons:

- *Cost of money.* The drawback is the recovery of duty already paid—a costly and time-consuming process. The Treasury Department does not expedite the repayment of duties already paid and, if it finally does, pays only 99 percent of the original amount, keeping 1 percent to cover administrative costs. If the duty had not been paid in the first place, that sum of money could have earned interest. The interest and administrative charges result in a cost of money that companies with high inventories could have avoided by using a foreign trade zone.

- *Cash flow.* The money paid to the Customs Service under the tariff schedule is money no longer available for other uses, even if that money is later recovered under drawback procedures. Using an FTZ to defer duty or taxes improves a cash flow position.

- *Reclamation.* There are many examples of reclamation within an FTZ that can provide a cost saving. In fact, the possibilities are limited only by the imagination of the user and the legality of the operation. Consider a computer manufacturer that imports chips from offshore (Asia or Mexico). Before importing them into the United States, the manufacturer conducts a quality assurance (QA) check within the FTZ. The firm reclaims the gold and other materials from the failed boards, sends the recovered material back to the offshore plant, and imports only the chips that pass QA, thus avoiding duty on the failed units.

- *Inverted tariff.* A foreign trade zone is the only method in U.S. law whereby an importer can choose between paying the duty rate of material parts or paying the rate of a finished product. The importer would, of course, make the choice that provided the greatest cost saving.

- *Lower insurance costs.* A foreign trade zone is required to be a secure area. It is fenced and alarmed and often guarded. For that reason and because the value of an inventory is not increased by the value added in the FTZ, the inventory stored within a zone is often charged at lower insurance rates.
- *Transportation time saving.* Goods destined for a foreign trade zone are not delayed on the dock for customs; rather, because they are considered in bond, they are usually given priority for pierside movement. Therefore those items destined for manipulation, reclamation, or repacking into smaller shipping units can be expedited by using the FTZ.
- *Reduced pierside pilferage and/or damage.* Because there are no dockside delays, there is less risk of theft, pilferage, and damage to the incoming goods.
- *Fine avoidance.* Goods imported into the United States with improper or incorrect labels are subject to fines. By checking the labels within an FTZ, the importer can avoid the fines.
- *Advantage over a bonded warehouse.* FTZ tenants avoid the cost of a bond, which is purchased by the zone operator.
- *Environmental protection.* Reclamation activities in an FTZ are centered within an enclosed area, using special machines, and can be carefully controlled.
- *General system of preferences (GSP).* The duty-free advantage of this multilateral trade agreement can be combined with the benefits of FTZs.
- *Customs Item 9802.00.80503.* Duty reduction can be obtained through incorporating this item of customs law (related to labor content) in offshore assembly.
- *Customs Item 9801.00.10108.* This item (related to packaging material content) offers duty-free treatment of U.S.-origin goods that are improved or advanced in condition or value while abroad.
- *State and local taxes.* Under federal law, tangible personal property imported into an FTZ, or tangible personal

property produced in the United States and held in an FTZ for export, is exempt from state and local ad valorem taxes.

- *Quota allocations.* Duty and charges against quota allocations can be avoided if shipments are rejected.
- *Duty elimination.* There is no duty on merchandise re-exported or destroyed in the zone.
- *Duty deferral.* Duty on foreign goods can be deferred until they leave the zone.
- *Indefinite storage.* Goods may be stored indefinitely while awaiting a more receptive market or more favorable sales conditions.

CUSTOMS BONDED WAREHOUSES

A bonded warehouse is a building or other secure area within the customs territory where dutiable foreign merchandise may be placed for a period up to five years without payment of duty. Only cleaning, repacking, and sorting may take place. The owner of the bonded warehouse incurs liability and must post a bond with the U.S. Customs Service and abide by those regulations pertaining to control and declaration of tariffs for goods on departure. The liability is canceled when the goods are removed.

Types of Bonded Warehouses

U.S. customs regulations authorize eight different types of bonded warehouses:

1. Storage areas owned or leased by the government to store merchandise undergoing customs inspection, under seizure, or unclaimed goods.
2. Privately owned warehouses used exclusively for the storage of merchandise belonging or consigned to the proprietor.
3. Publicly bonded warehouses used exclusively to store imported goods.
4. Bonded yards or sheds for the storage of heavy and bulky imported merchandise such as pens for animals—

stables and corrals—and tanks for the storage of imported fluids.

5. Bonded grain storage bins or elevators.

6. Warehouses used for the manufacture in bond, solely
for exportation, of imported articles.

7. Warehouses bonded for smelting and refining imported
metal-bearing materials.

8. Bonded warehouses created for sorting, cleaning,
repacking, or otherwise changing the condition of imported merchandise, but not for manufacturing.

How to Establish a Bonded Warehouse

Your Customs Service district office has all the needed information on how to get started, but in general, the following five
items must be fulfilled:

1. Submit an application to the district office giving the
location and stating the class of warehouse to be established. Such application should describe the general
character of the merchandise, the estimated maximum
duties and taxes that could become due at any one
time, and whether the warehouse will be used for private storage or treatment or as a public warehouse.

2. A fee of about $100.

3. A certificate that the building is acceptable for fire insurance purposes.

4. A blueprint of the building or space to be bonded.

5. A bond of $5000 or greater on each building, depending
on the class of the bonded area.

Bonded Warehouse or Foreign Trade Zone?

Table 8-4 compares the functions of a foreign trade zone and a
bonded warehouse.

Being aware of all the possibilities is a vital part of competing and winning the trade game. Not every importer or exporter will need countertrade or make use of a foreign trade
zone or a customs bonded warehouse, but proper and advanced

Table 8-4.   Comparison of FTZ and Bonded Warehouse

Function	Bonded warehouse	Zone
Customs entry	A bonded warehouse is within U.S. customs territory; therefore a customs entry must be filed to enter goods into the warehouse.	A zone is not considered within customs territory. Customs entry is, therefore, not required until merchandise is removed from a zone.
Permissible cargo	Only foreign merchandise may be placed in a bonded warehouse.	All merchandise, whether domestic or foreign, may be placed in a zone.
Customs bonds	Each entry must be covered by either a single-entry term bond or a general term bond.	No bond is required for merchandise in a zone.
Payment of duty	Duties are due prior to release from bonded warehouses.	Duties are due only upon entry into U.S. territory.
Manufacture of goods	Manufacturing is prohibited.	Manufacturing is permitted with duty payable at the time the goods leave the zone for U.S. consumption. Duty is payable on either the imported components or the finished product, whichever carries a lower rate.
Appraisal and classification	Immediately.	Tariff rate and value may be determined either at the time goods are admitted into a zone or when goods leave a zone, at the importer's discretion.
Storage periods	Not to exceed 5 years.	Unlimited.
Operations on merchandise destined for domestic consumption	Only cleaning, repackaging, and sorting may take place and under customs supervision.	Zone operations include sort, destroy, clean, grade, mix with foreign or domestic goods, label, assemble, manufacture, exhibit, sell, and repack.
Customs entry regulations	Apply fully.	Applicable only to goods actually removed from a zone for U.S. consumption.

planning is essential to take advantage of the subtleties of the trade laws. An appreciation of the capabilities of each of the business tools presented in this chapter could lead to the recognition of a winning opportunity.

The preceding two chapters have presented the elements that distinguish each side of the import/export transaction. In the next part of the book, five chapters are dedicated to understanding the basics of doing business in the major regions of the world: WTCs (world trade centers), NAFTA, Europe, Africa, and the Near East and Asia.

3

Doing Business
Worldwide

9

Doing Business Through World Trade Centers

MAKING WORLD TRADE CONNECTIONS CAN BE DIFFICULT BUT IT need not be, because there is a growing organization that can link you to other traders not only in other countries, but also in your own home area. That place is your nearest world trade center.

Founded in 1970, the World Trade Centers Association (WTCA) is a not-for-profit, nonpolitical association dedicated to the establishment and effective operation of world trade centers (WTCs) as instruments for trade expansion. To date, the WTCA membership represents 336 centers in 101 countries.

The World Trade Centers Association is the world's largest apolitical, private, international organization that is dedicated to providing services to those who develop and facilitate international trade. With its unique global mission and membership, the WTCA has been a world leader in creating innovative service for international business.

WTCs are located in over 170 cities with about 100 more centers in the planning stages. In other words, they are in virtually every major trading city in the world. The WTC Network links, by electronic trading, the centers and their clients and affiliates worldwide. Offers to buy or sell can be advertised on the WTC Network's bulletin board. Founded over 30 years ago, the WTCA continues in its stated purpose:

- To invite individual members.
- To promote mutual assistance and a cooperative exchange of services and information among members.
- To encourage the establishment of new centers and the development of improved services in existing centers.
- To promote international business relationships.
- To foster increased participation in world trade.

WHAT IS A WORLD TRADE CENTER (WTC)?

A WTC is a shopping center that puts all the services associated with international trade under one roof. It is the first stop for your import/export venture. WTCs complement and support the existing services of private and government agencies. Here are some of the services you will find at a WTC.

Trade Information

WTCs provide up-to-date information about their respective regions, including local products and services, market conditions, government regulations, and business culture. They also furnish detailed profiles of local business contacts, including manufacturers, distributors, and service providers. They also perform market research tailored to specific needs.

WTCA ON-LINE SERVICES

The WTCA's Web site (www.wtca.org) is a one-stop source for global business information. Through strategic alliances with leading information and service providers, WTCA On-Line offers the best international trade information and services at discount prices. These include:

- WTCA On-Line trade opportunities
- Trade flow pricing system
- STAT-USA's National Trade Data Bank
- WTCA On-Line catalog
- World Trade Library
- Directory of world trade center services
- Port Import Export Reporting Service (PIERS)

- World trade center events
- Access to WTCA online

World Trade Center Clubs

World trade center clubs feature comfortable lounge and dining services for members and their guests in an impressive centrally located address.

Trade Education Programs

Local WTCs sponsor practical workshops, seminars, and courses for credit on key local and global business issues.

Trade Mission Assistance

Each WTC helps businesses explore new markets by working with other WTCs to promote their products and services.

Display and Exhibit Services

Each WTC is equipped with professional staff and world-class facilities for media displays, product exhibitions, and more.

WTCA SERVICES AND BENEFITS TO MEMBERS

Every WTC is a member of the WTCA, and therefore enjoys the following benefits:

- Exclusive rights to use the WTCA's service marks and logo.
- Exclusive rights to market WTCA On-Line in the member's region.
- Access to information and services available through other WTCs.
- Reciprocal privileges for local members at all operating WTCs and world trade center clubs.
- Seminars on how to establish a successful WTC.
- Manuals on planning and operating specific WTC services.
- A monthly newsletter and many other useful publications.

- Annual general assemblies and regular committee meetings to promote a variety of special projects and mutual assistance programs.

The World Trade Center University

The World Trade Center University (WTCU), sponsored by the WTCA, is an international on-line educational program offering U.S.-accredited coursework and degrees. Participants download lectures, hold discussions, complete and submit assignments, take examinations, and gain access to an entire library of learning materials—all through their computers.

Each WTC is a potential regional learning center for the WTCU, providing administrative services and in-person student exams, which may be required upon completion of a course. For more information, call (213) 473-9820, fax (213) 473-9825, or go to www.wtcu.org.

Trade Card

Trade Card, the WTCA's electronic commerce system, automates the international trade process. E-commerce includes trade finance, preexport finance, inspection services, and on-line insurance.

For more information, contact the World Trade Centers Association, 1 World Trade Center, Suite 7701, New York, NY 10048; phone: (212) 432-2626; fax: (212) 488-0064; Web: www.wtca.org; e-mail: wtca@wtca.org.

The next chapter explains how to do business in the Americas and NAFTA.

10

Doing Business in the Americas and an Expanding NAFTA

TRADE AMONG THE 36 NATIONS OF THE AMERICAS (SEE TABLE 10-1) has always been brisk, but tariffs and other barriers have often stifled profitability and therefore economic growth. In recent years, incentives have been put in place to stimulate the potential market (see Table 10-2), bringing the promise of increased wealth to the Western hemisphere. Most notable among these efforts are the Caribbean Basin Initiative (CBI) of 1984, the U.S.-Canadian Free Trade Agreement of 1989, and the North American Free Trade Agreement (NAFTA) of 1994.

NAFTA is currently a single market composed of the three North American nations. However, integration of the other 31 nations (less Cuba) is being considered. At the "Miami Summit" held in December 1994, the leaders of 34 of the 35 democratic nations of the Americas signed a declaration to negotiate by the year 2005 a Free Trade Area of the Americas (FTAA).

This area of no trade barriers would embrace a market of almost a billion people and stretch from Alaska to the tip of Argentina. One method of achieving the FTAA is through the expansion of NAFTA. Another route being considered is the merger or linking of other, subregional trade arrangements with the FTAA.

Table 10-1. The Americas

Antigua and Barbuda	Dominican Republic	Paraguay
Argentina	Ecuador	Peru
Bahamas	El Salvador	St. Kitts-Nevis
Barbados	Grenada	St. Lucia
Belize	Guatemala	St. Vincent and the
Bolivia	Guyana	Grenadines
Brazil	Haiti	Surinam
Canada	Honduras	Trinidad and Tobago
Chile	Jamaica	United States of
Colombia	Mexico	America
Costa Rica	Nicaragua	Uruguay
Cuba	Panama	Venezuela
Dominica		

Table 10-2. Trading Potential in the Americas

		Purchasing Power Parity	
Country	Population (millions)	National Income ($ bil)	Per Capita Income
Canada	31	688	22,400
United States	273	8,500	31,500
Mexico	100	815	8,300
NAFTA totals	404	10,030	Avg. 20,733
Central/Latin America totals	569	2,678	Avg. 5,533

Source: *CIA Factbook 1999* (www.cia.gov).

Table 10-2 shows the potential of the total Americas market. The Central and Latin American markets, although smaller in gross domestic product (GDP), nevertheless have a growing middle class and offer excellent trade potential.

Each nation of the Americas has its own tariff schedule and each belongs to one or more regional trade arrangements that dictate a bloc tariff.

This chapter deals with two major elements of doing business in the Americas:

- NAFTA
- Maquiladora implications
- Other existing trade arrangements

NAFTA

The North American Free Trade Agreement (NAFTA) was signed by Canada, the United States of Mexico, and the United States of America. With 360 million people and per capita incomes of over $18,000 a year (about $8300 in Mexico), it represents the richest market in the world and has always been the first target for anyone doing international business.

NAFTA offers preferential tariff treatment for businesses trading within the newly created single market and is a major step toward stimulating regional trade. NAFTA rules are clear and understandable but require thought as they apply to a given firm's products. The tactical implications of NAFTA depend on a product-by-product analysis as well as on the position of the firm as an insider or outsider.

Key Provisions

The NAFTA document is over 1000 pages and its companion tariff schedule is even longer. Obviously, over the years there will be changes negotiated by the three countries, but those changes will be the result of users (exporters and importers) shoring up loopholes and finding better ways of doing business. The intent of the basic document will remain as follows:

- Phase-out of tariffs from applied rates in effect on July 1, 1991, including U.S. General System of Preferences (GSP) and Canadian General Preference Treatment (GPT) rates.
- Elimination of all tariffs between the United States and Canada.
- Phase-out and elimination of duties on U.S. and Canadian trade with Mexico within 15 years.
- Use of certificates of origin to prevent third-country intrusion.
- Elimination of customs user fees and duty drawbacks.
- Elimination of quotas unless grandfathered.

- Prohibition of product standards as a barrier to trade.
- Elimination of agricultural tariffs and subsidies.
- Elimination of Mexican tariffs on all U.S. exports within 10 years (corn and beans will have a 15-year phase-out).
- Expansion of government procurement markets.
- Elimination of discrimination on laws related to service providers.

National Treatment

NAFTA incorporates the fundamental "national treatment" obligation of the General Agreement on Tariffs and Trade (GATT). This commitment means that goods of other parties will be treated, in terms of tariffs and laws, as if they were domestic goods. "National treatment" extends to provincial and state measures as well.

Temporary Entry of Business Travelers

Taking into account the preferential trading relationship between the NAFTA countries, on a reciprocal basis the agreement commits to temporary entry into their respective territories of business travelers who are citizens of Canada, Mexico, or the United States.

Each country will grant temporary entry to four categories of business travelers:

- *Business visitors* engaged in international business for the purpose of conducting activities related to research and design, growth, manufacture and production, marketing, sales, distribution, after-sales service, and other general services.
- *Traders and investors* who carry on substantial trade in goods or services between their own country and the country they wish to enter, provided that such visitors are employed or operate in a supervisory or executive capacity or one that involves essential skills.
- *Intracompany transfers* who are employed in a managerial or executive capacity or one that involves special-

ized knowledge and who are transferred within their company to another NAFTA country.

- *Certain categories of professionals* who meet minimum educational requirements or who possess alternative credentials and who seek to engage in business activities at a professional level in the country they wish to enter.

HOT TIP: Temporary Entry Rules

Ordinary Business (Non NAFTA)

- U.S. citizens: No papers up to 72 hours and 48 miles.
- Tourist card or visa for longer stays.
- Mexican citizens: Valid border crossing card (USINS) up to 72 hours and 25 miles. Visa for longer stays.

NAFTA Business Visitors

- Proof of citizenship.
- Purpose documentation (i.e., must be international in scope).
- Employment outside territory of grantor.
- Each party grants temporary entry visa.

Duty-Free Temporary Admission of Goods

Business visitors covered by NAFTA's "temporary entry" provisions may bring into a NAFTA country "professional equipment" and "tools of the trade" on a duty-free, temporary basis. These rules also cover the importation of commercial samples, certain types of advertising films, and goods imported for sports purposes or for display and demonstration.

Other rules provide that after repair or alteration in another NAFTA country, all goods will reenter duty free.

Country-of-Origin Marking

Under NAFTA, country-of-origin marking is designed to minimize unnecessary costs, and to this end the following rules apply:

- Any reasonable method may be used (e.g., stickers, labels, tags, paint).
- Markings must be conspicuous and permanent.

HOT TIP: Marking Exemptions

- Item incapable of being marked.
- Item that cannot be marked prior to exportation without injury to goods.
- Item that cannot be marked except at great expense, which would discourage exportation.
- A crude substance.
- An original work of art.

Certificates of Origin

Each of the three countries has its own certificates for goods entering from non-NAFTA countries. However, there is also a common NAFTA *certificate of origin,* as shown in Figures 10-1 to 10-3. Note the key elements of the certificate:

Item 5	Description of goods
Item 6	Harmonized tariff classification number
Item 7	Preference
Item 8	Producer
Item 9	Net cost
Item 10	Country of origin

Rules of Origin (ROO)

Over a 15-year transition period, "NAFTA eliminates all tariffs on goods originating in Canada, Mexico, and the United States." This provision holds such financial benefit that foreign traders could be tempted to defeat preferential treatment by going around the free trade area and importing through the country that has the least external tariff. Thus NAFTA includes a rigorous set of rules of origin (ROO) that define which goods are eligible:

- Because each country maintains its own external tariffs on imports from other countries, ROO are required to prevent imports from third countries being shipped

DEPARTMENT OF THE TREASURY
UNITED STATES CUSTOMS SERVICE

NORTH AMERICAN FREE TRADE AGREEMENT
CERTIFICATE OF ORIGIN

Aproved through 12/31/96
OMB No. 1515-0204
See back of form for Paper-
work Reduction Act Notice.

Please print or type   19 CFR 181.11, 181.22

1. EXPORTER NAME AND ADDRESS	2. BLANKET PERIOD *(DD/MM/YY)*
	FROM
	TO
TAX IDENTIFICATION NUMBER:	
3. PRODUCER NAME AND ADDRESS	4. IMPORTER NAME AND ADDRESS
TAX IDENTIFICATION NUMBER:	TAX IDENTIFICATION NUMBER:

5. DESCRIPTION OF GOOD(S)	6. HS TARIFF CLASSIFICATION NUMBER	7. PREFERENCE CRITERION	8. PRODUCER	9. NET COST	10. COUNTRY OF ORIGIN

I CERTIFY THAT:

• THE INFORMATION ON THIS DOCUMENT IS TRUE AND ACCURATE AND I ASSUME THE RESPONSIBILITY FOR PROVING SUCH REP-
RESENTATIONS. I UNDERSTAND THAT I AM LIABLE FOR ANY FALSE STATEMENTS OR MATERIAL OMISSIONS MADE ON OR IN CON-
NECTION WITH THIS DOCUMENT;

• I AGREE TO MAINTAIN, AND PRESENT UPON REQUEST, DOCUMENTATION NECESSARY TO SUPPORT THIS CERTIFICATE, AND TO
INFORM, IN WRITING, ALL PERSONS TO WHOM THE CERTIFICATE WAS GIVEN OF ANY CHANGES THAT COULD AFFECT THE ACCU-
RACY OR VALIDITY OF THIS CERTIFICATE;

• THE GOODS ORIGINATED IN THE TERRITORY OF ONE OR MORE OF THE PARTIES, AND COMPLY WITH THE ORIGIN REQUIREMENTS
SPECIFIED FOR THOSE GOODS IN THE NORTH AMERICAN FREE TRADE AGREEMENT, AND UNLESS SPECIFICALLY EXEMPTED IN
ARTICLE 411 OR ANNEX 401, THERE HAS BEEN NO FURTHER PRODUCTION OR ANY OTHER OPERATION OUTSIDE THE TERRITORIES
OF THE PARTIES; AND

• THIS CERTIFICATE CONSISTS OF [   ] PAGES, INCLUDING ALL ATTACHMENTS.

11.	11a. AUTHORIZED SIGNATURE	11b. COMPANY	
	11c. NAME *(Print or Type)*	11d. TITLE	
	11e. DATE *(DD/MM/YY)*	11f. TELEPHONE ▷ NUMBER	:(Voice) :(Facsimile)

Customs Form 434 (121793)

Fig. 10-1. NAFTA certificate of origin

through one NAFTA partner into another in order to es-
cape a higher tariff.

• NAFTA reduces tariffs only for goods made in North
America.

• For duty-free treatment, goods must obtain substantial
North American content.

DEPARTMENT OF THE TREASURY
UNITED STATES CUSTOMS SERVICE

Aproved through 12/31/96.
OMB No. 1515-0204.   See
Customs Form 434 for Paper-
work Reduction Act Notice.

NORTH AMERICAN FREE TRADE AGREEMENT
CERTIFICATE OF ORIGIN CONTINUATION SHEET

19 CFR 181.11, 181.22

5. DESCRIPTION OF GOOD(S)	6. HS TARIFF CLASSIFICATION NUMBER	7. PREFERENCE CRITERION	8. PRODUCER	9. NET COST	10. COUNTRY OF ORIGIN

Customs Form 434A (121793)

Fig. 10-2. NAFTA certificate of origin (continuation sheet)

- ROO reward companies using North American parts and labor.
- ROO prevent "free riders" from benefiting through minor processing or transshipment.
- Mexico and Canada cannot be used as export platforms into the U.S. market.

- Goods containing nonregional components qualify if they are sufficiently transformed in the NAFTA region to warrant change of tariff classification.

How NAFTA Rules of Origin Work. Each product has a rule of origin that applies to it. The rules are set forth in the tariff schedule accompanying the NAFTA document. There are two types of ROO: tariff-shift and value-content (see Table 10-3).

Rules are organized according to the Harmonized Commodity Description and Coding System (HS). The first six digits of the HS classify products using the internationally recognized commodity code. To determine the tariff elimination schedule for a particular product, exporters must find out the product's HS number.

Examples of Specific Rules of Origin

CHAPTER 44: Wood and Articles of Wood
44.01 - 44.21:
   A change to heading 44.01 through 44.21 from any other heading, including another heading within that group.

CHAPTER 30: Pharmaceutical Products
30.04:
   A change to subheading 30.04.10 through 30.04.90 from any other heading, except from heading 30.03; or
   a change to subheading 30.04.10 through 30.04.90 from any other subheading within heading 30.04, whether or not there is a change from any other heading, provided there is a regional value of not less than:
      a. 60 percent; transaction value method
      b. 50 percent; net cost method

HOT TIP

Q: What is a good?
A: Whatever crosses the border.

Q: What is material?
A: The components (stuff) that make up a good.

How to Claim NAFTA Tariff

Using the customs entry document and the certificate of origin, follow these steps.

Instructions for the CF 434, as found on the form:

PAPERWORK REDUCTION ACT NOTICE: This information is needed to carry out the terms of the North American Free Trade Agreement (NAFTA). NAFTA requires that, upon request, an importer must provide Customs with proof of the exporter's written certification of the origin of the goods. The certification is essential to substantiate compliance with the rules of origin under the Agreement. You are required to give us this information to obtain a benefit.

Statement Required by 5 CFR 1320.21: The estimated average burden associated with this collection of information is 15 minutes per respondent or recordkeeper depending on individual circumstances. Comments concerning the accuracy of this burden estimate and suggestions for reducing this burden should be directed to U.S. Customs Service, Paperwork Management Branch, Washington DC 20229, and to the Office of Management and Budget, Paperwork Reduction Project (1515-0204), Washington DC 20503.

NORTH AMERICAN FREE TRADE AGREEMENT CERTIFICATE OF ORIGIN INSTRUCTIONS

For purposes of obtaining preferential tariff treatment, this document must be completed legibly and in full by the exporter and be in the possession of the importer at the time the declaration is made. This document may also be completed voluntarily by the producer for use by the exporter. Please print or type:

FIELD 1: State the full legal name, address (including country) and legal tax identification number of the exporter. Legal taxation number is: in Canada, employer number or importer/exporter number assigned by Revenue Canada; in Mexico, federal taxpayer's registry number (RFC); and in the United States, employer's identification number or Social Security Number.

FIELD 2: Complete field if the Certificate covers multiple shipments of identical goods as described in Field # 5 that are imported into a NAFTA country for a specified period of up to one year (the blanket period). "FROM" is the date upon which the Certificate becomes applicable to the good covered by the blanket Certificate (it may be prior to the date of signing this Certificate). "TO" is the date upon which the blanket period expires. The importation of a good for which preferential treatment is claimed based on this Certificate must occur between these dates.

FIELD 3: State the full legal name, address (including country) and legal tax identification number, as defined in Field #1, of the producer. If more than one producer's good is included on the Certificate, attach a list of additional producers, including the legal name, address (including country) and legal tax identification number, cross-referenced to the good described in Field #5. If you wish this information to be confidential, it is acceptable to state "Available to Customs upon request". If the producer and the exporter are the same, complete field with "SAME". If the producer is unknown, it is acceptable to state "UNKNOWN".

FIELD 4: State the full legal name, address (including country) and legal tax identification number, as defined in Field #1, of the importer. If the importer is not known, state "UNKNOWN", if multiple importers, state "VARIOUS".

FIELD 5: Provide a full description of each good. The description should be sufficient to relate it to the invoice description and to the Harmonized System (H.S.) description of the good. If the Certificate covers a single shipment of a good, include the invoice number as shown on the commercial invoice. If not known, indicate another unique reference number, such as the shipping order number.

FIELD 6: For each good described in Field #5, identify the H.S. tariff classification to six digits. If the good is subject to a specific rule of origin in Annex 401 that requires eight digits, identify to eight digits, using the H.S. tariff classification of the country into whose territory the good is imported.

FIELD 7: For each good described in Field #5, state which criterion (A through F) is applicable. The rules of origin are contained in Chapter Four and Annex 401. Additional rules are described in Annex 703.2 (certain agricultural goods), Annex 300-B, Appendix 6 (certain textile goods) and Annex 308.1 (certain automatic data processing goods and their parts). **NOTE: In order to be entitled to preferential tariff treatment, each good must meet at least one of the criteria below.**

Preference Criteria

A The good is "wholly obtained or produced entirely" in the territory of one or more of the NAFTA countries as referenced in Article 415. **Note: The purchase of a good in the territory does not necessarily render it "wholly obtained or produced".** If the good is an agricultural good, see also criterion F and Annex 703.2. *(Reference: Article 401(a) and 415)*

B The good is produced entirely in the territory of one or more of the NAFTA countries and satisfies the specific rule of origin, set out in Annex 401, that applies to its tariff classification. The rule may include a tariff classification change, regional value-content requirement, or a combination thereof. The good must also satisfy all other applicable requirements of Chapter Four. If the good is an agricultural good, see also criterion F and Annex 703.2. *(Reference: Article 401(b))*

224

C The good is produced entirely in the territory of one or more of the NAFTA countries exclusively from originating materials. Under this criterion, one or more of the materials may not fall within the definition of "wholly produced or obtained" as set out in Article 415. All materials used in the production of the good must qualify as "originating" by meeting the rules of Article 401(a) through (d). If the good is an agricultural good, see also criterion F and Annex 703.2. *Reference: Article 401(c).*

D Goods are produced in the territory of one or more of the NAFTA countries but do not meet the applicable rule of origin, set out in Annex 401, because certain non-originating materials do not undergo the required change in tariff classification. The goods do nonetheless meet the regional value-content requirement specified in Article 401 (d). This criterion is limited to the following two circumstances:

1. The good was imported into the territory of a NAFTA country in an unassembled or disassembled form but was classified as an assembled good, pursuant to H.S. General Rule of Interpretation 2(a), or

2. The good incorporated one or more non-originating materials, provided for as parts under the H.S., which could not undergo a change in tariff classification because the heading provided for both the good and its parts and was not further subdivided into subheadings, or the subheading provided for both the good and its parts and was not further subdivided.

NOTE: This criterion does not apply to Chapters 61 through 63 of the H.S. *Reference: Article 401(d)*

E Certain automatic data processing goods and their parts, specified in Annex 308.1, that do not originate in the territory are considered originating upon importation into the territory of a NAFTA country from the territory of another NAFTA country when the most-favored-nation tariff rate of the good conforms to the rate established in Annex 308.1 and is common to all NAFTA countries. *(Reference: Annex 308.1)*

F The good is an originating agricultural good under preference criterion A, B, or C above and is not subject to a quantitative restriction in the importing NAFTA country because it is a "qualifying good" as defined in Annex 703.2, Section A or B (please specify). A good listed in Appendix 703.2B.7 is also exempt from quantitative restrictions and is eligible for NAFTA preferential tariff treatment if it meets the definition of "qualifying good" in Section A of Annex 703.2. **NOTE 1: This criterion does not apply to goods that wholly originate in Canada or the United States and are imported into either country. NOTE 2: A tariff rate quota is not a quantitative restriction.**

FIELD 8: For each good described in Field #5, state "YES" if you are the producer of the good. If you are not the producer of the good, state "NO" followed by (1), (2), or (3), depending on whether this certificate was based upon: (1) your knowledge of whether the good qualifies as an originating good; (2) your reliance on the producer's written representation (other than a Certificate of Origin) that the good qualifies as an originating good; or (3) a completed and signed Certificate for the good, voluntarily provided to the exporter by the producer.

FIELD 9: For each good described in field #5, where the good is subject to a regional value content (RVC) requirement, indicate "NC" if the RVC is calculated according to the net cost method; otherwise, indicate "NO". If the RVC is calculated over a period of time, further identify the beginning and ending dates (DD/MM/YY) of that period. *(Reference: Articles 402.1, 402.5).*

FIELD 10: Identify the name of the country ("MX" or "US" for agricultural and textile goods exported to Canada; "US" or "CA" for all goods exported to Mexico; or "CA" or "MX" for all goods exported to the United States) to which the preferential rate of customs duty applies, as set out in Annex 302.2, in accordance with the Marking Rules or in each party's schedule of tariff elimination.

For all other originating goods exported to Canada indicate appropriately "MX" or "US" if the goods originate in that NAFTA country, within the meaning of the NAFTA Rules of Origin Regulations, and any subsequent processing in the other NAFTA country does not increase the transaction value of the goods by more than seven percent; otherwise "JNT" for joint production. *(Reference: Annex 302.2)*

FIELD 11: This field must be completed, signed, and dated by the exporter. When the Certificate is completed by the producer for use by the exporter, it must be completed, signed, and dated by the producer. The date must be the date the Certificate was completed and signed.

Fig. 10-3. NAFTA certificate of origin (instruction sheet)

225

Table 10-3. Examples of NAFTA Rules-of-Origin Types

Rule type	Description	Example
Tariff-shift	• All non-NAFTA inputs must be of a different tariff class than final product. • Rules state level of tariff shift required. • May require non-NAFTA input be a different HS chapter, heading or item number.	• Wood molding (HS 4409) made from (HS 4403) imported. Manufacturing process results in required HS heading shift.
Value-content	• Set percent of value must be North American. (Usually coupled with a tariff-shift requirement). • Some goods are subject to value-content rule only when they fail to pass tariff-shift test.	If medicaments (HS 3004), for example, fail tariff-shift rule, they must contain 50–60% North American content to get preferential treatment.

1. Classify the good.
2. Determine its HS number.
3. Tariff staging category (see Appendix C).
4. Is there a tariff difference?
5. Determine preference criteria A through F.
6. If preference B criteria then apply content calculation rules

    1. Tariff-shift?
    2. Tariff-shift + RVC?
    3. Regional value-content?

Preference Criteria

A. The good is "wholly obtained or produced entirely" in the territory of one or more of the NAFTA countries. *Note:* The purchase of a good in one territory does not necessarily render it "wholly obtained or produced." If the good is an agricultural good, see also criterion F.

B. The good is produced entirely in the territory of one or more of the NAFTA countries and satisfies the specific rule of origin, set out in Annex 401, that applies to its tariff classification. The rule may include tariff classification change, regional value-content requirement, or a combination thereof.

C. The good is produced entirely in the territory of one or more of the NAFTA countries exclusively from originating materials. Under this criterion, one or more of the materials may not fall within the definition of "wholly produced or obtained." All materials used in the production of the good must qualify as "originating."

D. Goods are produced in the territory of one or more of the NAFTA countries but do not meet the applicable rule of origin because certain nonoriginating materials do not undergo the required change in tariff classification. The goods do nonetheless meet the regional value-content requirement specified.

1. The good was imported into the territory of a NAFTA country in an unassembled or disassembled form but was classified as an assembled good.
2. The good incorporated one or more nonoriginating materials, provided for as parts under the HS, that could not undergo a change in tariff classification because the heading provided for both the good and its parts and was not further subdivided into subheadings, or the subheading provided for both the good and its parts and was not further subdivided.

E. Certain automatic data processing goods and their parts that do not originate in the territory are considered originating upon importation into the territory of a NAFTA country from the territory of another NAFTA country when the most-favored-nation tariff rate of the good conforms to the rate common to all NAFTA countries. (This criterion will go into effect when the NAFTA parties establish a Common External Tariff [CXT] Schedule.)

F. The good is an originating agricultural good under preference criterion A, B, or C above and is not subject to a

quantitative restriction in the importing NAFTA country because it is a "qualifying good" (as defined in NAFTA).

Content Calculation

- Tariff-shift: According to HS instructions
- Regional value-content (RVC) calculation
- *Transaction-value (TV) Method:* Based on price paid or payable for good.

$$RVC = \frac{TV - VNM}{TV} \times 100$$

- *Net cost (NC) method:* Based on total cost minus costs of royalties, sales promotion, and packing and shipping (sets limit on allowable interest).

$$RVC = \frac{NC - VNM}{NC} \times 100$$

- Either method may be used. However, net cost must be used when transaction value is not accepted under the WTO customs valuation code. Net cost must also be used for certain products, such as automotive goods.
- De minimus rule: If a good otherwise fails eligibility, it may still qualify if non-NAFTA content is no more than 7 percent of the price or total cost of good.

NAFTA by Industry

NAFTA goes beyond tariff reduction of general goods and specifies treatment by specific industries. The following is a cursory treatment.

Automotive Goods. NAFTA eliminates barriers to trade in North American automobiles, trucks, buses, and parts ("automotive goods") within the free trade area, and eliminates investment restrictions in this sector over a 10-year transition period.

Textiles and Apparel. NAFTA textiles and apparel provisions take precedence over any multifiber arrangement

(MFA) and other arrangements between NAFTA countries and provide:

- Immediate elimination or phase-out of duties over a maximum period of 10 years on goods that meet rules of origin.
- Immediate removal by the United States of import quotas on Mexican goods and gradual phase-out of import quotas that do not meet such rules.
- Immediate elimination by Mexico of tariffs on 20 percent of textile and apparel exports to the United States.
- Immediate duty-free treatment by Mexico of denim, underwear, sewing thread, and many household furnishings.

Textile and Apparel Rules of Origin. Specific rules of origin in NAFTA define when imported textile or apparel goods qualify for preferential treatment. For most products the "yarn forward" rule applies:

- *Yarn forward rule:* Goods must be made from yarn made in a NAFTA country in order to benefit from such treatment.
- *Fiber forward rule:* Goods must be produced from fiber made in a NAFTA country. The rule applies to certain goods such as cotton and synthetic fiber yarns.
- Preferential treatment is allowed for fabrics in short supply such as silk, linen, and certain shirting fabrics.

Energy and Basic Petrochemicals. NAFTA recognizes the desirability of strengthening the important role that trade in energy and basic petrochemical goods plays in the North American region and the need to enhance its role by sustained and gradual liberalization.

The energy provisions incorporate and build on WTO GATT disciplines regarding quantitative restrictions on imports and exports by providing that:

- A country may not impose minimum or maximum import or export price requirements, subject to the same exceptions that apply to quantitative restrictions.

- Each country may administer export and import licensing systems, provided that they are operated in a manner consistent with the provisions of the agreement.
- No country may impose a tax, duty, or charge on the export of energy or basic petrochemical goods unless the same tax, duty, or charge is applied to such goods when consumed domestically.
- Any import and export restrictions on energy trade will be limited to certain specific circumstances, such as to conserve exhaustible natural resources, deal with a short supply situation, or implement a price stabilization plan.
- Imports and exports may be restricted for national security reasons.
- Mexico reserves to the Mexican state goods, activities, and investments in Mexico in the oil, gas, refining, basic petrochemicals, nuclear, and electricity sectors.
- Investment in nonbasic petrochemical goods is governed by the general provisions of the agreement.

Agriculture

NAFTA sets out separate bilateral undertakings on cross-border trade in agricultural products: one between Canada and Mexico, and the other between Mexico and the United States. Both include a special transitional safeguard mechanism. The rules of the Canada-U.S. FTA will continue to apply to agricultural trade between Canada and the United States.

Technical Standards

NAFTA is designed to create a harmonization of technical standards in the three countries and prohibit countries from using technical standards as a barrier to market entry.

Government Procurement

The agreement opens a significant portion of the government procurement market in each NAFTA country on a nondiscriminatory basis to suppliers from other NAFTA countries for goods, services, and construction services.

Investment

NAFTA removes significant investment barriers, provides fair treatment of investors, eliminates government requirements that distort business decisions, and provides a dispute settlement mechanism for investors.

Services

NAFTA establishes a set of principles governing services trade. Virtually all services are covered with the exception of aviation, transport, maritime, and basic telecommunications.

Telecommunications

NAFTA provides that public telecommunications networks ("public networks") and services are to be available on reasonable and nondiscriminatory terms and conditions for firms or individuals who use those networks for the conduct of their business. These uses include the provision of enhanced or value-added telecommunications services and intracorporate communications. However, the operation and provision of public networks and services have not been made subject to NAFTA.

Financial Services

NAFTA establishes a principles-based approach to disciplining government measures regulating financial services. This section covers measures affecting financial institutions in the banking, insurance, and securities sectors as well as other financial services. These principles are:

- Commercial Presence and Cross-Border Services: May establish in any NAFTA country.
- Nondiscriminatory Treatment: Must provide both national and MFN treatment.
- Procedural "Transparency": Must make procedures transparent to applicants from other NAFTA countries. Guidelines include:

- Inform interested persons of its requirements.
- Provide information on status of application.
- Make administrative determination within 120 days.
- Allow interested persons opportunity to comment.

Intellectual Property

NAFTA embraces copyright, patent, and intellectual property laws, binding the three countries to existing international agreements and builds upon WTO and other international treaties.

Transformation: Maquiladora, FTZ, Bonded Warehouse

To claim NAFTA tariff, goods must, in general, have 60 percent North American content. Transformation of goods to obtain this content can be achieved in three ways: in a Maquiladora, a foreign trade zone, or a bonded warehouse. (The FTZ and bonded warehouse were explained in Chapter 8.) The Mexican Maquiladora Program, created in 1966 and still in effect, creates free zones in any location in Mexico where labor may be added to a production-sharing process. It is a business form in which goods and capital equipment can be imported into Mexico duty free. Duties on the exported product originally were imposed only on the value-added labor content. However, now all products must meet the 60 percent regional content (average), and duties no longer are assessed on value added.

MAQUILADORA IMPLICATIONS

The Mexican Maquiladora Program was instituted as a means of promoting investment in Mexico's border region (Programa de Industrialization Fronteriza). Companies that qualify under Mexico's current Maquiladora decree gain significant tax and duty deferral benefits. Under the current decree, a Maquiladora operating under this production-sharing program can sell into the Mexican domestic market up to 70 percent of its prior year's export volume. This amount increases 5 percent per year until January 1, 2001.

The second stage of NAFTA takes effect on January 1, 2001. As of that date, all Maquiladora production may be sold into the domestic market of Mexico; however, there will be restrictions on the duty relief available on materials originating outside of NAFTA. Raw materials incorporated into the assembly or manufacture of the finished good will pay the lesser of:

- The total amount of Mexican duties.
- The amount of import duties paid to the United States or Canada.

For additional information, visit www.doc.gov.

OTHER EXISTING TRADE ARRANGEMENTS

Trade among Central and Latin American nations has skyrocketed in recent years, rising fivefold from $7 billion in 1983 to $35 billion in 1999. Much of the gains can be attributed to the movement to reduce tariffs regionally. In addition to NAFTA, there are a growing number of regional trade arrangements, as described below:

Andean Common Market. The Andean Pact, which began with the Cartagena Agreement in 1969, is one of the oldest free trade agreements in existence. The original membership of Bolivia, Chile (since withdrawn), Colombia, Ecuador, and Peru now includes Venezuela. This market of 80 million, finalized in 1993, establishes a four-level common external tariff.

Caribbean Basin Initiative (CBI). This trade arrangement, dating from 1984, is intended to stimulate U.S. trade with about 20 Caribbean nations. The centerpiece is that almost all goods imported from the region without regard for quotas can enter the United States tariff free. Contact Office of Latin America and Caribbean (OLAC) Facts in a Flash for CBI Information, phone (202) 482-2521 or 482-2527.

Association of Caribbean States. Launched on January 1, 1995, this 200 million market provides preferential tariffs to Antigua and Barbuda, Cuba, Mexico, Dominica, Nicaragua, Bahamas, Dominican Republic, Barbados, Paraguay, Belize, El Salvador, Grenada, St. Kitts-Nevis, St. Lucia, Guyana, St. Vincent and the Grenadines, Haiti, Surinam, Colombia, Honduras, Trinidad and Tobago, Costa Rica, and Venezuela.

Caribbean Common Market (Caricom). This market of 7 million consumers was created on July 4, 1973, and includes Antigua and Barbuda, Bahamas, Barbados, Belize, Dominica, Grenada, Guyana, Jamaica, St. Vincent and the Grenadines, and Trinidad and Tobago. For additional information, visit www.caricom.org.

Caricom-Bolivia Free Trade Agreement. This free trade arrangement on selected products was launched January 1, 1995, and includes most of the same nations as the Caribbean Common Market (Caricom) plus Bolivia.

Caricom-Venezuela Free Trade Agreement. Again applying only to certain products, this arrangement is the same as Caricom with the addition of Venezuela.

Central American Common Market. This customs union comprising a market of 28 million people began December 13, 1960, and includes Costa Rica, El Salvador, Guatemala, Honduras, and Nicaragua.

Group of Three. This free trade area of 145 million includes only Mexico, Colombia, and Nicaragua.

Latin American Integration Association (LAIA). This trade preference association was formed in August 1980. Its market of 400 million people consists of Argentina, Bolivia, Brazil, Chile, Colombia, Ecuador, Mexico, Paraguay, Peru, Uruguay, and Venezuela.

Mercosur (Southern Cone Common Market). Mercosur is composed of Brazil, Argentina, Paraguay, and Uruguay and was launched on March 26, 1991. For more information, visit www.mercosur.org.

Organization of Eastern Caribbean States. This customs union encompasses Antigua and Barbuda, Dominica, Grenada, Montserrat, St. Kitts-Nevis, St. Lucia, and St. Vincent and the Grenadines.

The next chapter explains how to do business in an expanding Europe.

11

Doing Business in an Expanding Europe

OPPORTUNITY AWAITS IN A CHANGING EUROPEAN MARKET, including expansion of the European Union (EU) to include many of the newly independent states of Central and Eastern Europe. Visit www.europa.eu.int/index.htm for more information. The trade potential of Western Europe alone is a bonanza, as shown in Table 11-1.

This chapter discusses the following important elements of doing business in Europe.

- The European Union
- The European Free Trade Association (EFTA)
- Trade potential of the newly independent states
- Enlargement of the EU
- How to do business in the single market
- Doing business in Russia

For additional information, go to www.doc.gov or call (800) USA-TRADE.

THE EUROPEAN UNION

The original European Union (EU) consisting of Belgium, France, West Germany, Italy, Luxembourg, United Kingdom, Spain, Netherlands, Denmark, Greece, Portugal, and Ireland

Table 11-1.   Western European Trading Potential

Country	Population (millions)	Purchasing Power Parity National Income ($ bil)	Purchasing Power Parity Per Capita Income
European Union (EU)			
Germany	82	1,813	22,100
France	59	1,320	22,600
United Kingdom	59.1	1,250	21,200
Italy	56.7	1,180	20,800
Spain	39.1	645.6	16,500
Netherlands	15.8	348.6	22,200
Belgium/Luxembourg	10.1	236	23,300
Denmark	5.3	124.4	23,300
Greece	10.7	143	13,400
Portugal	9.9	144.8	14,600
Ireland	3.6	67.1	18,600
Sweden	8.9	175	19,700
Austria	8.1	184.5	22,700
Finland	5.2	103.6	20,100
Total	373.4	7,735.6	Avg. 20,078
European Free Trade Association (EFTA)			
Switzerland	7.3	191.8	26,400
Sweden	8.9	175	19,700
Austria	8.1	184.5	22,700
Finland	5.2	103.6	20,100
Norway	4.4	109	24,700
Iceland	0.27	6.06	22,400
Total	66.17	13,189.6	Avg. 22,667

Source: *CIA World Fact Book 1999* (www.cia.gov).

(now 15 members) established a single market when members agreed to a common external tariff (CXT) about 1968. Subsequently they harmonized most internal tariff and non-tariff rules related to their so-called four freedoms: free movement of goods, services, people, and capital.

These four freedoms amount to a principle that individual EU member states may not adopt measures that have the effect of restricting or interfering with intracommunity trade, subject to specific exceptions provided by EU law.

In practice, the European Union is a modern evolution of a customs union that expanded to a common market and then a political union with the signing of the Maastricht Treaty in 1992.

HISTORY NOTE: The European Union had its beginning in 1951, when the *Treaty of Paris* established the Coal and Steel Community between Belgium, France, the Federal German Republic, Italy, Luxembourg, and Holland. In 1957 the European Economic Community (ECC) was formed when the members of the Coal and Steel Community signed the *Treaty of Rome*. The more popular term European Community (EC) is the organization that resulted from the 1967 *Treaty of Fusion* that merged the secretariat (the "Commission") and the intergovernmental executive body (the "Council") of the older European Economic Community (EEC) with those of the European Coal and Steel Community (ECSC) and the European Atomic Energy Community (EURATOM), which was established to develop nuclear fuel and power for civilian purposes.

THE EUROPEAN FREE TRADE ASSOCIATION (EFTA)

The European Free Trade Association (EFTA) is a regional grouping established in 1960 by the Stockholm Convention, headquartered in Geneva. EFTA now comprises Austria, Iceland, Norway, Sweden, and Switzerland, with Finland as an associate member. Two charter members, Denmark and the United Kingdom, withdrew to join the European Union in 1973. Portugal, also a former member, withdrew in 1986 to join the European Union. EFTA member countries have gradually eliminated tariffs of manufactured goods originating and traded within EFTA. Agricultural products, for the most part, are not included on the EFTA schedule for internal tariff reductions. Each member country maintains its own external tariff schedule and each has concluded a trade agreement with the European Union that provides for the mutual elimination of tariffs for most manufactured goods except for a few sensitive products. As a result, the European Union and EFTA form what is now called the de facto European Economic Area (EEA).

TRADE POTENTIAL OF THE NEWLY INDEPENDENT STATES

The breakup of the Soviet Union offers practically virgin territory and excellent opportunities for expansion of markets.

The peaceful revolution of 1989 saw the beginning of a movement from Marxism toward market theory. But in Central and Eastern Europe perestroika is suffering in its attempt to leap forward from state enterprise to private ownership. Because there are few entrepreneurs and little private capital, more likely the immediate mechanism adopted by these nations will be a hybrid of Marxist-market theory that takes the best of the two approaches for the good of the economic growth of the regional nations. The ultimate change to privatization could take three or more decades.

The year 1989 was one of the most significant of the twentieth century. It was the year the Berlin Wall crumbled, signifying the peaceful revolution of Central European nations retreating from nonmarket economics. Even more significant was 1991. It was the year the Soviet Union splintered into its individual parts. It was the year the world sifted into two worlds: the industrial "haves" and the underdeveloped "have nots." The new free markets of Central and Eastern Europe are shown in Table 11-2.

ENLARGEMENT OF THE EU

The four fundamental freedoms of the European Union provide the framework for limitless boundary expansion and formation of a new Europe. Over the next decades the EU will welcome new members, the alacrity depending on economic and political reforms in Eastern Europe and the republics of the former Soviet Union.

Standing in the wings to join the EU are many nations that see benefits to the economic integration. Members of the European Free Trade Association (EFTA) as well as nations of Central Europe are candidates.

The agreement forming the European Economic Area between the EU and EFTA countries signifies the next step toward the economic integration of all Europe. Already three EFTA nations—Sweden, Finland, and Austria—have formally

Table 11-2.   The New Free Market Nations of Europe

	Population (millions)	Purchasing Power Parity GDP ($ bil)	Per Capita GDP
Central Europe			
Poland	38.6	263	6,800
Czech Republic	10.3	116.7	11,300
Slovakia	5.4	44.5	8,300
Slovenia	1.9	20.4	10,300
Hungary	10.2	75.4	7,400
Romania	22.3	90.6	4,050
Serbia/Montenegro	11.2	25.4	2,300
Croatia	4.7	23.6	5,100
Bosnia/Herzegovina	3.5	5.8	1,720
Bulgaria	8.2	33.6	4,100
Albania	3.3	5	1,490
Total	119.6	Total 704	Avg. 5,714
Eastern Europe			
Estonia	1.4	7.8	5,500
Latvia	2.4	9.7	4,100
Lithuania	3.6	17.6	1,640
Belarus	10.4	53.7	5,200
Ukraine	49.8	108.5	2,200
Georgia	5	11.2	2,200
Moldova	4.5	10	2,200
Russia	146.3	593	4,000
Azerbaijan	7.9	12.9	1,640
Kazakhstan	16.8	52.9	3,100
Kyrgyzstan	4.5	9.8	2,200
Tajikistan	6.1	6	990
Turkmenistan	4.3	7	1,630
Uzbekistan	24.1	59.2	2,500
Total	287.1	Total 957	Avg. 2,700

Source: *CIA World Fact Book 1999* (www.cia.gov).

joined the EU. Applications to join the EU are pending for Turkey and Switzerland. The people of Norway have rejected joining. Five formerly Communist countries are in the fast track into the Union—Poland, Hungary, the Czech Republic, Estonia, and Slovenia—as is Cyprus. Others waiting in line are Bulgaria, Latvia, Lithuania, Romania, and Slovakia. It is likely that the EU will expand to a customs union of at least 20 countries early in this century. A "Greater Europe," stretching from the Atlantic to the Urals, will develop into an organized power only if it is built around a stable nucleus capable of speaking and acting as one.

HOW TO DO BUSINESS IN THE SINGLE MARKET

The Single European Act (SEA) of 1992 contained a series of amendments to the Treaty of Rome that made it easier to negotiate the directives needed to make the single market work. The key innovation in the SEA was to extend the use of majority voting in place of unanimity in the EU's main decision-making body. Without majority voting, it would have been impossible to pass the more than 280 separate items of legislation that were required to eliminate internal EU frontiers and have the single market ready by the end of 1992. The measures already adopted relate to:

- The liberalization of public procurement.
- The harmonization of taxation.
- The liberalization of capital markets.
- Standardization (thanks to a new approach to certification and testing) and mutual recognition of the equivalence of national standards.
- The abolition of technical barriers (freedom to exercise an activity and recognition of the equivalence of training qualifications) and physical barriers (elimination of border checks) to the free movement of individuals.
- The creation of an environment that encourages business cooperation by harmonizing company law and approximating legislation on intellectual and industrial property.

National Treatment

A white paper issued in 1985 consolidated the principle of mutual recognition of national laws and regulations. The pronouncement eliminated the need to create a new uniform body of EU regulations. Harmonization at the EU level was necessary only when basic issues of health, safety, or the environment were too divergent.

Customs Duties

The European Union established a common commercial policy toward third countries through adoption of a common customs tariff (CCT), which applies equally to all non-EU goods entering any part of the EU for the first time. The imported product will be eligible for "free circulation" within the EU once customs duties have been paid and all customs formalities completed. Free circulation means that the goods will be treated in the same manner as goods of EU origin and may move within the EU without incurring further liability to customs import charges. Steps in assessing customs duties include:

- Identify the tariff classification of the goods in the CCT and the rate which applies for that classification;
- Establish the value of the goods for customs purposes; and
- Apply the CCT rate to the customs value of the goods, subject to any preferential rates which may exist if the goods originate from particular countries.

Valuation

European community valuation is based upon the principles of the World Trade Organization (WTO) valuation code. The customs value is usually based on CIF (cost, insurance, and freight) and should include all payments by the buyer as a condition of the sale of the goods. This usually means that royalties, license payments, or sales commission accruing to the exporter on resale of the goods by the importer are included in the valuation. There are six methods of ascertaining the value, and each must be applied in turn until a suitable valuation is achieved. These alternative methods ensure that a value can be put on goods that are, for instance, sold at an undervalue, either because the sale is part of a barter transaction or because it is between related companies.

Customs Procedures

The EU has adopted the international harmonized system of commodity description and coding, and applies the annex on rules of origin to the International Convention on the

Simplification and Harmonization of Customs Procedures. The test is as follows: when two or more countries are involved in the manufacture of a product, origin is determined by where the last substantial process or operation that is economically justified was performed. Proof of origin rests with the importer.

As of 1988, the free movement of goods meant they were no longer subject to checks. Some 30 documents had been reduced to one—the so-called Single Administrative Document (SAD). However, on January 1, 1993, the SAD was no longer required for internal movement, but is required for goods crossing an EU external border with a nonmember country.

Nonmember Documentation

The usual documents on commercial shipments to the EU countries, irrespective of value or means of transport, are the commercial invoice, bill of lading, certificate of origin (when requested by the importer or required for certain items), packing list, and depending on the nature of the goods being shipped, or on the request of the importer, various special certificates (health, sanitary, etc.).

Commercial invoices should provide a clear and precise description of the product, terms of sale, and all details necessary to establish the full CIF price.

Rules of Origin

The European Union has established rules of origin to provide within the context of its common external commercial policy a key to any differential treatment applied to imports from nonmember countries. For example, the origin of goods is a necessary concept to apply preferential tariff treatment, to charge antidumping duties, or to enforce quantitative quotas.

The question of origin is relevant for trade outside the EU, at importation as well as at exportation, but not for intra-EU trade, which is subject to specific rules (free circulation). In intra-EU trade the question of origin can be pertinent only in the case where measures of commercial policy (surveillance or protective measures) are decided by the EU as regards certain goods originating in third countries and put into free circulation in one of the member states.

Under the EU rules of origin, originating products are (1) products that are obtained in one party to the agreement in question without using third-country products or (2) products that are obtained with use of third-country products but that have supported sufficient processing so as to cause the final product to be classified under a different tariff heading from the raw materials of semifinished goods processed.

The rules of origin applicable at importation into the European Union or at exportation of goods from the EU belong in two different categories: preferential and nonpreferential.

Preferential Rules. The European Union has some 24 different preferential trading regimes covering more than 150 countries. The major groups are as follows:

- The EC-EFTA agreements (Iceland, Norway, and Switzerland), which cover both exports and imports.

- The Mediterranean Agreements, covering all the Mediterranean countries (including Jordan and the Palestinian Authority), except for Libya and Turkey. All cover imports and three also cover exports (Cyprus, Malta, and Israel).

- The Lome Convention and the linked arrangement for some overseas countries and territories. These two cover most of Africa south of the Sahara (except the Republic of South Africa), the Caribbean islands (formerly dependent on EU member states), and former dependencies in the Pacific—all of these in relation to imports.

- The General System of Preferences (GSP) for the remaining developing countries.

Nonpreferential Rules. The nonpreferential rules of origin, which also have to be applied when preferential rules are not fulfilled in a preferential context of exchanges, are laid down in Regulation (EEC) No. 802/68 of June 27, 1968. The principles are as follows:

- Goods wholly obtained or produced in one country shall be considered as originating in that country.

- For goods produced in more than one country, origin is established in that country in which *"the last substantial process or operation* that is *economically justified* was performed, having been carried out in an *undertaking equipped for the purpose,* and *resulting in the manufacture of a new product or representing an important stage of manufacture."* The four conditions in italics are cumulative and to be taken in conjunction with one another.

Certificates of origin (CO) are not required on most commercial and industrial goods exported from the United States to Europe. However, Spain requires certificates of origin on all products, with the exception of motor vehicles, and other countries require it on certain other goods (e.g., textile products in France).

VAT Harmonization

Each EU member has a standard value-added tax (VAT), which is assessed on the sale of both domestic and imported products. The VAT is a sales or consumption tax imposed on buyers upon the sale of goods, from the beginning of the production and distribution cycle to the final sale to the consumer.

The EU exporter or importer of any given item is required to file a declaration with the VAT authority in the home country. The VAT authorities in the member states are to cooperate closely to ensure that frauds are not being committed. The standard VAT rate is between 15 and 25 percent, with a range of exceptions. Essential goods—such as food, medicines, books, and transport—qualify for a lower rate. Table 11-3 shows these rates for the 15-member EU. The VAT is paid in the country of origin, so that firms can buy, sell, and invest in any member state without having to go through checks or formalities when crossing intra-EU borders.

Citizens may obtain goods for their own use in any EU member state and may take them across borders without being subject to controls or liable for tax.

For importers from non-EU nations the VAT should be applied on the cost, insurance, and freight (CIF) value plus the duty charged on the particular good. Thus CIF + duty (CIF × duty rate) + VAT = Total cost to importers.

Recovery of VAT. Inasmuch as the VAT must be paid on entry into the EU and again collected at the point of sale, the nonmember exporter may (with exceptions) recover any VAT paid on entry.

Table 11-3.   VAT Rates in the 15-Member European Union

	Standard[1]	Reduced[2]	Increased[3]	Other[4]
Belgium	19.5%	12%		
Denmark	25%			
France	18.6%	5.5%		
Germany	15%	7%		
Greece	18%	8%		
Ireland	21%	10%		0%
Italy	19%	9%	38%	
Luxembourg	15%	6%		
Netherlands	17.5%	6%		
Portugal	16%	5%	30%	
Spain	15%	6%	28%	
United Kingdom	17.5%			0%

[1]A standard rate applies on most products. Exceptions are noted in other footnotes, below.
[2]Reduced rates are levied on basic necessities, such as foodstuffs, electricity, heat, lumber, and books, but items affected and rates vary between countries.
[3]Increased rates are generally levied on luxury items, including perfumes, jewelry, hi-fi and stereo equipment, cameras, and cars.
[4]Zero rates of duty are applied by some EU countries on foodstuffs and medicines.

Common Currency

The European Union has a common currency. The euro is a basket of the 15 currencies, dominated by a 30 percent share for the German mark and a 20 percent share for the French franc. All other currencies are represented, but in shares ranging from as much as 12 percent for the British pound to as little as 1 percent for the Portuguese escudo.

How the EU Standards Process Works

The European Union has developed hundreds of new product standards that are an important condition of sale. In fact, standards are one of the principal pieces of the internal market program. European-wide standards are replacing divergent national product standards. The advantage is that a manufacturer will have to meet only one European-wide standard and not have to make costly changes to meet 15 different national standards.

Mutual recognition of national standards applies to non-safety aspects of unregulated products (those not covered by EU-wide directives); examples are paper and furniture. Mutual recognition applies to trade both within the EU and between the EU and other countries.

Markings. For products within their scope, the EU "new approach" directives require that a CE mark be affixed to the product (or its packaging, under certain circumstances) to signify that the product complies with all relevant EU legal requirements specified in appropriate directives.

Products bearing the CE mark are guaranteed free circulation within the European Union. It does not eliminate the need to obtain other marks for the product, which may be recognized or expected by purchasers. These include performance marks, product or process quality marks, and marks indicating environmental friendliness or recyclability.

Quality System Registration. While the EU new approach legislation focuses on product approval, there are many instances in which the independent assessment of a manufacturer's design and/or production process is also an important factor in marketing in the EU. Process approval in Europe generally means registration by an independent third party to the relevant standard in the ISO 9000 series (quality management and quality assurance standards). ISO 9000 registration is becoming increasingly important in EU markets, both in legal terms and as a competitive factor. Compliance with ISO 9000 standards is referenced in specific EU product safety directives as a component of the product approval process. In a growing number of sectors, European purchasers may require suppliers to attest that they have an approved quality system in place as a condition for purchase. ISO 9000 registration may also be a competitive factor in product areas where safety or liability is a concern.

Checklist: EU Standards, Testing, and Certification

- Obtain copies of applicable EU-wide directives or regulations.
- Determine if EU-wide regulations cover your product.
- Check the EU technical requirements.
- Check if European national standards apply.

- Check if any European standards are referenced.
- Check international standards.
- Obtain copies of European standards (see Chapter 7).

Distribution

Great care should be taken in selecting an importing distributor in Europe, because in many EU countries statutory provisions or traditionally developed doctrines exist that restrict the freedom of contract in the distributorship area. One of such restrictions is the rule that a distributorship agreement may not be terminated or renewed, even in accordance with its terms, without payment of special compensation to the distributor unless the distributor has been found to have committed certain statutorily defined breaches. EU law is clear in that it forbids absolute territorial limits and resale price maintenance provisions in distribution contracts.

A sales subsidiary is an alternative that should be considered in lieu of an importing distributor. With the advent of the single market, a foreign exporter need not be established in each European country. Rather, a sales subsidiary in one country can transship to the entire EU and may be more profitable in the long run.

DOING BUSINESS IN RUSSIA

Russia is the most politically powerful of the independent states of the former Soviet Union and it has instituted sweeping economic reforms, including broad privatization. It is a nation with precious natural resources, a huge consumer market, and an educated work force. With massive shortages of consumer as well as capital goods, Russia is seeking many joint-venture opportunities. Investors may now buy hard currency and repatriate profits and dividends. Foreign trade activity has not only been authorized, it is encouraged. Russia is a member of the International Monetary Fund and the World Bank. That means, in practical terms, there is hard-currency credit available for imports. Nevertheless, many transactions still involve barter trade.

Highest Potential Imports to Russia

Russia has an almost insatiable market for data processing machines, telecommunications equipment, medical supplies, pollution control equipment, agricultural machinery, and computer software. Of course, grain and other agricultural products such as animal feed, wheat, and maize are mainstays of Russia's importing business. Goods imported from the United States receive most-favored-nation rates. The Russian government imposes a value-added tax (VAT) on most goods sold in Russia, including imported goods. The standard VAT is 23 percent, but the VAT on imported goods is calculated as a percentage of the sum of the customs value of the good, the imported tariff, and the excise tax. Exemptions are available for certain investors.

Exports from Russia

Russia is a nation rich in natural resources. Hydrocarbons, 40 percent of the world's natural gas, 50 percent of the world's timber, and inorganic chemicals are available as well as iron ore, metals, and an excellent machinery production capacity. Companies exporting from Russia are required to pay an average export tariff of about 20 percent on goods and services sold in cash transactions and about 30 percent on goods and services sold in noncash (barter) transactions.

Banks

In addition to Vnesheconombank, the former state bank of the Soviet Union, many foreign banks now have offices in Moscow: Bank of America, Chase Manhattan, Credit Lyonnais, Italian Commerica, Societe General, Generale Bank, and Deutsche Bank.

Export Platforms

To assist investors and joint ventures, Russia has established a major free trade zone in Kaliningrad, a Baltic Sea port, and has established a U.S.-Russian economic development organization.

Entry Requirements

A visa is required for business travel. For visa applications, contact the Russian Consulate, 1825 Phelps Place NW, Washington, DC 20008; phone: (202) 939-8907.

FURTHER READING

From Single Market to European Union, Commission of the European Communities, Luxembourg, 1992.

The Single Market in Action, Commission of the European Communities, Luxembourg, 1992.

European Union, Commission of the European Communities, Luxembourg, 1992.

The European Community 1992 and Beyond, Commission of the European Communities, Luxembourg, 1992.

The European Financial Common Market, Commission of the European Communities, Luxembourg, 1992.

European Trade Fairs: A Key to the World for U.S. Exporters, U.S. Department of Commerce, ITA, February 1993.

Europe in Ten Lessons, Commission of the European Communities, Luxembourg, 1992.

The European Community as a Publisher, 1992–93, Office for Official Publications of the European Communities, Luxembourg, 1992.

A Single Market for Goods, Commission of the European Communities, Luxembourg, 1992.

European Community and Europe: A Legal Guide to Business Development, California Chamber of Commerce and California Trade and Commerce Agency, 1993.

The ABC of Community Law, Office for Official Publications of the European Communities, Luxembourg, 1992.

EC 1992: A Commerce Department Analysis of European Community Directives, Volume 1, U.S. Department of Commerce, International Trade Administration, May 1989.

EC 1992: A Commerce Department Analysis of European Community Directives, Volume 2, U.S. Department of Commerce, International Trade Administration, September 1989.

EC 1992: A Commerce Department Analysis of European Community Directives, Volume 3, U.S. Department of Commerce, International Trade Administration, March 1990.

"EC Single Market Opens to Business," *Business America,* U.S. Department of Commerce, March 8, 1993.

International Trade Resources Guide, California Chamber of Commerce and California Trade Commerce Agency.

U.S. Department of Commerce, ITA Document, "Chemicals and European Community Directives," October 1, 1991.

U.S. Department of Commerce, ITA Document, "The European Community and Environmental Policy and Regulations," April 1, 1991.

U.S. Department of Commerce, ITA Document, "EC Labor Policy—An Integral Part of 1992," October 1, 1991.

U.S. Department of Commerce, ITA Document, "EC Product Standards Under the Internal Market Program," February 10, 1993.

Saunders, Mary, "Obtaining EC-Wide Certification for Industrial Products," *Business America,* March 8, 1993, pp. 28–31.

Hagigh, Sara E., and Mary Saunders, "Europe 1992: Preparing for the Europe of Tomorrow," *Business America,* February 24, 1992, pp. 6–8 and 30–33.

"Global Standards: Building Blocks for the Future," report prepared by Linda Garcia, Office of Technology Assessment, U.S. Congress, March 1992.

The next chapter discusses how to do business in Africa.

12

Doing Business in Africa

AFRICA IS NOT A COUNTRY. IT IS A CONTINENT with more than 40 sovereign nations—the second-largest trading area in the world with an estimated population of over 700 million people. More than 800 languages are spoken in Africa, representing an equally vast number of different cultures. However, most business continues to take place in the urban areas and there, for the sake of business, the various cultures become fused.

AFRICAN TRADING POTENTIAL

Always rich in natural resources (diamonds, cobalt, copper, gold, manganese, and uranium), the nations of Africa are just coming into their own as international traders. They are accomplishing this by moving into new industries and taking advantage of new competencies.

Do keep in mind that most African nations were once European colonies; therefore, throughout the continent there are strong remnants of those cultures interlaced with the new. Lingering sensitivities make it wise to avoid discussions of colonialism in conversation. Concentrate on international politics and the positive, recent achievements of the country you are visiting. Table 12-1 shows the trading potential of the African continent.

Table 12-1.   African Trading Potential

Country	Population (millions)	Purchasing Power Parity	
		National Income ($ bil)	Per Capita Income
North Africa			
Algeria	31	140.2	4,600
Egypt	63	188	2,850
Libya	5	38	6,700
Morocco	29.6	107	3,200
Tunisia	9.5	49	5,200
Total	138.1	Total 522.2	Avg. 4,510
Central Africa			
Burundi	5.7	4.1	740
Cameroon	15.5	29.6	2,000
Central African Republic	3.5	5.5	1,640
Chad	7.6	7.5	1,000
Congo Republic	2.7	3.9	1,500
Dem. Rep. of Congo	50.5	34.9	710
Gabon	1.2	7.7	6,400
Rwanda	8.1	5.5	690
Total	98.8	Total 97.7	Avg. 1,835
East Africa			
Ethiopia	59.6	32.9	560
Kenya	28.8	43.8	1,550
Somalia	7.1	4	600
Sudan	34.5	31.2	830
Uganda	22.8	22.7	1,020
Total	152.8	Total 134.6	Avg. 912
West Africa			
Benin	6.3	7.6	1,300
Gambia	1.3	1.3	1,000
Ghana	18.9	33.6	1,800
Guinea	7.5	8.8	1,180
Liberia	2.9	2.8	1,000
Mali	10.4	8	790
Mauritania	2.6	4.7	1,890
Niger	9.9	9.4	970
Nigeria	114	106.3	960

Table 12-1.   African Trading Potential (Continued)

Country	Population (millions)	Purchasing Power Parity National Income ($ bil)	Per Capita Income
Senegal	10	15.6	1,600
Sierra Leone	5.3	2.7	530
Togo	5.1	8.2	1,670
Total	194.2	Total 209	Avg. 1,224
Southern Africa			
Angola	11.2	11	1,000
Botswana	1.5	5.25	3,600
Lesotho	2.1	5.1	2,400
Mozambique	19.1	16.8	900
Namibia	1.6	6.6	4,100
South Africa	43.5	290.6	6,800
Swaziland	0.985	4	1,200
Tanzania	31.2	22.1	730
Zambia	9.6	8.3	880
Zimbabwe	11	26.2	2,400
Total	131.78	Total 395.95	Avg. 2,701
Continent total	715.7	Total 1,359.5	Avg. 2,236.4

Source: CIA World Fact Book 1999 (www.cia.gov).

HOT TIP: All African countries except Liberia, Eritrea, Gabon, Nigeria, Mauritania, and Sudan are eligible for the General System of Preferences (GSP).

AMERICAN PARTNERSHIP FOR ECONOMIC GROWTH

The Partnership for Economic Growth and Opportunity in Africa is an American initiative to recognize the achievements of many countries in sub-Saharan Africa (SSA) that are pursuing economic and political reform. Through this partnership, the United States seeks to provide support for accelerated growth and development by offering the opportunity to take part in an assistance program allowing for participation at one of three different levels.

Level 1 Participation

Enhanced Market Access. (1) Less-developed countries that are GSP-eligible will continue to receive basic GSP benefits—that is, duty-free access to U.S. markets for about 4000 product groups. (2) Least-developed countries that are GSP-eligible will receive enhanced GSP, which includes approximately 1800 additional products.

Investment Support. The Overseas Private Investment Corporation (OPIC) offers guarantees for a proposed $150 million fund investing in the region, sponsored by private sector participants. In addition, OPIC will work to secure partial guarantees for special infrastructure investment funds with aggregate capital of up to $500 million, concentrating on economic infrastructure projects such as telecommunications, power, transportation, and financial services.

Support for Regional Integration. Up to $25 million annually will be provided under USAID's Initiative for Southern Africa (ISA) for private sector and trade-related activities in areas of regional concern, including investment policy harmonization, regional business ties, financial sector development, privatization, and facilitating cooperation between the private sector and regional governments.

Support for American-African Business Relations. Up to $1 million annually from USAID is available to help catalyze relations between U.S. and African firms.

Level 2 Participation

To provide additional support to those countries pursuing accelerated growth-through-reform programs, the U.S. government offers, at the discretion of the president, the following package of opportunities.

Further Enhanced Market Access. An expanded GSP program will include some product groups that are presently statutorily excluded or products that have traditionally been excluded.

Debt Reduction. (1) The U.S. government supports an approach that leads to the extinction of concessional bilateral debt for the poorest countries. (2) The World Bank and IMF boards are urged to provide maximum relief for eligible countries in support of their growth-promotion efforts. The United States will seek comparable action from other creditor countries.

U.S.-Africa Economic Cooperation Forum. A cabinet/minister-level forum is scheduled to meet once a year in order to raise the level and caliber of dialogue between Africa's strongest reformers and the United States, and to highlight successes and obstacles.

Bilateral Technical Assistance to Promote Reforms. Up to $5 million annually may be made available from USAID to finance short-term technical assistance to help African governments liberalize trade and promote exports; bring their legal regimes into compliance with World Trade Organization standards pursuant to joining the WTO; and make financial and fiscal reforms. The U.S. Department of Agriculture will provide technical assistance to promote agribusiness linkages.

Support for Agricultural Market Liberalization. Under the new multiyear Africa Food Security Initiative, up to $15 million may be designated annually to support agricultural market liberalization, export development, and agribusiness investment.

Trade Promotion. The Trade Development Agency (TDA) will increase the number of reverse trade missions focusing on growth-oriented countries.

Reprogramming Commodity Assistance. To support countries experiencing budget shortfalls in the course of their growth-through-reform programs, and to encourage more effective spending on human resource development and agricultural policy reform, the United States is committed to focusing PL-480 Title I assistance on growth-oriented countries in SSA, and to exploring the possibilities of increasing funding for Title III assistance from within PL-480.

Support for Economic Policy Reform. Up to $10 million annually may be made available from USAID to finance specific growth-oriented programs.

Level 3 Participation

In the future, and as appropriate, the United States will be open to pursuing free trade agreements with strong-performing, growth-oriented SSA countries.

USEFUL NATION-BY-NATION BUSINESS INFORMATION

This section is organized into five regions: North Africa, Central Africa, East Africa, West Africa, and Southern Africa. These groupings lend themselves to condensed statements about business and economic conditions that are useful for the foreign businessperson. Much of the information in this section is taken from Carl A. Nelson, *Protocol for Profit: A Manager's Guide to Competing Worldwide* (1998), with the permission of Thomson Learning Business Press, London.

North Africa

In the North African region—which includes Algeria, Egypt, Libya, Morocco and Tunisia—you can expect business to cease five times a day for Islamic prayers. Visitors of all religions are encouraged to face Mecca out of respect. The ninth month of the Islamic calendar is called Ramadan, and during this period all work stops before noon. Thursday or Friday is the Muslim day of rest. It is common in all these states to eat with the right hand, but not to eat pork or drink alcohol.

Algeria. Oil and natural gas form the backbone of the Algerian economy. Hydrocarbons account for nearly all export receipts. The current government has continued efforts to admit private enterprise to the hydrocarbon industry, but has instituted reforms, including privatization of some public sector companies.

Egypt. Egypt, the land of the Pyramids, has one of the largest public sectors of all the North African states—most industrial plants are owned by the government. As Egypt and its Middle Eastern neighbors pursue regional peace, foreign companies are pitching in to help meet their economic development goals. The main airports are at Heliopolis, near Cairo, and at Alexandria. Egypt's marine ports are Port Said and

Suez and a free industrial zone located in northern Sinai; all are serviced by inland waterways. The telecommunications system is undergoing intensive upgrading.

Libya. Libya is one of the most ancient of countries—it existed before the Romans ruled and even before the Phoenicians, Carthaginians, and Greeks. Today it is an Islamic, socialist-oriented economy that depends primarily upon oil-related revenues. The oil sector contributes practically all export earnings and about one-third of GDP. Per capita GDP of about $5410 is the highest in Africa. Libya imports about 75 percent of its food requirements. The non-oil manufacturing and construction sectors have expanded from processing mostly agricultural products to include petrochemicals, iron, steel, and aluminum.

Morocco. In 1992 the Moroccan government embarked on privatizing 112 state-owned companies. It now plans to shift its program into higher gear in a bid to reverse recent setbacks to the largely agricultural economy. The most important ports in terms of cargo volumes are Casablanca, Mohammedia, Jor Lasfa, and Safi. Morocco has a good telecommunications system and several international airports. Morocco is an associate member of the European Union.

Tunisia. The Tunisian economy came back strongly in the 1990s as a result of good harvests, continued export growth, and higher domestic investment. The government appears committed to implementing its structural adjustment program, with International Monetary Fund (IMF) support, and to servicing its foreign debt.

Central Africa

The Central African states include Burundi, Cameroon, Central African Republic, Chad, Congo Republic, Democratic Republic of the Congo, Gabon, and Rwanda.

Burundi. Burundi will not be ready for business until its longstanding genocidal warfare ceases. A landlocked, resource-poor country in an early stage of economic development, Burundi is predominately agricultural with only a few basic industries. As part of its economic reform agenda, the government launched, with IMF and World Bank support, an effort to diversify its agricultural exports and attract foreign investment in industry. Several state-owned coffee companies have been privatized.

Cameroon. Because of its offshore oil resources, Cameroon has one of the highest incomes per capita in tropical Africa. With support from the IMF and World Bank, the Cameroon government has begun to introduce reforms designed to spur business investment, increase efficiency in agriculture, and recapitalize the nation's banks.

Central African Republic. Subsistence agriculture, including forestry, is the backbone of the Central African Republic's economy. Agricultural products account for about 60 percent of export earnings and the diamond industry for 30 percent. Multilateral and bilateral development assistance, particularly from France, plays a major role in providing capital for new investment.

Chad. Chad's industry is based almost entirely on the processing of agricultural products, including cotton, sugar cane, and cattle. Chad is highly dependent on foreign aid. Oil companies are exploring areas north of Lake Chad and in the Doba basin in the south.

Congo Republic. Officially the Republic of the Congo, this country has an economy that mixes village agriculture and handicrafts, along with a beginning industrial sector based largely on oil and supporting services. Oil has supplanted forestry as the mainstay of the economy, providing about two-thirds of government revenues and exports. The government, responding to pressure from business and the electorate, is reducing bureaucracy and regulation.

Democratic Republic of the Congo. Ethnic violence continues to plague the country once known as Zaire. Although short-term prospects for improvement are dim, improved political stability would boost the country's long-term potential to effectively exploit its vast wealth of mineral and agricultural resources.

Gabon. Located along the Equator, Gabon is rich in natural resources and is one of the most secure and stable countries on the continent. The economy, previously dependent on timber and manganese, is now dominated by the oil sector. The high oil prices of the early 1980s contributed to a substantial increase in per capita national income, stimulated domestic demand, reinforced migration from rural to urban areas, and raised the level of real wages to among the highest in sub-Saharan Africa.

Rwanda. Rwanda will not be ready for business until it overcomes deep-seated genocidal conflict. Almost 50 percent of Rwanda's GDP comes from the agricultural sector; coffee and tea make up 80 to 90 percent of total exports. The industrial sector in Rwanda is small, contributing only 17 percent to GDP. Manufacturing focuses mainly on the processing of agricultural products. The Rwandan economy remains dependent on coffee exports and foreign aid.

East Africa

East Africa includes the states of Ethiopia, Kenya, Somalia, Sudan, and Uganda.

Ethiopia. Ethiopia seems to be on the way to recovery after more than two decades of war. Its economy is based on subsistence agriculture. The manufacturing sector is heavily dependent on inputs from the agricultural sector. Over 90 percent of large-scale industry, but less than 10 percent of agriculture, is run by the state; the government is considering selling off a portion of state-owned plants. Since 1992, because of some easing of civil strife and aid from the outside world, the economy has substantially improved.

Kenya. Kenya's annual population growth rate—one of the highest in the world—presents a serious problem for the country's economy. GDP growth in the near term has kept slightly ahead of population, annually averaging 4.9 percent. There are international airports at Nairobi, Mombassa, and Kisumu, as well as several export processing zones. Telecommunications are considered among the best in Africa.

Somalia. Clan warfare blocks the way to doing business in Somalia. With few resources, Somalia is one of the world's poorest and least developed countries; much of the economy has been even more devastated by the civil war. Agriculture is the most important sector, with livestock accounting for about 40 percent of GDP and about 65 percent of export earnings. The main export crop is bananas; sugar, sorghum, and corn are grown for the domestic market. The small industrial sector is based on the processing of agricultural products and accounts for less than 10 percent of GDP. Somalia is the only non-Arab member of the League of Arab Nations.

Sudan. Sudan is buffeted by civil war, chronic political instability, adverse weather, high inflation, a drop in remittances from abroad, and counterproductive economic policies. The economy is dominated by government entities that account for more than 70 percent of new investment. The private sector's main areas of activity are agriculture and trading, with most private industrial investment predating 1980. The economy's base is agriculture, which employs 80 percent of the work force. Industry mainly processes agricultural items.

Uganda. Uganda has substantial natural resources, including fertile soils, regular rainfall, and sizable deposits of copper and cobalt. In recent years, this economy has turned in a solid performance based on continued investment in the rehabilitation of infrastructure, improved incentives for production and exports, and gradual improvements in domestic security. Agriculture is the most important sector of the economy, employing over 80 percent of the work force. Coffee is the major export crop and accounts for the bulk of export revenues.

West Africa

The West African states include Benin, Gambia, Ghana, Guinea, Liberia, Mali, Mauritania, Niger, Nigeria, Senegal, Sierra Leone, and Togo.

Benin. With a stable democracy in place, the Benin government has undertaken to improve its poorly developed infrastructure and make sweeping market-oriented reforms. Agriculture accounts for about 35 percent of GDP, employs about 60 percent of the labor force, and generates a major share of foreign exchange earnings. Port facilities and the international airport near Cortonou are being upgraded to serve as a hub for Benin's many landlocked neighbors.

Gambia. This country's official name is the Gambia. Although politically stable, it has no important mineral or other natural resources and has a limited agricultural base. About 75 percent of the population is engaged in crop production and livestock raising, which contribute 30 percent to GDP. Small-scale manufacturing activity—processing peanuts, fish, and hides—accounts for less than 10 percent of GDP. Tourism is a growing industry. The Gambia imports one-third of its food, all fuel, and most manufactured goods. Exports are concentrated on peanut products (about 75 percent of total value).

Ghana. Supported by substantial international assistance, Ghana has been implementing a steady economic rebuilding program, including moves toward privatization and relaxation of government controls. Ghana is heavily dependent on cocoa, gold, and timber exports and is encouraging foreign trade and investment. Ghana opened a stock exchange in 1990.

Guinea. Guinea possesses many natural resources and considerable potential for agricultural development. Thanks to its rich mineral and other natural resources, it is now one of the few African nations whose standard of living is on the rise. Exports of bauxite and alumina accounted for about 70 percent of total exports in 1998.

Liberia. Liberia will be ready for international business only when it overcomes civil warring and other conflicts. Richly endowed with water, mineral resources, forests, and a climate favorable to agriculture, Liberia is a producer and exporter of basic products. Manufacturing, mainly foreign owned, is small in scope. Liberia's merchant ship registry is known for having little or no restrictions (almost no inspection requirements or safety standards).

Mali. Landlocked Mali is the largest country in West Africa, but among the poorest countries in the world, with about 70 percent of its land area desert or semidesert. Economic activity is largely confined to the riverine area irrigated by the Niger. About 10 percent of the population live as nomads and some 80 percent of the labor force is engaged in agriculture and fishing. Industrial activity is concentrated on processing farm commodities. In consultation with international lending agencies, the government has adopted a structural adjustment program, aiming at GDP annual growth of 4.6 percent, inflation of no more than 2.5 percent on average, and a substantial reduction in the external current account deficit.

Mauritania. A majority of the Mauritanian population still depends on agriculture and livestock for a livelihood, even though most of the nomads and many subsistence farmers have been forced into the cities by recurrent droughts.

Mauritania has extensive deposits of iron ore, which account for almost 50 percent of total exports. The nation's coastal waters are among the richest fishing areas in the world. The country's first deepwater port opened near Nouakchott in 1986. The government has begun the second stage of an economic reform program in consultation with the World Bank, the IMF, and major donor countries.

Niger. Niger is one of 14 landlocked countries in Africa and is the world's sixth-largest uranium producer. The economy depends heavily on exploitation of these large uranium deposits. About 90 percent of the population is engaged in farming and stock raising, activities that generate almost half the national income. France is a major customer, while Germany, Japan, and Spain also make regular purchases.

Nigeria. Prior to adopting democratic elections and becoming a civil society, Nigeria was plagued with crime and scams—it was the world's major drug-smuggling and money-laundering center. Although Nigeria is Africa's leading oil-producing country, it remains very poor. The government has set ambitious targets for expanding oil production capacity and is offering foreign companies more attractive investment incentives.

Senegal. Senegal is a country ready to do international business. It has been stable since independence and the government has relaxed trade and investment restrictions. The agricultural sector accounts for about 12 percent of GDP and provides employment for about 80 percent of the labor force. About 40 percent of the total cultivated land is used to grow peanuts, an important export crop. Another principal economic resource is fishing, which brought in about 23 percent of total foreign exchange earnings in 1999. Mining is dominated by the extraction of phosphate, but production has faltered because of reduced worldwide demand for fertilizers in recent years. Over the past 10 years tourism has become increasingly important to the economy. There is an international airport and a free-trade zone at Dakar, the capital as well as the second-largest maritime port in West Africa. Senegal enjoys most-favored-nation trading status with the United States under the General System of Preferences and reduced rates with the European Union under the Lome Convention.

Sierra Leone. Recent government stabilization gives indications of a turnaround for Sierra Leone, a country that seems to be ready to do business. However, the economic and social infrastructure is not well developed. Subsistence agriculture dominates the economy, generating about one-third of GDP and employing about two-thirds of the working population. Industry, which accounts for roughly 10 percent of GDP, consists mainly of the processing of raw materials and of light manufacturing for the domestic market. Diamond mining provides an important source of hard currency. The economy suffers from high unemployment, rising inflation, large trade deficits, and a growing dependency on foreign assistance. Liberian rebels in southern and eastern Sierra Leone have severely strained the economy and have undermined efforts to institute economic reforms.

Togo. The economy of Togo is heavily dependent on subsistence agriculture, which accounts for about 33 percent of GDP and provides employment for 78 percent of the labor force. Primary agricultural exports are cocoa, coffee, and cotton, which together account for about 30 percent of total export earnings. Togo is self-sufficient in basic foodstuffs when harvests are normal. In the industrial sector phosphate mining is by far the most important activity, with phosphate exports accounting for about 40 percent of total foreign exchange earnings. Togo serves as a regional commercial and trade center. The government, with IMF and World Bank support, has been implementing a number of economic reform measures to encourage foreign investment and bring revenues in line with expenditures.

Southern Africa

The Southern African states include Angola, Botswana, Lesotho, Mozambique, Namibia, South Africa, Swaziland, Tanzania, Zambia, and Zimbabwe.

Angola. Still feeling the effects of war, Angola is nevertheless ready to do business in the global economy. Subsistence agriculture provides the main livelihood for 80 to 90 percent of the population, but accounts for less than 15 percent of GDP. Oil production is vital to the economy, contributing about 60 percent to GDP. For the long run, Angola has the advantage of rich natural resources in addition to oil—notably, gold, diamonds, and arable land.

Botswana. The economy of Botswana has historically been based on cattle raising and crops. Agriculture today provides a livelihood for more than 80 percent of the population, but produces only about 50 percent of food needs. The mining industry, mostly on the strength of diamonds, has gone from generating 25 percent of GDP in 1980 to 50 percent in 1991. No other sector has experienced such growth, especially not agriculture, which is plagued by erratic rainfall and poor soils.

Lesotho. Small, landlocked, mountainous, and completely surrounded by South Africa, Lesotho has no important natural resources other than water. Its economy is based on agriculture, light manufacturing, and remittances from laborers employed in South Africa. The great majority of households gain their livelihoods from subsistence farming and migrant labor. Manufacturing depends largely on farm products to support the milling, canning, leather, and jute industries; other industries include textile, clothing, and construction. A major water improvement project is under way to permit the sale of water to South Africa.

Mozambique. Mozambique has sizable agricultural, hydropower, and transportation resources. The economy depends heavily on foreign assistance to keep afloat. Continuation of civil strife dims the chances of foreign investment.

Namibia. Namibia is the fourth-largest exporter of non-fuel minerals in Africa and the world's fifth-largest producer of uranium. Alluvial diamond deposits are among the richest in the world, making Namibia a primary source for gem-quality diamonds. Namibia also produces large quantities of lead, zinc, tin, silver, and tungsten. More than half the population depends on agriculture (largely subsistence farming) for its livelihood.

South Africa. Within the continent, the nation of South Africa is without question the economic powerhouse, with a GDP of about $290 billion. Political reform and political stability have turned South Africa into a hot market. Many of the white one-seventh of the South African population enjoy incomes, material comforts, and health and educational standards equal to those of Western Europe. In contrast, most of the remaining population suffers from the poverty patterns of the less developed countries, including unemployment and lack of job skills.

The main strength of the South African economy lies in its rich mineral resources, which provide two-thirds of exports. Economic developments in the future will be driven partly by the changing relations among the various ethnic groups. Local economists estimate that the economy must grow between 5 percent and 6 percent in real terms to absorb the more than 300,000 workers entering the labor force annually. There are international airports at Johannesburg and Cape Town and marine ports at all the major coastal cities. Telecommunications as well as road and rail services are extensive.

Swaziland. The economy of Swaziland is based on subsistence agriculture, which occupies most of the labor force and contributes nearly 25 percent to GDP. Manufacturing, which includes a number of agroprocessing factories, accounts for another quarter of GDP. Exports of sugar and forestry products are the main earners of hard currency. Surrounded by South Africa, except for a short border with Mozambique, Swaziland is heavily dependent on South Africa, from which it receives 75 percent of its imports and to which it sends about half its exports.

Tanzania. An economic recovery program announced in the mid-1980s has generated notable increases in agricultural production. The World Bank, the International Monetary Fund, and bilateral donors have provided funds to rehabilitate Tanzania's deteriorated economic infrastructure. Subsequent growth features a pickup in industrial production and a substantial increase in output of minerals, led by gold. Inland waterways and two railways connect Tanzania's several air and maritime ports.

Zambia. The Zambian economy has been in decline for more than a decade with falling imports and growing foreign debt. Some of the world's largest copper mines lie in this country; however, economic difficulties stem from a chronically depressed level of copper production. A high inflation rate has added to Zambia's economic woes in recent years.

Zimbabwe. Agriculture   employs   three-fourths   of Zimbabwe's labor force and supplies almost 40 percent of exports. The manufacturing sector, based on agriculture and mining, produces a variety of goods and contributes 35 percent to GDP. Mining accounts for only 5 percent of both GDP and employment, but supplies of minerals and metals account for about 40 percent of exports.

TRADE BLOCS AND SPECIAL TREATIES

Through its well-developed infrastructure and deepwater ports, South Africa handles much of the trade for the whole Southern African region. In order to counter the economic dominance of South Africa in the region, the countries to the north have organized themselves into various economic groupings.

Southern African Customs Union (SACU)

Formed in 1970, SACU enables Botswana, Swaziland, Lesotho, and Namibia to share in the customs revenue from their trade passing through South African ports.

Southern African Development Conference (SADC)

Member states include those of SACU as well as Angola and its oil-rich enclave of Cabinda, Mozambique on the east coast, and three countries of south-central Africa: Zimbabwe, Zambia, and Malawi.

Treaty for Enhanced East African Cooperation

In the eastern region of Africa the countries of Kenya, Uganda, and Tanzania recently agreed to allow for the free flow of goods and people.

Economic Community of Central African States

Members are Cameroon, Central African Republic, Chad, Equatorial Guinea, oil-rich Congo and Gabon, and the vast Democratic Republic of the Congo.

Economic Community of West African States (ECOWAS)

This solid geographical bloc of 15 states extends from Nigeria in the east to Mauritania in the west. The countries of

Mauritania, Mali, and Niger are located in the southern stretch of the Sahara Desert while the remaining countries are splayed out along the coastline. As a result of their respective colonial histories, these countries are divided into French- and English-speaking states. French is the official language of the republics of Benin, Burkina Faso, Togo, Côte d'Ivoire (Ivory Coast), Guinea, and Senegal, while the remaining states of Nigeria, Ghana, Liberia, Sierra Leone, and Gambia have English as their official language. Guinea Bissau is a Portuguese-speaking republic to the south of Senegal.

FUNDING SOURCES

This section is not an exhaustive list of financial institutions and programs but serves as an excellent guide to sources for African investment.

Export-Import Bank of the United States (EXIMBank)

The Export-Import Bank of the United States has implemented a $200 million Africa pilot program, designed to make available short-term export credit insurance in 16 countries, including 11 countries where routine EXIMBank financing has previously been unavailable. Some $100 million of the proposed $200 million will support U.S. export sales to Nigeria, based on current projected demand for financing exports to that country. The remaining $100 million will be allocated on a first-come, first-served basis to the other 15 countries. The one-year pilot program went into effect on August 1, 1999.

The public and/or private sectors of the sub-Saharan countries impacted by the new Africa pilot program are Burkina Faso, Cameroon, Côte d'Ivoire, Chad, Equatorial Guinea, Gambia, Guinea, Madagascar, Malawi, Mali, Mauritania, Mozambique, Nigeria, São Tomé and Principe, Tanzania, and Togo.

Under this pilot program, EXIMBank will help small and medium-size companies in many African markets purchase the U.S. goods and services needed in order to participate in the global economy. In particular, businesses can obtain financing for the purchase of U.S.-made spare parts, raw materials, and agricultural commodities. The short-term export credit insurance will generally be made available in the private sector through irrevocable letters of credit from creditworthy banks in the respective countries. Coverage will be provided primarily under EXIMBank's short-term "bank letter of credit policy."

Calvert New Africa Fund

This fund has no sector-specific requirements; a participating country must have liquid capital exchange. Areas of investment include tourism, cottage industry, minerals, and technology (75 percent in South Africa). The minimum investment is $2000. The only restriction is that the fund can invest a maximum of 5 percent of holdings in one company. Contact: Maceo K. Sloan, Manager, Calvert New World Fund, Inc., 103 W. Main Street, 4th Floor, Durham, NC 27707; phone: (800) 548-7786 or (919) 688-0620/8092; fax: (919) 688-9095.

Commonwealth Africa Investment Fund (COMAFIN)

This private equity fund provides risk capital for equity investments. It channels investment to privatized/privatizing companies, new ventures, and small to medium-size private sector businesses in Africa's 19 commonwealth nations. Fund size is $62.5 million to $70 million. The focus is on resource-based projects—particularly agribusiness, minerals, manufacturing, power, telecommunications, and services (including tourism)—as well as on infrastructure and property development. Special emphasis is placed on ventures that encourage the growth of communication and trade in African commonwealth countries. Zimbabwe contacts—phone: 011-263-70-68-59; fax: 011-263-4-70-55-03. London contact—phone: 011-44-171-828-44-88; fax: 011-44-171-828-65-05.

Morgan Stanley Africa Investment Fund

This nondiversified, closed-end fund invests in African government debt securities and in equity securities of firms organized in Africa or firms with Africa as a principal trading partner. The fund targets countries with functioning stock markets such as Botswana, Côte d'Ivoire, Egypt, Ghana, Kenya, Mauritius, Namibia, Swaziland, South Africa, and Zimbabwe. Fund size is $323.6 million. Contact: Morgan Stanley Asset Management, Inc., 1221 Avenue of the Americas, New York, NY 10020; phone: (800) 221-6726.

Development Finance Company of Uganda

Managed by the Commonwealth Development Corporation, this $3.4 million fund is invested in 11 Ugandan companies, including a fish processing plant and the country's first rose exporting business. Contact: Development Finance Company of Uganda Limited, P.O. Box 2767, Crusader House, Portal Avenue, Kampala, Uganda; phone: 011-256-41-25-61-25.

New South Africa Fund

This nondiversified, closed-end fund invests primarily in South African issues and to a lesser extent in issues of other countries in Southern Africa. It targets industries across the board in South Africa, Botswana, Lesotho, Mauritius, Namibia, Swaziland, and Zimbabwe. Fund size is $67.8 million. Contact: Jerome Davies, Bear Stearns Funds Management, 245 Park Avenue, 15th Floor, New York, NY 10167; phone: (212) 272-3550; fax: (212) 272-3098.

Southern Africa Fund, Inc.

A nondiversified, closed-end company investing in individual stocks of various South African companies, this fund targets industries across the board in Angola, Botswana, Lesotho, Malawi, Mozambique, Namibia, South Africa, Swaziland, Zambia, and Zimbabwe. Fund size is $90 million. Contact: Alliance Capital Management Information Line, 1345 Avenue of the Americas, New York, NY 10105; phone: (800) 247-4154.

Mauritius Venture Capital Fund (MVCF)

MVCF invests in situations from early-stage and start-up projects to expansions, buyouts and buy-ins, and privatizations in the form of equity or quasi-equity amounts ranging from $100,000 to $1 million. Contact: Mauritius Equity Investment Management Limited, 6th Floor, Sir William Newton Street, Port Louis, Mauritius; phone: 011-230-211-4949; fax: 011-230-211-9393; e-mail: 101663.764@compuserve.com.

Enterprise Fund—South Africa

This fund provides development capital to medium-scale enterprises as equity and quasi-equity investment. It will support small and medium-size businesses in connection with the transfer of ownership and management of businesses to previously disadvantaged sectors of the economy. Fund size is $27 million. Contact: Capital Fund, P.O. Box 11177, 55 Fax Street, Johannesburg 2001, South Africa; phone: 011-27-11498-21-52; fax: 011-27-11-498-21-38.

Tanzania Venture Capital Fund (TVCF)

TVCF and its associated company, Equity Investment Management Ltd., now invest in 16 diverse projects ranging from exports of cut flowers to a regularly scheduled private charter airline. In 1998 TVCF capital exceeded $7.61 million, with disbursements and commitments totaling $4.1 million. Contact: Tanzania Venture Capital Fund (TVCF), Equity Management Ltd., Plot 1404/45, Ghana Avenue, P.O. Box 8020, Dar es Salaam, Tanzania; phone: 011-255-51-444/51-348-83; fax: 011-255-51-444-440.

Cauris Investment

A regional venture capital fund for countries of the Union Economique et Monetaire Ouest Africane (West African Economic and Monetary Union), Cauris targets small and medium-size majority-owned African companies in the areas of food, manufacturing, or services with potential for superior earnings. It provides such businesses with debt, equity, or lease financing. Contact: Patrick Mestrallet, Advisor to the Director of Financial Institutions and Industries Department, Banque Ouest Africane de Développement, B.P. 1172 Lome, Togo; phone: 011-228-21-42-44; fax: 011-228-21-72-69.

Enterprise Fund

Sponsored by the European Union for small and medium-size businesses, this $4 million fund supplies up to $100,000 per company. Contact: John Ababio, Manager, Venture Fund Management Co., Ltd., 5th Floor Tower Block, Box 2617, SSNIT Pension House, Liberia Road, Accra, Ghana; phone: 011-233-21-66-61-65; fax: 011-233-21-66-40-55.

Ghana Venture Capital Fund (GVCF)

GVCF targets equity and loan investments of up to $500,000 with an equity stake of 10 to 40 percent. A credit return of at least 20 percent per year net of inflation is desired. All companies must be based in Ghana. Contact: John Ababio, Manager, Venture Fund Management Co., Ltd., 5th Floor Tower Block, Box 2617, SSNIT Pension House, Liberia Road, Accra, Ghana; phone: 011-233-21-66-61-65; fax: 011-233-21-66-40-55.

Africinvest

This start-up venture capital firm targets small and medium-size businesses in Senegal with equity investments of 5 to 20 percent. Contact: Beal et Compagnie Internationale, B.P. 2969, Dakar, Senegal; phone: 011-221-214-474; fax: 011-221-214-897/222-095.

Société Financiàre—SENIVEST

Sponsored by CBAO Bank in Dakar, SENIVEST targets small to medium-size businesses operating in Senegal with potential for rapid growth. The director general is a member of the West African Enterprise Network. Contact: SENIVEST, 3 Place de l'Indépendance, B.P. 129 Dakar, Senegal; phone: 011-221-231-000.

Bankers Association for Foreign Trade (BAFT)

BAFT is an association of banks that promote U.S. exports, international trade, and international investment. Its Access to Export Capital (AXCAP) program catalogs the services offered by banks and other institutions that are involved in trade finance. AXCAP also has a national inventory of services of government export credit agencies like EXIMBank, OPIC, and the SBA. Contact: Mary Condeelis, Executive Director, Bankers Association for Foreign Trade, 2121 K Street NW, Suite 701, Washington, DC 20037; phone: (202) 452-0952; fax: 202-452-0959; e-mail: mary@baft.org.

Commonwealth Development Corporation (CDC)

Based in the United Kingdom, CDC has venture capital funds operating in eight sub-Saharan African countries, including Ghana, Tanzania, and Uganda. Contact: Commonwealth Development Corporation, 1 Bessborough Gardens, Pimlico, London, W1V2JQ, UK; phone: 011-44-171-828-4488.

KEY CONTACTS AND WEB SITES

Let there be no doubt, Africa is changing. One sure indication is the availability and openness of information. Here are just some of the ways to gain information about African markets.

African Development Bank (ADB). U.S. companies may contact the U.S. commercial liaison officer with the African Development Bank for further assistance. Call 225-21-46-16, fax 225-22-24-37, or go to www.afdb.org/.

Mailing address:
American Embassy—Abidjan
U.S. Department of State
Washington, DC 20520-2010

Street address:
Commercial Liaison to African Development Bank
U.S. and Foreign Commercial Service
Ambassade des Etats-Unis d'Amerique
5 Rue Jesse Owens
01 B.P. 1712 Abijan 01
Côte d'Ivoire

Common Market of Eastern and Southern Africa (COMESA). Members include Angola, Burundi, Comoros, Democratic Republic of the Congo, Eritrea, Ethiopia, Kenya, Madagascar, Malawi, Mauritius, Namibia, Rwanda, Seychelles, Sudan, Swaziland, Tanzania, Uganda, Zambia, and Zimbabwe. Web: www.comesa.int/.

Greater Horn Information Exchange. Members include Sudan, Eritrea, Ethiopia, Somalia, Kenya, Tanzania, Burundi, Rwanda, and Uganda. Web: 198.76.84.1/HORN/.

Multilateral Investment Guaranty Agency (MIGA) Investment Promotion Network. Affiliated with the World Bank, MIGA promotes foreign investment in emerging markets, information sharing, and marketing opportunities. Web: www.ipanet.net.

South African Development Community (SADC). Members include Angola, Botswana, Lesotho, Malawi, Mozambique, Namibia, South Africa, Swaziland, Tanzania, Zambia, and Zimbabwe. Web: www.sadcexpo.org.

United Nations—Africa Economic Recovery. Web: www.un.org/ecosocdev/geninfo/afrec/.

United Nations—Africa Policy. Web sites:

www.africapolicy.org/featdocs/central.htm
www.africapolicy.org/featdocs/east.htm
www.africapolicy.org/featdocs/north.htl
www.africapolicy.org/featdocs/southern.htm
www.africapolicy.org/featdocs/west.htm

National Minority Business Council—*Business Person's Guide to Africa.* The council offers a one-stop guide to the economic, political, and cultural information necessary for conducting business in 13 very important African countries: Algeria, Botswana, Côte d'Ivoire, Ghana, Kenya, Morocco, Nigeria, Senegal, South Africa, Tanzania, Tunisia, Uganda, and Zimbabwe. Contact: National Minority Business Council, Inc., 235 East 42d Street, New York, NY 10017, ATTN: International Trade Department; phone: (877) ASK-NMBC or (212) 573-2385; e-mail: nmbc@msn.com; Web: www.nmbc.org.

The next chapter is about doing business in the Near East and Asia.

13

Doing Business in the Near East and Asia

BY FAR THE LARGEST TRADING REGION IN THE world, Asia covers over 17 million miles and has a population of over 3 billion people. To the east it includes Australia and New Zealand as well as Japan, which is the richest; to the west it extends to Turkey and Israel. China and India are the most populous nations, with 1.2 billion and 900 million people respectively, and the whole area has potential for regional economic integration.

This chapter concentrates on Japan, the People's Republic of China, Hong Kong and Taiwan—two of the four Tigers of Asia (with South Korea and Singapore)—and the Pacific Basin as a whole. Additional information is available by calling (800) USA-TRADE (872-8723) or the Pacific Rim hotline at (202) 482-3875, or by visiting www.doc.gov.

JAPAN

This nation of dynamic people has a population of about 126 million, a GDP of about $3 trillion, and a per capita GNP of over $23,000. That makes Japan a prime target for international market expansion.

Import Policies

The average Japanese tariff is low—about 3.4 percent—but on certain items, such as foodstuffs and leather goods, tariffs and quotas are quite restrictive of trade. Duties are assessed on the CIF value at ad valorem or specific rates, and in a few instances are charged on a combination of both.

Taxes

Since April 1989, the Japanese commodity tax has been replaced with a general consumption tax of 3 percent (6 percent on autos). The tax is levied on the CIF plus duty value.

Marketing Strategy

The key to marketing success in Japan is commitment and persistence. You must ensure that your product is of the highest quality and has excellent after-sales service. Without these two qualities, a product that might sell satisfactorily in other countries may not do well in Japan.

Japan External Trade Organization (JETRO)

The Japan External Trade Organization is a nonprofit, government-supported organization dedicated to promoting mutually beneficial trade between businesses of other nations. Generally speaking JETRO's services are free of charge and should be the first stop for any firm contemplating doing business in or with Japan. JETRO is headquartered in Tokyo but maintains a network of 30 offices in Japan as well as in 77 overseas offices in 57 countries. To make contact with the seven offices in the United States, go to www.jetro.org. Or call the office in New York at (212) 997-0400 or fax (212) 819-7781; Houston at (713) 0759-9595; Los Angeles at (213) 624-8855; San Francisco at (415) 392-1333 or fax (415) 788-6927; Atlanta at (404) 681-0660; Chicago at (312) 527-9000; and Denver at (303) 629-0404.

Distribution and Sales Channels

The Japanese distribution system is as inefficient as it is complex. Typically multiple layers of middlemen are involved in a system of highly institutionalized marketing channels linking producers, retailers, and end users.

If the market for your product has a large number of end users, it may be better to rely on an existing network of wholesalers. On the other hand, if your buyers are concentrated, a single intermediary may be your best marketing method. Setting up your own distribution system is very expensive initially, but more efficient over the long term.

Information

The U.S. Department of Commerce has set up a special Japan Export Information Center. To make contact, call (202) 482-2425 or try the Japan Export Promotion hotline fax at (202) 482-4565.

PEOPLE'S REPUBLIC OF CHINA

The People's Republic of China (PRC) is one of the fastest-growing economies in the world, and the driving force has been world trade. Foreign trade as a percentage of GNP has been as much as 38 percent. To make contact, try www.china.com.

China is a nation moving toward a market system. State-owned enterprises, banking, taxation, social security, and foreign trade are all in a state of reform.

In the past, trade with China was conducted by the Ministry of Foreign Trade within the overall plans and guidelines established by the relevant economic policymaking bodies, such as the State Economic and Financial Commission, the State Planning Commission, and the State Energy Commission.

China's foreign trade structure has undergone significant change and is still fluid. In recent times there has been a major shift to private enterprise. About 6000 foreign trading corporations (FTCs) have been granted trading rights. About 300 specialized FTCs remain under the direct control of the Ministry of Foreign Trade and Economic Cooperation (MOFTEC), which formulates centralized plans for a small portion of state-critical products.

Development Zones and Free Trade Zones

Over the years of reform the government has promoted foreign trade by establishing special economic zones (SEZs) in about 20 coastal provinces and free zones in most coastal cities. These zones provide preferential treatment, including tax holidays, import/export duty exemption, low income tax rates, and other incentives to induce technology and export-oriented foreign investment.

Negotiating a Contract

Negotiations with China tend to be more technical, more detailed, and more time-consuming than with other countries. For time-conscious Westerners, the pace of Chinese negotiations—characterized by patience and attention to the greatest detail—is extremely frustrating. The Chinese are excellent negotiators, well aware of the bargaining ploys and tactics used all over the world, and they employ these with varying degrees of subtlety. Chinese businesspeople place emphasis on getting to know their trading partners and maintaining relationships with "old friends."

Payment

Chinese sellers prefer to be denominated in their own currency—renminbi (RMB). Most sales and purchase transactions in the China trade typically call for payment by irrevocable letters of credit (L/Cs) against presentation of sight draft and shipping documents. Chinese end users must be able to acquire foreign currency for imports. They can do so three ways: (1) the government can allocate hard currency for a specific deal; (2) the importer can use retained foreign currency from previous deals; or (3) the importer can request assistance from an FTC, which buys the goods in its own foreign currency and then sells the product to the end user in RMB.

Value-Added Tax

Exporters are subject to China's value-added tax (VAT), which, together with the new consumption tax, replaces the 1958 consolidated industrial and commercial tax. Customs duty is first calculated, then consumption tax (if applicable) is determined, and finally, VAT is computed.

Hong Kong China

Long noted for its huge reexport trade, as entrepôt to the world, Hong Kong is a "special administrative region" of China. The Chinese government has stated that it will not change the arrangement for 50 years. More than 38,000 trading companies are registered on the tiny island, and all are eager to do business with outsiders. These companies are typically small and tend to specialize in importing or exporting or reexporting. Many companies that wish to foray into the China market begin by establishing operations in Hong Kong.

The best way to make contact is to try www.hongkong.com or write or phone the Chinese consulate nearest your city. Address your inquiry to the Foreign Trade Officer and ask to be put in contact with the appropriate office in China.

Another approach is to call (202) 482-3583 and ask for the fax "Everything you want to know about exporting to China" or use the Pacific Rim flashfax at (202) 482-3875.

You may also order the excellent annual publication *The China Business Guide* by calling (202) 512-1800 with order number 003-009-00637-6. The cost is about $5.

TAIWAN CHINA

Trading with Taiwan, or the Republic of China (ROC), has become easier and more convenient thanks to dedicated efforts of government, private enterprise, and trade-related organizations. Rules have been simplified, infrastructure improved, and trade services enhanced. Taiwan uses the Harmonized Tariff System, with an average nominal tariff rate of 8.64 percent and an average effective rate of 3.62 percent.

The best way to make contact is through CETRA, the premier trade promotion agency of the ROC. This nonprofit organization, sponsored by domestic associations and exporters, has a staff of over 700 in its Taipei headquarters, as well as additional personnel in offices located in major cities around the world. It offers a wide range of information and services to both domestic and foreign firms. Contact: CETRA, 4-7 Fl. Cetra Tower, 333 Keelung Road, Sec. 1, Taipei, Taiwan, 110, Republic of China; phone: 886-2-2725-5200; fax: 886-2-2757-6653; Web:

www.cetra.org.tw. Other valuable contacts are www.tai-wantrade.com and www.tradeweb.com.tw/home.htm.

PACIFIC BASIN

The Pacific Basin is the fastest-growing trade region of the world. It is also the most widely dispersed. As a coherent trade area, it is weakened by its geography (see Figure 13-1), and the economic gap is even more formidable. For instance, Indonesia's per capita GDP is about $600 million, while Singapore's is about $91.5 billion.

Made up mainly of islands strung north and south across the Pacific Ocean, the region includes Australia, Brunei, Cambodia, China, Canada, Chile, Hong Kong, Indonesia, Japan, North Korea, South Korea, Laos, Malaysia, Mexico, New Zealand, Philippines, Singapore, Papua New Guinea, Singapore, Taiwan, Thailand, Vietnam, and the United States.

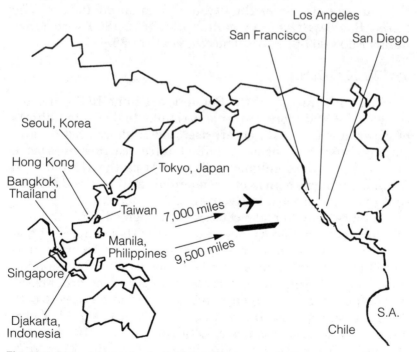

Fig. 13-1. Dispersement of potential Asian bloc

The Four Tigers—Hong Kong, South Korea, Singapore, and Taiwan—are best known for their extraordinary economic progress during the second half of the twentieth century. Of course, Japan stands alone as the major trading nation of Asia, but since 1960, for example, South Korea's economy has grown by about 1500 percent and its per capita income has risen nearly eightfold.

The entire Pacific Basin region, which already accounts for 40 percent of world trade, is now poised to grow at the rates previously attributed only to the Tigers.

Regional Integration

The idea of a single Pacific Basin trade bloc similar to NAFTA and the European Union is difficult to grasp, but there is the distinct possibility that a third major trade area may be formed. The Asian bloc would then become the largest trade area, with a total population of over 3 billion compared with the EU (about 350 million) and NAFTA (about 400 million). The Association of South East Asian Nations (ASEAN), formed in 1975, has considered expanding to become the Asia-Pacific Economic Cooperation (APEC) trade bloc or possibly the East Asia Economic Caucus (EAEC), an arrangement similar to APEC but without Canada, New Zealand, Australia and the United States. Until an Asian regional trade area is in fact formed, business practices continue to be conducted on a nation-by-nation basis.

APEC

At the Asia-Pacific Economic Cooperation (APEC) summit held in September 1999, 18 Pacific Basin nations agreed to remove trade and investment barriers by the year 2010 for industrialized countries and 10 years later for developing economies.

Table 13-1 shows the membership of this potential bloc.

HELPFUL PUBLICATIONS AND INFORMATION

- *Destination Japan: A Business Guide for the 1990s* (2d ed.) and China and Hong Kong business publications. U.S. Government Printing Office. Call (202) 512-1800 or go to GPO.gov.

Table 13-1. APEC (Asia-Pacific Economic Cooperation)

Country	Population (millions)	Purchasing Power Parity National Income ($ bil)	Per Capita Income
ASEAN (Association of South East Asian Nations)			
Indonesia	216	602	2,830
Malaysia	21.4	215.4	10,300
Philippines	79.3	270.5	3,500
Singapore	3.5	91.5	26,300
Thailand	60.6	369	6,100
Total	380.8 Total	1,548.4 Avg.	10,372
Other Pacific Basin			
Australia	18.8	394	21,200
Brunei	0.323	5.4	17,000
Canada	31	688	22,400
Chile	15	185	12,400
China	1,250	4,420	3,600
Hong Kong	6.8	168.1	25,100
Japan	126	2,900	23,100
Mexico	100	815.3	8,300
New Zealand	3.7	61.1	17,000
Papua New Guinea	4.7	11.1	2,400
South Korea	46.8	585	12,600
Taiwan	22	362	16,500
United States	275	8,600	31,500
Total	2,280.9 Total	20,743.4 Avg.	14,720

Source: *CIA World Fact Book 1999* (www.cia.gov).

- Africa, Near East, and South Asia documents. Call fax number (202) 482-0878.
- South Asia automated information. Call fax number (202) 482-4453.

The next chapter offers 20 tips to gain import/export success and big profits.

14

20 Keys to
Import/Export Success

SUCCESS IN THE INTERNATIONAL MARKETPLACE IS MEASURED IN profits and market share. It is also measured in the satisfaction you feel in reaching new horizons and visiting places that previously were only dreams. You and your firm can be successful if you act on these 20 critical points:

1. The most important key to success is commitment by you, the decision maker, to enter the global market. You'll reap tax advantages, sales volume advantages, the excitement of the international experience, and lots of profit. Change your game and get into the global competition. Get to work and earn a share of the more than $7 trillion that's out there waiting for enthusiastic entrepreneurial Americans.

2. Get beyond cultural obstacles. Accept the fact that the rest of the world isn't just like the United States. Other countries like their way of doing things, or they would change it. Get used to the idea that cultural differences exist, but be assured that the differences can be learned and even understood. At a minimum, the differences can be appreciated and respected. Remember, there are more similarities among peoples of the world than there are differences.

The Japanese like cars, and they don't dislike American cars. The problem is that American car manufacturers just haven't figured out how to satisfy the Japanese car consumer, who is used to a different style and, above all, different service considerations. The world is becoming more and more internationalized.

3. Plan, plan, plan, but do not treat international trade as a stand-alone process.   Plan for success. Assuming that your initial market research revealed some demand for your product as is or with minor redesign, develop a strategic plan for your business. From the beginning, *write* the plan. What is your competitive advantage? What are your geographical and product-line priorities? How are you going to penetrate the market?

4. The market, the market, the market.   An early investigation of the market is the key to success. Get an estimate of the demand for the products that you already manufacture. The best information will come from your own industry—here and overseas. Talk to those who have experience. Don't overlook available statistics and library resources. Lay out a map of the world and apply some logic. If you plan to export, divide the world into export regions and prioritize the regions according to broad assumptions of their need for your product and their ability to pay. Based on your common understanding of the various regions—their languages, environment, and cultures—select one or more target countries for start-up. Do consider the political and financial stability of the country. Use the same logic for imports. Examine a map of the United States or your region and divide it into target segments. Do not try to sell to the entire world, all of the Americas, or even one entire foreign country immediately. Just remember that nothing happens until you sell something.

5. Information is critical.   Research is critical to the success of your market plan. Begin with a list of the information you will need to support your analysis. What do you need to know about the regions of the United States (imports) or the foreign country (exports) you have selected? What level of detail will you require? Next, organize a list of the potential sources of your research. Classify your sources and begin to sort the material logically. Again, you can gain the most accurate and meaningful information by traveling to the potential market.

6. Define your market goals. Develop a well-researched, solidly reasoned market plan; it should include a background review, an analysis of the market environment, and a description of your goals in terms of your company.

7. Where there are competitors, there is a market. Take a close look at the competition. It will be to your favor to discover that there is competition. Why? Because where there is competition, there is a market.

8. Be persistent—don't give up. Don't become discouraged if you find that your product is ahead of its time in the international marketplace. Don't give up on exporting. WD-40 and Coca-Cola created a global market for their products. Search for products that do have an overseas market and are similar to yours.

9. Adapt the product to the market. Learn what products your customers like and *how* they like the products, whether you are importing an article for American tastes or exporting a product for a foreign market. Be ready to adapt your product to the market. Redesign your product and compete.

10. Budget for success. Include international goals in your financial plan. Treat import/export start-up as you would any other entrepreneurial venture. Budget from the beginning and keep good books. Watch your costs and cash flow. As with any new business, expect short-term losses, but plan for long-term gains.

11. Manage for success. Develop the tactical plans that implement your overall strategic plan, such as a personnel plan, an advertising policy, a market entry point, and a sales approach. Motivate your personnel by emphasizing team work.

12. Be patient in developing international trade. International trade takes a little longer than domestic trade. After all, there are oceans in between, and the transportation systems are slower. Every transaction will require financing. International financing and banking methods are sophisticated and generally excellent, but negotiations and transactions across borders take more time than domestic business.

13. The best long-term investment is a well-planned trip. Things go right when the boss checks everything out.

And in international business that means international travel. After you have developed your strategic plan, visit the overseas sources or markets you have chosen. There is nothing like getting firsthand information. You will find it interesting, rewarding, and essential to meet the people you will be doing business with. Even after you have established a successful sales and distribution network, you or representatives of your company should visit at least twice a year.

14. Walk on two legs. Choose a good international banker, freight forwarder, and customs house broker. Talk with them to learn the language of international business—pricing, quotations, shipping, and getting paid. Establish a good relationship, then stick with it. Deal with a bank that has personnel who are experienced in the international marketplace.

15. Proper communication gets sales results. Provide customer service the international way by communicating often, clearly, and simply. Keep your overseas business partners on the team by being particularly sensitive to communications, letters, faxes, and phone calls. Above all, develop a Web site and use the Internet.

16. Expert counsel saves money. Minimize your inevitable mistakes by asking for help. Banks, customs house brokers, freight forwarders, and the U.S. Department of Commerce are sources of free information. And most private consultants ask reasonable fees.

17. Selection of distributors is critical. Your objective is to get your product in front of your buyer—the decision-making unit (DMU). The wrong distributor can stifle your market efforts and tie you up legally.

18. Stick to a marketing strategy. Don't chase orders. Of course, fill the over-the-counter orders, but be proactive rather than reactive. Establish an effective marketing effort according to your market plan.

19. Treat international partners and customers the same as domestic counterparts. It may surprise some people that foreign bad debt ratios are often less than half of U.S. bad debt ratios. The reason is that in the United States credit is a way of life. In overseas markets, credit is still something to be earned as a result of having a record of prompt payment. Use common sense in extending credit to overseas customers, but don't use tougher rules than you do for American clients.

20. Don't fret about the international business cycle. Don't worry about booms or busts, just do it. International trade is exciting and profitable because there are so many side benefits. Think of traveling to such diverse places as Hong Kong and Vienna—and writing off the trip as an expense to the company.

OK, you've found the sources, developed the markets, and written the business plan. You have the entrepreneurial spirit to make your own import/export business a success. The time to get into the import/export market is now—and make lots of money!

Good Luck

Appendix A

ATA Carnet Countries and Their Customs Territories (2000)

Algeria (DZ)
Andorra (AD)
Australia (AU)
Austria (AT)
Balearic Isles
Belgium (BE)
Botswana (BW)
Bulgaria (BG)
Canada (CA)
Canary Islands
Ceuta
China (CN)
Corsica
Croatia (HR)
Cyprus (CY)
Czech Republic (CZ)
Denmark (DK)
Estonia (EE)
European Union (EU)

Finland (FI)
France (FR)
French Guiana (GF)
French Polynesia (PF), including Tahiti
Germany (DE)
Gibraltar (GI)
Greece (GR)
Guadeloupe (GP)
Bailiwick of Guernsey
Hong Kong (HK)
Hungary (HU)
Iceland (IS)
India (IN)
Ireland (IE)
Isle of Man
Israel (IL)
Italy (IT)
Ivory Coast (CI)

Japan (JP)
Jersey
Korea (KR)
Lebanon (LB)
Lesotho (LS)
Liechtenstein
Luxembourg (LU)
Macedonia (MK)
Macao
Malaysia (MY)
Malta (MT)
Martinique (MQ)
Mauritius (MU)
Mayotte
Melilla
Miguelon
Monaco (MC)
Morocco (MA)
Namibia (NA)
Netherlands (NL)
New Caledonia (NC)
New Zealand (NZ)
Norway (NO)
Poland (PL)
Portugal (PL)
Puerto Rico

Reunion Island (RE)
Romania (RO)
St. Barthelemy
St. Martin, French part
St. Pierre
Senegal (SN)
Singapore (SG)
Slovakia (SK)
Slovenia (SI)
South Africa (ZA)
Spain (ES)
Sri Lanka (LK)
Swaziland (SZ)
Sweden (SE)
Switzerland (CH)
Tahiti
Tasmania
Taiwan   (TW)   TECRO/AIT
    Carnets only
Thailand (TH)
Tunisia (TN)
Turkey (TR)
United Kingdom (GB)
United States of America
    (US)

Appendix B

U.S. Government Bookstores

U.S. Government Bookstore
First Union Plaza
999 Peachtree St. NE Ste.
   120
Atlanta, GA 30309-3964
(404) 347-1900
Fax (404) 347-1897

U.S. Government Bookstore
O'Neill Building
2021 3d Ave. N
Birmingham, AL 35210-1159
(205) 731-1056
Fax (205) 731-3444

U.S. Government Bookstore
Thomas P. O'Neill Building
10 Causeway St. Rm. 169
Boston, MA 02222-1047
(617) 720-4180
Fax (617) 720-5753

U.S. Government Bookstore
One Congress Center
401 South State St. Ste. 124
Chicago, IL 60605-1225
(312) 353-5133
Fax (312) 353-1590

U.S. Government Bookstore
Federal Building
1240 E 9th St. Rm. 1653
Cleveland, OH 44199-2001
(216) 522-4922
Fax (216) 522-4714

U.S. Government Bookstore
Federal Building
200 N High St. Rm. 207
Columbus, OH 43215-2408
(614) 469-6956
Fax (614) 469-5374

U.S. Government Bookstore
Federal Building
1100 Commerce St. Rm. IC50
Dallas, TX 75242-1027
(214) 767-0076
Fax (214) 767-3239

U.S. Government Bookstore
1660 Wynkoop St. Ste. 130
Denver, CO 80202-1144
(303) 844-3964
Fax (303) 844-4000

U.S. Government Bookstore
Federal Building
477 Michigan Ave. Ste. 160
Detroit, MI 48226-2500
(313) 226-7816
Fax (313) 226-4698

U.S. Government Bookstore
Texas Crude Building
801 Travis St. Ste. 120
Houston, TX 77002-5727
(713) 228-1187
Fax (713) 228-1186

U.S. Government Bookstore
100 West Bay St. Ste. 100
Jacksonville, FL 32202-3811
(904) 353-0569
Fax (904) 353-1280

U.S. Government Bookstore
120 Bannister Mall
5600 E Bannister Rd.
Kansas City, MO 64137
(816) 765-2256
Fax (816) 767-8233

U.S. Government Printing
Office
Retail Sales Outlet
8660 Cherry Ln.
Laurel, MD 20707-4907
(301) 953-7974
(301) 792-0262
Fax (301) 496-8995

U.S. Government Bookstore
ARCO Plaza C-Level
505 S. Flower St.
Los Angeles, CA 90071-2101
(213) 239-9844
Fax (213) 239-9848

U.S. Government Bookstore
310 W. Wisconsin Ave. Ste.
  150W
Milwaukee, WI 53203-2228
(414) 297-1304
Fax (414) 297-1300

U.S. Government Bookstore
Federal Building
26 Federal Plaza Rm. 2-120
New York, NY 10278-0004
(212) 264-3825
Fax (212) 264-9318

U.S. Government Bookstore
Robert Morris Building
100 N 17th St.
Philadelphia, PA 19103-2736
(215) 636-1900
Fax (215) 636-1903

U.S. Government Bookstore
Federal Building
1000 Liberty Ave. Rm. 118
Pittsburgh, PA 15222-4003
(412) 395-5021
Fax (412) 395-4547

U.S. Government Bookstore
1305 SW 1st Ave.
Portland, OR 97201-5801
(503) 221-6217
Fax (503) 225-0563

U.S. Government Bookstore
Norwest Banks Building
201 W 8th St.
Pueblo, CO 81003-3038
(719) 544-3142
Fax (719) 544-6719

U.S. Government Bookstore
Marathon Plaza
303 2d St. Rm. 141-S
San Francisco, CA 94107-
1366
(415) 512-2770
Fax (415) 512-2276

U.S. Government Bookstore
Federal Building
915 2d Ave. Rm. 194
Seattle, WA 98174-1001
(206) 553-4270
Fax (206) 553-6717

U.S. Government Bookstore
U.S. Government Printing
   Office
710 N Capitol St. NW
Washington, DC 20401
(202) 512-0132
Fax (202) 512-1355

U.S. Government Bookstore
1510 H St. NW
Washington, DC 20005-1008
(202) 653-5075
Fax (202) 376-5055

Appendix C

Staging Codes

Staging Code	Definition
A	Immediate and full duty elimination (1-1-94)
B	Five equal annual duty reductions to zero, starting 1-1-94
BA	Duties removed in five annual stages
BP	Duties removed in three annual stages, starting 1-1-97
By	Duties removed in five annual stages from a base of five percent beginning 1-1-94
D	Duties removed in seven stages, the first on 1-1-94, then annually beginning 1-1-96
B6	Duty reduction on 1-1-94 equal, in percentage terms, to the base rates. Then elimination in five equal stages beginning 1-1-95
B8	Duties removed in two equal stages on 1-1-98 and 1-1-2001
C	Duties removed in ten equal stages, starting 1-1-94
CQ	Sets quota amounts that may enter Mexico duty-free each calendar year beginning 1-1-94 (tariffs for above-quota shipments are subject to Code C schedule)
CM	Duties removed in three stages, 1-1-94, 1-1-98, and 1-1-2003
C8	Duties removed in eight annual stages, starting 1-1-94
C10	Duties removed in nine stages, starting 1-1-94, then annually beginning 1-1-96
C12	Duties removed in three stages, 1-1-94, 1-1-2000, and 1-1-2005
C+	Duties removed in 15 annual stages beginning 1-1-94
C15	Duties removed in 13 stages, starting 1-1-94, then annually beginning 1-1-97
N	Section 22 cotton item covered in the agriculture tariff schedule
D	Duty-free prior to the agreement and will remain so after NAFTA takes effect

Glossary

COMMONLY USED TRADE TERMS

International trade, like other specialized fields, has developed its own distinctive vocabulary, which can mystify newcomers. Many businesspeople stumble over the commonly used terms and acronyms that guide, regulate, and facilitate trade. Lack of precision in the language impedes communication, causes misunderstandings, and delays transactions. Undoubtedly, it loses sales for global companies.

Arranged alphabetically, this glossary of terms frequently used in global trade was sourced from the U.S. Information Agency, U.S. Departments of Commerce, State, and Treasury, U.S. International Trade Commission, Office of the U.S. Trade Representative, World Trade Organization, and UNCTAD Secretariats in Geneva. It also includes other terms, researched by the author, that are particularly applicable to the scope of this book.

acceptance A bill of exchange accepted by the drawee, as evidenced by the drawee's signature on the face of the bill. The drawee commits to pay the bill at maturity. (The payee must be sure that the drawee has the means and the will to make payment.)

acceptance draft A sight draft document against acceptance. See **documents against acceptance, sight draft.**

acceptance letter of credit An L/C available by acceptance calling for a *time draft* (or *usance draft,* in international parlance). Drawn on an intermediate accepting bank, these L/Cs are popular when both buyer and seller need interim financing to facilitate cash flow.

ad valorem   According to value. See **duty.**

advance payment   An arrangement in which the buyer delivers cash to the seller before the seller releases the goods. Some sellers ask for such partial payment to show good faith on the part of the buyer and also to enhance their cash flow related to the sale of a particular custom-made item. It may not mean exactly the same as *payment in advance.*

advising bank   The bank, usually in the country of the exporter, that notifies the availability of the letter of credit to the exporter. The advising bank is responsible for authenticating and forwarding the L/C but makes no commitment to pay unless it agrees to act as confirming bank. See also **negotiating bank.**

advisory capacity   A term indicating that a shipper's agent or representative is not empowered to make definitive decisions or adjustments without approval of the group or individual represented. Compare **without reserve.**

affreightnemt (contract of)   An agreement between a steamship line (or similar carrier) and an importer or exporter in which cargo space is reserved on a vessel for a specified time and at a specified price. The importer or exporter is obligated to make payment whether or not the shipment is made.

after date   A phrase indicating that payment on a draft or other negotiable instrument is due a specified number of days after presentation of the draft to the drawee or payee. Compare **after sight, at sight.**

after sight   A phrase indicating that the date of maturity of a draft or other negotiable instrument is fixed by the date on which it was drawn, a specified number of days after presentation of the draft to the drawee or payee. Compare **after date, at sight.**

agent   See **representative.**

air waybill   The carrying agreement between shipper and air carrier that is obtained from the airline used to ship the goods. Technically, it is a nonnegotiable instrument of air transportation that serves as a receipt for the shipper, indicating that the carrier has accepted the goods listed therein and obligates itself to carry the consignment to the airport of destination according to specified conditions. Compare **inland bill of lading, ocean bill of lading, through bill of lading.**

all-risks clause   An insurance clause providing additional coverage to an *open cargo policy,* usually for an additional premium. Contrary to its name, the clause does not protect against all risks. The more common perils it does cover are theft, pilferage, nondelivery, fresh water damage, contact with other cargo, breakage, and leakage. Loss of market and losses caused by delay are not covered.

alongside   A phrase referring to the side of a ship. Goods to be delivered "alongside" are placed on the dock or lighter within reach of the transport ship's tackle so that they can be loaded aboard.

amendment—letter of credit   A change in the terms, amount, or expiration date of a letter of credit usually in the interest of the beneficiary. (Exporters should check Art. 9.d.iii of UCP 500 very carefully, especially regarding adverse amendments.)

applicant   The party, usually an importer, requesting the issuing bank to issue the letter of credit.

arbitrage   The process of buying foreign exchange, stocks, bonds, and other commodities in one market and immediately selling them in another market at higher prices.

assignment of proceeds   A document signed by the beneficiary under a letter of credit assigning the rights to proceeds from an L/C drawing to a third party. From the perspective of the assignee, an assignment differs radically from a *transferable letter of credit.* The latter conveys a right to the transferee to present documents under an L/C; the former does not.

ATA   A French abbreviation signifying temporary admission.

ATA carnet   A customs document that enables the holder to carry or send goods temporarily into certain foreign countries without paying duties or posting bonds.

at sight   A phrase indicating that payment on a draft or other negotiable instrument is due upon presentation or demand. Compare **after date, after sight.**

authority to pay   A document comparable to a *revocable* letter of credit but under whose terms the authority to pay the seller stems from the buyer rather than from a bank.

baby letter of credit The second of two L/Cs in a *back-to-back letter of credit* arrangement.

back-to-back letter of credit A baby letter of credit in which the issuing bank is secured by a *master letter of credit*. The applicant of the baby becomes the beneficiary of the master, and the terms of the two L/Cs are such that documents presented under the baby can obtain payment under the master. Back-to-backs are popular among middlemen who want to protect their position between the buyer and manufacturer.

balance of trade The balance between a country's exports and imports.

bank affiliate trade association A trade association partially or wholly owned by a banking institution.

banker's acceptance (B/A) A draft bearing the acceptance of a drawee bank, thus qualifying for financing in the liquid U.S. dollar banker's acceptance market. It is a useful vehicle for fixed-term, fixed-rate financing, especially for banks without access to low-cost U.S.-dollar funds.

banker's bank A bank that is established by mutual consent by independent and unaffiliated banks to provide a clearinghouse for financial transactions.

bank holding company (BHC) Any company that directly or indirectly owns or controls, with power to vote, more than 5 percent of the voting shares of another bank.

barratry Negligence or fraud on the part of a ship's officers or crew resulting in loss to the owners. See **open cargo policy.**

barter Trade in which merchandise is exchanged directly for other merchandise without use of money. Barter is an important means of trade with countries using currency that is not readily convertible.

beneficiary The person, usually an exporter, in whose favor a letter of credit is issued or a draft is drawn.

bill of exchange A written, unconditional demand, signed by the drawer and addressed to the drawee, to pay a sum of money upon presentation or at some future date (*x* days after "sight" or *x* days after "bill of lading date") to the order of the payee, or to the bearer. Frequently known as a draft or bill. See **draft.**

bill of lading (B/L)   A document that provides the terms of the contract between the shipper and the transportation company to move freight between stated points at a specified charge. Usually prepared by the shipper on forms issued by the carrier, it serves as a document of title, a contract of carriage, and a receipt of goods. It is the primary evidence of shipment of goods and the exporter's key to prompt payment. See also **charter party bill of lading, transport document.**

blanket policy   See **open cargo policy.**

blocked currency   Exchange that cannot be freely converted into other currencies. Cash deposits that cannot be transferred to another country because of local regulations or a shortage of foreign exchange.

bonded warehouse   A building authorized by customs authorities under bond or guarantee of compliance with revenue laws for the storage of goods without payment of duties until removal.

booking   An arrangement with a steamship company for the acceptance and carriage of freight.

broker   See **export broker.**

Brussels Tariff Nomenclature   See **Customs Cooperation Council Nomenclature.**

buying agent   An agent who buys in a country for foreign importers, especially for such large foreign users as mines, railroads, governments, and public utilities. Synonymous with *purchasing agent.*

carnet   A customs document allowing special categories of goods to cross international borders without payment of duties.

carrier   A transportation line that hauls cargo.

cash against documents (CAD)   Payment for goods in which a commission house or other intermediary transfers title documents to the buyer upon payment in cash.

cash in advance (CIA)   Payment for goods in which the price is paid in full before shipment is made. This method is usually used only for small purchases or when the goods are built.

cash with order (CWO)   Payment for goods in which the buyer pays when ordering and in which the transaction is binding on both parties.

certificate of free sale   A certificate, required by some foreign governments, stating that the goods for export, if products under the jurisdiction of the U.S. Food and Drug Administration, are acceptable for sale in the United States—that is, the products are sold freely without restriction. The FDA will issue shippers a "letter of comment" to satisfy foreign requests or regulations.

certificate of inspection   A document in which certification is made as to the good condition of the merchandise immediately prior to shipment. The buyer generally designates the inspecting organization, usually an independent inspection firm or government body.

certificate of manufacture   A statement by a producer, sometimes notarized, certifying that manufacture has been completed and that the goods are at the disposal of the buyer.

certificate of origin   A certificate stating the origin of goods, usually signed by the importing country's embassy in the country of the exporter.

C&F   Cost and freight. See **CFR.**

CFR Cost and Freight   Incoterm indicating that the sale price includes all costs of shipment and freight up to the port of destination. The buyer must insure the cargo from the port of loading, for if the cargo is lost the buyer will bear the consequence. See **Incoterms 2000.**

chamber of commerce   An association of businesspeople whose purpose is to promote commercial and industrial interests in the community.

charter party   A written contract, usually on a special form, between the owner of a vessel and a "charterer" who rents use of the vessel or a part of its freight space. The contract generally includes the freight rates and the ports involved in the transportation.

charter party bill of lading   A B/L issued subject to a charter party arrangement. Charter party B/Ls are not acceptable under letters of credit unless allowed explicitly (See Art. 25.a of UCP 500).

C&I   Cost and insurance. A pricing term indicating that these costs are included in the quoted sale price.

CIF   Cost, insurance, and freight. Incoterm indicating that all costs of shipment and insurance and freight up to the port of destination are included in the quoted sale price. The seller must insure the cargo as far as the port of delivery, for if the cargo is lost the seller will bear the consequence. See **Incoterms 2000.**

CIF&C   Cost, insurance, freight, and commission. A pricing term indicating that these costs are included in the quoted sale price.

CIF&E   Cost, insurance, freight, and exchange (currency) A pricing term indicating that these costs are included in the quoted sale price.

clean bill of lading   A B/L signed by the transportation company indicating that the shipment has been received in good condition with no irregularities in the packing or general condition of all or any part of the shipment. Compare **foul bill of lading.**

clean draft   A draft to which no documents have been attached.

collecting bank   Bank in the importer's country involved in processing a collection.

collection   The procedure involved in a bank's collecting money for a seller against a draft drawn on a buyer abroad, usually through a correspondent bank.

collection papers   All documents (invoices, bills of lading, etc.) submitted to a buyer for the purpose of receiving payment for a shipment. Also, the documents submitted by the buyer, usually with a draft or against a letter of credit, for payment of an export shipment.

combined transport bill of lading   A B/L used when more than one carrier is involved in a shipment, for example when a consignment travels by rail and by sea. Sometimes referred to as a *multimodal bill of lading.*

commercial attaché   The commercial expert on the diplomatic staff of a country's embassy or large consulate in a foreign country.

commercial invoice   The seller's itemized list of goods shipped, with descriptions, details, prices, and costs, addressed to the buyer. The invoice should represent a complete record of the business transaction between the exporter and the foreign importer with regard to the goods sold. It is also a document of content and, therefore, must fully identify the overseas shipment as well as serve as the basis for the preparation of all other documents covering the shipment. Some countries may require further documentation, such as quality certificates, certificates of origin, certificates of free sale, and customs invoices.

commercial letter of credit   U.S. parlance for documentary letter of credit, or DC, as it is known elsewhere. See **letter of credit.**

commission agent   See **foreign sales representative, purchasing agent.**

commission representative   See **foreign sales representative.**

commodity credit corporation   A corporation controlled by a government's department or ministry of agriculture that provides financing and stability to the marketing and exporting of agricultural commodities.

common carrier   An individual, partnership, or corporation that transports people or goods for compensation.

compensation   A form of countertrade in which the seller agrees to take full or partial payment in goods or services generated from the sale.

conference line   A member of a steamship conference. See **steamship conference.**

confirmation   The act of a bank to add its commitment to that of the issuing bank to pay the beneficiary for compliant documents. Under Article 9.b of UCP 500, confirming banks must be requested or authorized by the issuing bank to "add their confirmation" to the L/C. Note that the act of confirmation does not relieve the issuing bank of its obligation to the beneficiary.

confirmed letter of credit.   An L/C issued by a bank abroad whose validity and terms are confirmed to the beneficiary in the home bank. A letter of credit bearing the confirmation, or commitment to pay, of a second bank, most often in the country of the exporter. Confirmations are the exporter's insurance against nonpayment by the issuing bank for most reasons other than a *discrepancy*.

confirming bank   A bank adding its commitment to pay for compliant documents to that of the issuing bank, usually at the request of same. Confirming banks are very often correspondents of issuing banks. L/C beneficiaries should understand clearly how soon the confirming bank will pay after presentation of conforming export documents.

consignee   The person, firm, or representative to whom a seller or shipper sends merchandise and who, upon presentation of the necessary documents, is recognized as the owner of the merchandise for the purpose of the payment of customs duties. Also, the person to whom goods are shipped, usually at the shipper's risk, when an outright sale has not been made. See **consignment.**

consignee marks   See **marks.**

consignment   A payment method in which the buyer pays for goods after selling them. The exporter retains title to the goods until they are sold (as well as 100 percent risk of nonpayment by the buyer).

consolidator's bill of lading   A B/L issued by the consolidator (forwarder) to a shipper as a receipt for goods to be consolidated with other cargoes prior to shipment.

consul   A government official residing in a foreign country who is charged with representing the interests of his or her country and its nationals.

consular declaration   A formal statement, made to the consul of a foreign country, describing goods to be shipped.

consular invoice   A detailed statement regarding the character of goods shipped, duly certified by the consul of the importing country at the port of shipment.

consulate   The official premises of a foreign government representative.

contingency insurance   Insurance taken out by the exporter complementary to insurance bought by the consignee abroad.

control of goods   Of vital interest to all parties involved in trade, control of goods is exercised through the *transport document*. It determines whether the buyer will be able to clear an inbound shipment without the transport document (and thus without paying for the documents held at the bank).

correspondent bank   An overseas bank with which a local bank has a relationship. Relationships between banks are just one factor that determine appetite for confirmation and thus have relevance to importers and exporters.

counterpurchase   One of the most common forms of countertrade in which the seller receives cash but contractually agrees to buy local products or services as a percentage of cash received and over an agreed period of time.

countertrade   International trade in which the seller is required to accept goods or other instruments of trade, in partial or whole payment for its products.

countervailing duty   An extra duty imposed by the importing country to offset export grants, bounties, or subsidies paid to foreign suppliers in certain countries by the government of those countries as an incentive to export.

country of origin   The country where a product is made, as determined by the amount of work done on the product in the country and attested by a *certificate of origin*.

credit risk insurance   A form of insurance that covers the seller against loss from nonpayment on the part of the buyer.

customs   The duties levied by a country on imports and exports. Also, the procedures and organization involved in such collection.

customs (house) broker   A firm representing the importer in dealings with customs, responsible for obtaining and submitting documents for clearing merchandise through customs, arranging inland transport, and paying related charges.

Customs Cooperation Council Nomenclature (CCCN) The customs tariff used by many countries worldwide, including most European nations. It is also known as the Brussels Tariff Nomenclature. Compare **Standard Industrial Classification, Standard International Trade Classification, tariff schedule.**

D/A   See **documents against acceptance.**

date draft   A draft drawn to mature on a specified number of days after the date it is issued, with or without regard to the date of acceptance.

DC   A popular acronym outside the Americas for documentary letter of credit. The U.S. equivalent is the L/C, or more properly the commercial L/C. See **letter of credit.**

deferred payment letter of credit   An L/C available "by deferred payment" calling for a *time draft* (or *usance draft* in international parlance) drawn on the issuing bank. It is popular in cases of supplier credit.

delivery point   See **specific delivery point.**

demurrage   A storage fee for inbound merchandise held beyond the free time allowed by the shipping company. Excess time taken for loading or unloading a vessel as a result of a shipper. Charges are assessed by the shipping company.

department of commerce   An agency of government whose purpose it is to promote commercial industrial interests in the country.

devaluation   The official lowering of the value of one country's currency in terms of one or more foreign currencies. Thus, if the U.S. dollar is devaluated in relation to the French franc, $1 will "buy" fewer francs than before.

discrepancy   An instance in which documents presented do not conform to the L/C. Article 13.a of UCP 500 states that "banks must examine all documents stipulated in the credit with reasonable care." In fact, banks exercise extreme care and international standard banking practice dictates that exporters must exercise detailed vigilance in preparing documents under letters of credit if they are not to be frustrated by delays in obtaining payment.

discount (financial)   A deduction from the face value of commercial paper in consideration of cash by the seller before a specified date.

dishonor   Refusal on the part of the drawee to accept a draft or pay upon maturity.

dispatch   An amount paid by a vessel's operator to a charterer if loading or unloading is completed in less time than stipulated in the *charter party*.

distributor   A firm that sells directly for a manufacturer, usually on an exclusive contract for a specified territory, and who maintains an inventory on hand.

dock receipt A receipt issued by an ocean carrier or its agent, acknowledging that the shipment has been delivered, or received at the dock or warehouse of the carrier.

documentary collection An order written by the seller to the bank to deliver *documents against payment* or *documents against acceptance* to the buyer. The seller's bank will act on the instruction of the seller in a principal/agent relationship and remit the documents to a branch, or a correspondent, in the country of the buyer, with instructions for collection. A key factor in the effectiveness of such collections is the *control of goods* exercised through the *transport document.*

documentary draft A draft to which documents are attached.

documentary letter of credit (D/C) See **letter of credit.**

documentation documents See **shipper's documents.**

documents against acceptance (D/A) A type of payment for goods in which the documents transferring title to the goods are withheld until the buyer has accepted the draft issued against the buyer.

documents against payment (D/P) A type of payment for goods in which the documents transferring title to the goods are withheld until the buyer has paid the value of a draft issued against the buyer.

domicile The place where a draft or an acceptance is made payable.

D/P See **documents against payment.**

draft The same as a *bill of exchange.* A written order for a certain sum of money to be transferred on a certain date from the person who owes the money or agrees to make the payment (the drawee) to the creditor to whom the money is owed (the drawer of the draft). See **date draft, documentary draft, sight draft, time draft.**

drawback (import) The repayment, up to 99 percent, of customs duties paid on merchandise that later is exported, as part of a finished product. Also, a refund of a domestic tax that has been paid upon exportation of imported merchandise.

drawee   One on whom a draft is drawn, and who owes the stated amount. See **draft.**

drawer   One who "draws" a draft, and receives payment. See **draft.**

dumping   Exporting merchandise into a country at prices below the prices in that country's domestic market.

duty   The tax imposed by a government on merchandise imported from another country.

EDI   Electronic data interchange. The exchange between computers of trade documentation. EDI can take two forms, financial and documentary, and suffers from a curse common in the world of computers: at least two message format standards. They are ANSI (popular in the United States) and EDIFACT (popular elsewhere).

EMC   See **export management company.**

ETC   See **export trading company.**

eurodollars   U.S. dollars on deposit in any branch of any bank located outside the United States. Likewise, euroyen are Japanese yen on deposit in banks outside Japan, and may be outside of Europe, too. Any "eurocurrency" is a foreign currency deposit and should be treated with care if offered as a form of payment. For example, a U.S. exporter offered U.S. dollars to be delivered in some countries may face a challenge to convert these eurodollars to U.S. dollars.

evergreen clause   A provision in an L/C for the expiration date to extend without requiring an amendment.

EX (point of origin)   A pricing term (EXF = ex factory, EXW = ex warehouse, etc.) under which the seller agrees to place the goods at the buyer's disposal at the agreed place, with costs from that point being paid by the buyer.

exchange   A pricing term indicating that these costs are included in the price.

exchange permit   A government permit sometimes required to enable an importer to convert its own country's currency into foreign currency with which to pay a seller in another country.

exchange rate   The price of one currency expressed in terms of another. Exchange rates may be quoted spot (for delivery within two working days) or forward (for delivery at some future time). They are apt to fluctuate. Any international trader with an eye for profit will be aware of the currency circumstances affecting a partner.

exchange regulations/restrictions   Restrictions imposed by an importing country to protect its foreign exchange reserves. See **exchange permit.**

excise tax   A domestic tax assessed on the manufacture, sale, or use of a commodity within a country. It is usually refundable if the product is exported.

EXIMBank   Export-Import Bank of the United States.

expiration date   The final date upon which the presentation of documents and drawing of drafts under an L/C may be made.

export   To send goods to a foreign country or overseas territory.

export broker   A person or firm that brings together the exporter and importer for a fee and then withdraws from the transaction.

export declaration   A formal statement made to the collector of customs at a port of exit declaring full particulars about goods being exported.

export license   A government permit required to export certain products to certain destinations.

export management company (EMC)   A firm that acts as local export sales agent for several noncompeting manufacturers, usually without taking title to the goods. Also called "manufacturer's export agent." Compare **export trading company.**

export merchant   A producer or merchant who sells directly to a foreign purchaser without going through an intermediary such as an export broker.

export trading company (ETC)   A firm formed under the Export Trading Company Act of 1982 that buys domestic products for sale overseas taking title to the goods. Compare **export management company.**

factor   A finance company willing to purchase a receivable at a discount, either with recourse to the seller or without. In exchange for immediate payment, the seller will transfer title to the receivable to the factor. Factoring is a convenient but expensive alternative to other methods of converting receivables to cash.

FAS   Free Alongside Ship. Incoterm indicating that the sale price includes the cost of transport to the port of embarkation, but not the costs of loading, export clearance, ocean freight, or insurance. The buyer must insure the cargo as far as the port of delivery, for if the cargo is lost the buyer will bear the consequence. See **Incoterms 2000.**

FCIA   See **Foreign Credit Insurance Association.**

FI   Free in. A pricing term indicating that the charterer of a vessel is responsible for the cost of loading goods into the vessel.

FIO   Free in and out. A pricing term indicating that the charterer of a vessel is responsible for the cost of loading and unloading goods from the vessel.

floating policy   See **open cargo policy.**

FO   Free out. A pricing term indicating that the charterer of a vessel is responsible for the cost of loading goods from the vessel.

FOB   Free on board. Incoterm indicating that the sale price includes the cost of transport to and loading at the port of embarkation, but not the costs of export clearance, ocean freight, or insurance. The buyer must insure the cargo as far as the port of delivery, for if the cargo is lost the buyer will bear the consequence. See **Incoterms 2000.**

force majeure   A standard clause in marine contracts exempting the parties for nonfulfillment of their obligations as a result of conditions beyond their control, such as earthquakes, floods, or war.

Foreign Credit Insurance Association (FCIA)   An association of 50 insurance companies that operate in conjunction with EXIMBank to provide comprehensive insurance for exporters against nonpayment. FCIA underwrites the commercial credit risks. EXIMBank covers the political risk and any excessive commercial risks.

foreign currency account   An account maintained by a bank in foreign currency and payable in that currency.

foreign distribution   See **distributor.**

foreign exchange   A currency or credit instrument of a foreign country. Also, transactions involving purchase and/or sale of currencies.

foreign freight forwarder   See **freight forwarder.**

foreign sales agent   An individual or firm that serves as the foreign representative of a domestic supplier and seeks sales abroad for the supplier.

foreign sales corporation (FSC)   An American territorial tax scheme whereby a corporation within a U.S. possession, such as the Virgin Islands, or within a qualifying jurisdiction, such as Barbados, may exempt 15 to 30 percent of export profits from U.S. corporate tax. To qualify for special tax treatment, an FSC must be a foreign corporation, maintain a summary of its permanent books of account at the foreign office, and have at least one director resident outside of the United States. A portion of the foreign sales corporation's income (generally corresponding to the tax-deferred income of the domestic international corporation) is exempt from U.S. tax at both the FSC and the U.S. corporate parent levels. This exemption is achieved by allowing a domestic corporation that is an FSC shareholder a 100 percent deduction for a portion of dividends received from an FSC attributable to economic activity actually conducted outside U.S. customs territory. Interest, dividends, royalties, or other investment income of an FSC are subject to U.S. tax.

foreign sales representative   A representative residing in a foreign country who acts as a sales agent for a U.S. manufacturer, usually for a commission. Sometimes referred to as a "sales agent" or "commission agent." See also **representative.**

foreign trade zone (FTZ)   U.S. term for a site sanctioned by the authorities in which imported goods are exempted from duties until withdrawn for domestic sale or use. An FTZ can be used for commercial warehousing, assembly plants, and re-export. See also **free trade zone.**

forfeit   The sale of a term debt against a discounted cash payment in which the seller forfeits the right to future payments by the debtor. A popular method for exporters of capital equipment to dispose of long-term overseas debt.

forward exchange The purchase or sale of a foreign currency, usually for an equivalent amount of local currency, for delivery at some future date. Compare **spot exchange.**

forwarder's bill of lading A B/L issued by forwarder to shipper, a receipt for merchandise to be shipped.

foul bill of lading A receipt for goods issued by a carrier bearing a notation that the outward containers or goods have been damaged. Compare **clean bill of lading.**

FPA Free of particular average. A clause used in marine insurance indicating that partial loss or damage to a foreign shipment is not covered. (Loss resulting from certain conditions, such as the sinking or burning of the ship, may be specifically exempted from the effect of the clause.) Compare **WA.**

fraud All too common in international trade, especially transactional deals handling commodities, and a perfect reason why any sensible importer, exporter, or middleman will develop a relationship with a competent trade bank.

free port An area generally encompassing a port and its surrounding locality into which goods may enter duty free or subject only to minimal revenue tariffs.

free sale See **certificate of free sale.**

free trade zone A term used by all countries (except the U.S.A.) for a site sanctioned by the authorities in which imported goods are exempted from duties until withdrawn for domestic sale or use. The site can be used for commercial warehousing, assembly plants, and reexport. See also **foreign trade zone.**

freight forwarder A company that books shipment of goods, often as an agent for an airline. Usually, many small shipments are combined to take advantage of bulk discounts. Forwarders may provide other services, such as trucking, warehousing, and document preparation.

FSC See **foreign sales corporation.**

FTZ See **foreign trade zone.**

General Agreement on Tariffs and Trade (GATT). A Geneva-based organization that governed world trade until the formation of the World Trade Organization (WTO) in 1995. Formed by 23 countries at a conference in Geneva in

1947 to increase trade by lowering duties and quotas, the General Agreements on Tariffs and Trade is a multilateral trade treaty among governments, embodying rights and obligations. The detailed rules set out in the agreement constitute a code that the parties to the agreement agreed upon to govern their trading relationships.

general license (export)   Government authorization to export without specific documentary approval.

gross weight   Total weight of goods, packing, and container, ready for shipment.

guarantee letter   A commitment popular outside the United States guaranteeing payment in the event of nonperformance by the applicant. Compare **standby letter of credit.**

handling charges   The forwarder's fee to a shipper client.

harmonized code   Harmonized Commodity Description and Coding System. An international classification system that assigns identification numbers to specific products. The code ensures that all parties use a consistent classification for purposes of documentation, statistical control, and duty assessment.

horizontal trade association   A trade association that exports a range of similar or identical products supplied by a number of manufacturers or other producers. An association of agricultural cooperatives is a prime example. Compare **vertical trade association.**

ICC   See **International Chamber of Commerce.**

import   To bring merchandise into a country from another country or overseas territory.

import license   A government document that permits the importation of a product or material into a country where such licenses are necessary.

in bond   A term applied to the status of merchandise admitted provisionally into a country without payment of duties. See **bonded warehouse.**

inconvertibility   The inability to exchange the currency of one country for the currency of another.

Incoterms 2000   Terms of sale indicating costs and responsibilities included in the price under a sales contract (e.g.,

EXW, FOB, CFR, CIF, DDP). Defined under ICC 460, these worldwide, standardized terms transcend borders and should be clearly understood by all parties negotiating an international sales contract. (The year 2000 refers to the latest revision to the Incoterms.)

inherent vice An insurance term indicating defects or characteristics of a product that could lead to deterioration without outside influence. See **all-risks clause.**

inland bill of lading A B/L used in transporting goods overland to the exporter's international carrier. Although a through B/L can sometimes be used, it is usually necessary to prepare both an inland B/L and an ocean B/L for export shipments. Compare **air waybill, ocean bill of lading, through bill of lading.**

inland carrier A transportation line that handles export or import cargo between the port and inland points.

insurance certificate A certificate furnished, usually in duplicate, whenever the seller provides ocean marine insurance. The certificate is a negotiable document and must be endorsed before submission to the bank. The seller can arrange to obtain an *open cargo policy* that the freight forwarder maintains.

International Chamber of Commerce (ICC) A nongovernment organization serving worldwide business. Members in 123 countries represent tens of thousand of business organizations and companies and promote world trade and investment based on free and fair competition. Many of its publications are de facto standards in global commerce, including Uniform Customs and Practices for Documentary Credits (UCP 500), Uniform Rules for Collections (URC 522), and Incoterms 2000 (ICC 460).

international freight forwarder See **freight forwarder.**

invoice See **commercial invoice.**

irrevocable An adjective attached to an L/C to denote an instrument that cannot be amended or canceled without the agreement of all parties (including the beneficiary). The adjective is popular and redundant: Under Article 6 of UCP 500, credits shall be deemed to be irrevocable unless otherwise indicated. In most circumstances, *revocable* L/Cs are worthless and, as a consequence, are very rare.

joint venture   A commercial or industrial arrangement in which principals of one company share control and ownership with principals of another.

latest shipment date   The last day on which goods may be shipped (as evidenced by the "on board" date on a B/L or flight date on an air waybill).

legal weight   The weight of the goods plus the immediate wrappings that go along with the goods. An example is the contents of a tin can together with its can. Compare **net weight.**

letter of credit (L/C)   An undertaking written by the issuing bank to pay the beneficiary a stated sum of money, within a certain time, against the presentation of conforming documents. Other parties to a letter of credit may be the advising bank, the confirming bank, the negotiating bank, the paying bank, and the reimbursing bank. The main contract of payment remains between the issuing bank and the beneficiary. Since the issuing bank is very often located in a separate country from the beneficiary, the latter relies on the advising bank, locally, for notification of the arrival of the L/C and for authentication. Conforming documents may consist of various export documents, as in a *documentary letter of credit,* or a simple statement by the beneficiary, as in a standby letter of credit.

license   See **export license, import license, validated license.**

licensing   The granting of technical assistance, service, and/or the use of product rights (such as a trademark) in return for royalty payments.

lighter   An open or covered barge towed by a tugboat and used mainly in harbors and inland waterways.

lighterage   The loading or unloading of a ship by means of a barge or lighter because of shallow water, which prevents the ship from coming to shore.

marine bill of lading   A B/L for shipment by sea.

marine insurance   Insurance that will compensate the owner of goods transported on the seas in the event of loss that cannot be legally recovered from the carrier. Also covers air shipments.

marks   A set of letters, numbers, and/or geometric symbols, generally followed by the name of the port of destination, placed on packages for export for identification purposes.

master letter of credit   The first of two L/Cs in a *back-to-back letter of credit* arrangement.

maturity date   The date upon which a draft or acceptance becomes due for payment.

MEA   Manufacturer's export agent. See **export management company.**

most-favored-nation status   Designation of a country's status in relation to a trading partner. All countries having most-favored-nation status receive equal treatment with respect to customs and tariffs.

multimodal bill of lading   A B/L used when more than one mode of transport is involved in a shipment—for example, when a consignment travels by rail and by sea. Sometimes referred to as a combined transport bill of lading.

named point   See **specific delivery point.**

negotiable bill of lading   A B/L consigned to the order of, and endorsed in blank by, the shipper. Whoever carries a negotiable bill of lading possesses the document of title to the goods.

negotiating bank   The bank that checks the exporter's documents under the L/C and advances cash to the exporter, at a small discount, in the expectation of reimbursement by the issuing bank.

net weight   The weight of the goods alone without any immediate wrapping. An example is the weight of the contents of a tin can without the weight of the can. Compare **legal weight.**

nomenclature of the Customs Cooperation Council   See **Customs Cooperation Council Nomenclature.**

ocean bill of lading   A B/L indicating that the exporter consigns a shipment to an international carrier for transportation to a specified foreign market. Unlike an inland B/L, the ocean B/L also serves as a collection document. If it is a "straight B/L," the foreign buyer can obtain the shipment from the carrier by simply showing proof of identity. If a "negotiable B/L" is used, the buyer must first pay for the goods, post a bond, or meet other conditions agreeable to the seller. Compare **air waybill, inland bill of lading, through bill of lading.**

offset   A variation of countertrade in which the seller is required to assist in or arrange for the marketing of locally produced goods.

on board bill of lading   A bill of lading in which a carrier acknowledges that goods have been placed on board a certain vessel.

open account   A trade arrangement in which goods are shipped to a foreign buyer without guarantee of payment. The obvious risk to the supplier makes it essential that the buyer's integrity be unquestionable.

open cargo policy   Synonymous with "floating policy." An insurance policy that binds the insurer automatically to protect with insurance all shipments made by the insured from the moment the shipment leaves the initial shipping point until it is delivered at destination. The insuring conditions include clauses naming such risks insured against as perils of the sea, fire, jettison, forcible theft, and barratry. See **all-risks clause, barratry, perils of the sea.**

opening bank   Banker's terminology for the *issuing bank* in the L/C process.

open insurance policy   A marine insurance policy that applies to all shipments made by an exporter over a period of time rather than to one shipment only.

OPIC   Overseas Private Investment Corporation. A wholly owned government corporation designed to promote private investment in developing countries by promoting political risk insurance and some financing assistance.

"order" bill of lading   A negotiable bill of lading made out to the order of the shipper.

packing credit   Common parlance internationally, especially in Asia, for *preexport finance* provided against a letter of credit.

packing list   A list prepared by the seller itemizing goods shipped, quantities, sizes, weights, and packing marks. Very common in trade finance, the packing list should be prepared so as to be consistent with other documents, especially under a letter of credit.

parcel post receipt   The postal authority's signed acknowledgment of receipt of a shipment made by parcel post.

paying bank   The bank nominated in the L/C to pay out against conforming documents, without *recourse*. Exporters interested in their cash flow should understand whether the paying bank is in their own country or that of their customer, the importer.

payment in advance   An arrangement in which the buyer delivers cash to the seller before the seller releases the goods. Often referred to as cash in advance, or CAD, it may not mean exactly the same as *advance payment.*

perils of the sea   A marine insurance term used to designate heavy weather, straining, lightning, collision, and sea water damage.

phytosanitary inspection certificate   A certificate, issued to satisfy import regulations of foreign countries, indicating that a shipment has been inspected and is free from harmful pests and plant diseases.

piggybacking   The assigning of export marketing and distribution functions by one manufacturer to another.

port marks   See **marks.**

preexport finance   U.S. bankers' terminology for a loan to an exporter to finance the accumulation of materials and subsequent manufacture, assembly, production, packaging, and transport of physical goods to fulfill an export order. Such financing is commonly guaranteed by EXIMBank or SBA Working Capital Guarantee programs.

presentation period   The time allowed after issue of transport documents to present such documents under an L/C.

presenting bank   The bank in a documentary collection process presenting export documents to the drawee for payment. The exporter and the presenting bank behave in a principal/agent relationship. Therefore it is wise for the uncertain exporter to ensure that the collection is presented by some bank other than the importer's bank.

procuring agent   See **purchasing agent.**

pro forma invoice   A provisional invoice written by the seller that serves as a quotation to the buyer. Following negotiations, a document issued by the exporter to confirm product details, prices, shipping, and payment terms. This is the starting point for further documentation.

purchasing agent   An agent who purchases goods in his or her own country on behalf of large foreign buyers such as government agencies and large private concerns.

quota   The total quantity of a product or commodity that may be imported into a country. Most quotas are imposed to protect a domestic market. In the United States, sugar, wheat, cotton, tobacco, textiles, and apparel are governed by quotas.

quotation   An offer to sell goods at a stated price and under stated terms.

rate of exchange   The basis upon which money of one country will be exchanged for that of another. Rates of exchange are established and quoted for foreign currencies on the basis of the demand, supply, and stability of the individual currencies. See also **exchange.**

received for shipment bill of lading   A B/L indicating goods received for shipment (but not "on board"). It is unacceptable under an L/C arrangement unless the B/L is specifically allowed by the letter of credit or unless it is marked "on board" with a date and signature.

recourse   A term indicating that the paying party retains the right to the funds in the event that reimbursement (from another party) is not forthcoming. Recourse is an important concept in trade finance.

red clause letter of credit   An L/C allowing the beneficiary to draw down an advance payment prior to shipment, usually against presentation of a simple receipt. So called because this clause was traditionally written in red ink. Its purpose is to finance the seller during the preparation of the export order. The applicant remains liable for any drawings even if goods are never shipped. This is one reason that importers should expect red clause L/Cs to be collateralized differently from plain import L/Cs.

reimbursing bank   The bank empowered by the issuing bank (i.e., with a bank balance) to charge the account of the issuing bank and pay to the bank collecting funds under a letter of credit.

remitting bank   The role played by the exporter's bank in a documentary collection process. The remitting bank sends export documents to a correspondent bank in the country of the importer (the drawee in the collection process).

representative   An individual or firm that acts on behalf of a supplier. The word "representative" is preferred to "agent" in writing, since agent, in an exact legal sense, connotes more binding powers and responsibilities than representative. See also **foreign sales representative.**

revocable   An adjective attached to an L/C indicating that it can be altered or canceled after the buyer has opened the L/C through his or her bank. Compare **irrevocable.**

revolving letter of credit   An L/C that reinstates automatically. It may revolve in relation to time or value, the latter being cumulative or noncumulative.

royalty payment   The share of the product or profit paid by a licensee to a licensor. See **licensing.**

SA   Société anonyme. French expression for a corporation.

sales agent   See **foreign sales representative.**

sales representative   See **foreign sales representative.**

sanitary certificate   A certificate that attests to the purity or absence of disease or pests in the shipment of food products, plants, seeds, and live animals.

S/D   See **sight draft.**

shipper's documents   Commercial invoices, bills of lading, insurance certificates, consular invoices, and related documents.

shipper's letter of credit   An L/C issued by the exporter to the freight forwarder covering key details of the transaction, shipping terms, and other applicable instructions that the freight forwarder must follow.

ship's manifest   A true list in writing of the individual shipments comprising the cargo of a vessel, signed by the captain.

SIC   See **Standard Industrial Classification.**

sight draft (S/D)   A draft so drawn as to be payable upon presentation to the drawee or at a fixed or determinable date thereafter. See also **documents against acceptance, documents against payment.**

SITC   See **Standard International Trade Classification.**

specific delivery point   A point in sales quotations that designates specifically where and within what geographical locale the goods will be delivered at the expense and responsibility of the seller. An example is FAS (named vessel) at (named port of export).

spot exchange   The purchase or sale of foreign currency, usually against an equivalent amount of local currency, for immediate delivery (i.e., within two working days after the agreement). Compare **forward exchange.**

Standard Industrial Classification (SIC)   A numerical system developed by the U.S. government for the classification of commercial services and industrial products. SIC also classifies establishments by type of activity.

Standard International Trade Classification (SITC)   A numerical system developed by the United Nations to classify commodities used in international trade and in reporting trade statistics.

standby letter of credit   An L/C popular in the United States that guarantees payment in the event of nonperformance by the applicant. It is similar in method to the commercial L/C and subject to UCP 500 but different in three significant aspects: (1) The beneficiary's statement or claim of default suffices to draw (in contrast to a pile of detailed export documents under the commercial L/C); thus (2) the discrepancy rate is between low and zero; therefore (3) banks collateralize standby L/Cs somewhat differently from commercial L/Cs (i.e., 100 percent).

state-controlled trading company   In a country with a state trading monopoly, a trading entity empowered by the country's government to conduct export business.

steamship conference   A group of vessel operators joined together for the purpose of establishing freight rates. A shipper may receive reduced rates if it enters into a contract to ship on vessels of conference members only.

steamship guarantee A guarantee issued by a bank to a steamship line against financial loss arising from the release of a consignment without the appropriate *transport document*. Such a guarantee is popular because goods frequently arrive at the port of discharge before documents are available to clear them.

stocking distributor A distributor that maintains an inventory of goods of a manufacturer.

straight bill of lading A B/L consigned directly to a party who holds title to the goods. Such consignment is discomforting to bankers if the consignee party is not the bank. A straight B/L cannot be endorsed to another party. Compare **negotiable bill of lading.**

swap arrangements A form of countertrade in which the seller sells on credit and then transfers the credit to a third party.

SWIFT Society for Worldwide Interbank Financial Telecommunication. A cooperative owned by a consortium of banks designed to carry formatted messages between them in a secure environment. The messages all relate to financial transactions between banks and their customers.

switch arrangements A form of countertrade in which the seller sells on credit and then transfers the credit to a third party.

tare weight The weight of packing and containers without the goods to be shipped.

tariff schedule A schedule or system of duties imposed by a government on goods imported or exported. The rate of duty imposed in a tariff.

tenor The time fixed or allowed for payment, as in the tenor of a draft.

TEU Twenty-foot equivalent unit. A measurement of cargo based on a standard ocean shipment container, which is 20 feet in length.

through bill of lading A single B/L covering both the domestic and international carriage of an export shipment. An air waybill, for instance, is essentially a through B/L used for air shipments. Ocean shipments, on the other hand, usually require two separate documents—an inland B/L for domestic carriage and an ocean B/L for international carriage. Through bills of lading, therefore, cannot be used. Compare **air waybill, inland bill of lading, ocean bill of lading.**

time draft A draft so drawn as to mature at a certain fixed time after presentation or acceptance.

trade acceptance A *time draft* in which the drawee signs the word "accepted" across the face and thus commits to pay the holder upon maturity. The instrument is as valuable as the creditworthiness of the accepting party.

trade development program (TDP) A program designed to promote economic development abroad and the sale of a nation's goods and services to developing countries.

trade mission A mission to a foreign country organized to promote trade through the establishment of contracts and exposure to the commercial environment. Trade missions are frequently organized by federal, state, or local agencies.

tramp steamer A ship not operating on regular routes or schedules.

transport document A bill of lading, an air waybill, a truck receipt, or any other document acting as a receipt for goods and a contract of carriage. Of all these transport documents, only a B/L is a document of title.

transshipment Shipment of merchandise to a destination abroad on more than one vessel. Liability may pass from one carrier to the next, or it may be covered by a *through bill of lading* issued by the first carrier.

trust receipt Release of merchandise by a bank to a buyer in which the bank retains title to the merchandise. The buyer, who obtains the goods for manufacturing or sales purposes, is obligated to maintain the goods (or the proceeds from their sale) distinct from the remainder of his or her assets and to hold them ready for repossession by the bank.

turnkey A method of construction whereby the contractor assumes total responsibility from design through completion.

UCP 500 Uniform Customs and Practice for Documentary Credits, Publication No. 500 of the International Chamber of Commerce. The indisputable authority on letters of credits, recognized internationally, UCP 500 serves as the self-regulation of the L/C industry and renders L/Cs a more reliable form of payment. Importers and exporters are advised to be particularly careful of any L/C that does not clearly state (usually in the final paragraph) it is subject to UCP 500.

unconfirmed letter of credit   An L/C that does not carry any confirmation by a second bank, usually located in the country of the beneficiary. Exporters intent on collecting payment under such L/Cs should hold a view as to risk of non-payment for various reasons.

URC 522   Uniform Rules for Collections, Publication No. 522 of the International Chamber of Commerce. It is an internationally recognized code for the handling of collections, clean or documentary.

usance   Bankers' terminology, in use more commonly overseas than in the United States, indicating the time allowed for payment of a *bill of exchange.* Compare **at sight.**

usance draft   More often referred to in the United States as a *time draft.* See also **documents against acceptance.**

usance letter of credit   Sometimes referred to in the United States as a time L/C.

validated license   A government document authorizing the export of commodities within limitations set forth in the document.

vertical trade association   A trade association that integrates a range of functions taking products from suppliers to consumers. Compare **horizontal trade association.**

visa   A signature of formal approval on an entree document obtained from a consulate.

WA   With average. A marine insurance term meaning that a shipment is protected from partial damage whenever the damage exceeds a given percentage.

warehouse receipt   A receipt issued by a warehouse listing goods received for storage.

wharfage   The charge assessed by a carrier for handling incoming or outgoing ocean cargo.

without reserve   A term indicating that a shipper's agent or representative is empowered to make definitive decisions and adjustments abroad without approval of the group or individual represented. Compare **advisory capacity.**

INTERNET TERMS

Don't be intimidated by Web jargon. Here, in simple English, are explanations of basic terms you will encounter as you wander on the Web.

applet   A small program or application, usually written in *Java* language. Applets run on a Web browser and power most of the fancier features, from animations to calculators.

bandwidth   A measure of the amount of information that can be transmitted over a connection. The lower the bandwidth, the slower the downloading of material, especially pictures. (Slang: A person with low bandwidth is slow on the uptake.) A very high bandwidth connection is known as a broadband connection.

bookmark   A direct link to an often-visited site that is saved on a Web browser for easy access. See also **hyperlink.**

bot   Slang for robot. A utility that performs a function on the Web automatically or electronically. A site that seeks out the cheapest prices for clothes is a shopping bot.

browser   A program that allows users to interact with the World Wide Web. Examples are Netscape Navigator and Microsoft Explorer.

cache   High-speed memory set aside on a computer to store frequently accessed data.

chat room   A variation on the message board. A site for live on-line conversation.

cookie   The programming code from a Web site, stored on the user's computer. When the site is visited again, the cookie is sent back to the Web site to remind it of the user's preferences.

cyberspace   A general term for the Internet and anything else on-line. The universe in which people interact by means of connected computers.

domain name   A unique name that identifies a Web site. See **URL.**

download   To transfer a file from a remote computer to a local computer. Compare **upload.**

hacker   The highwayman of the Internet highway. A person who uses a computer to gain unauthorized access to other networks and protected Web servers. Some hackers are crooks; others just annoying pranksters.

hit   A visit to a Web site, no matter how brief. Leading portal Yahoo has 37 million hits a month.

home page   A Web site's main or central page, or, alternatively, the page that appears on a browser when the user logs on.

HTML   Hypertext markup language. The programming language for most Web pages.

hyperlink   A connection, or just plain "link," to another site. It usually appears underlined and in a different color on screen. Clicking on a link transports the user to another Web page.

ISP   Internet service provider. A company that provides Internet access, usually for a monthly fee. Examples are AOL, Earthlink, and At Home.

Java   A programming language, from Sun Microsystems, used to create *applets*.

message board   A place where people can post, read, and respond to computer messages written by other users.

plug-in   An add-on program that enhances the capabilities of a Web browser, such as the ability to hear live audio feeds and see video clips. Examples are RealPlayer and Shockwave.

server   A computer that controls a network of computers or powers a Web site. The speed of a server is slowed by high Web traffic, no matter how fast the Internet connection.

snail mail   Slang term for conventional mail delivery.

spam   Unwanted e-mail advertisements or solicitations. As too much of that processed meat can clog the arteries, so too much electronic spam can clog an e-mail box and slow everything down to a crawl.

streaming   Audio or video that accompanies a Web transmission. Examples are live tickers and radio broadcasts.

surf   An overused Web term to describe the action of moving from one Web site to another to another and another.

upload   To transfer a file from a local computer to a remote computer. Compare **download.**

URL   Universal resource locator. The Internet address typed into a browser window. Most begin with "http://www." and end with ".com" (commercial sites), ".gov" (government sites), or ".edu" (educational sites).

virus   A program usually hidden in a file or e-mail that infects a computer by altering or deleting files.

Index

A

ABI, 178, 179
Absolute quotas, 196
Accounting, 131, 132
ADB, 272
ADS, 157
Advertising, 40, 73
Africa, 251–273
  American partnerships for
    economic growth, 253–256
  central, 257–259
  contacts/web sites, 272, 273
  east, 259, 260
  funding sources, 267–272
  north, 256, 257
  southern, 263–266
  trade blocs/special treaties,
    266, 267
  trading potential, 251–253
  west, 260–263
Africa Food Security Initiative, 255
African Development Bank (ADB),
  272
Africinvest, 271
Agency/distributor agreements,
  104, 105
Agency for International
  Development (AID), 86
Agent Distributor Service (ADS),
  157
Agreeing to a contract, 43

AID, 86
Air cargo agents, 163
Air transportation, 106
Air waybill, 125, 126
Algeria, 256
Americas, 216
  (See also NAFTA)
Andean Common Market, 233
Angola, 263
APEC, 281, 282
Arbitration clauses, 105
Asia-Pacific Economic
  Cooperation (APEC), 281, 282
Asian tigers, 281
Assignment of proceeds, 95, 96,
  98–100
Association of Caribbean States,
  233
At sight, 90
ATA carnet, 63, 289, 290
Attitudes, 48
Authority to purchase, 88, 90
Automated Brokerage Interface
  (ABI), 178, 179
Avoiding risk, 86–105
  agency/distributor agreements,
    104, 105
  bad debts, 99–102
  commercial risk, 87–102
  foreign exchange risk, 103, 104
  payment, 87–99

Avoiding risk (*Cont.*):
  political risks, 102, 103
  shipping risks, 102
AXCAP, 271

B
B/A, 83
Back-to-back L/C, 96, 98, 101
Bad debts, 99
BAFT, 271, 272
Bank draft, 88–90
Bank financing, 82–84
Banker's acceptance (B/A), 83
Bankers Association for Foreign
  Trade (BAFT), 271, 272
Bargaining, 42–46
Barter, 44
Basic Guide to Exporting, 161
Beaucoup, 75
Benin, 260
Berra, Yogi, 110
Bill of lading, 121, 125–128
Body language, 47, 48, 51
Bonded warehouses, 204–206
Bonds:
  continuous, 195
  general, 195
  surety, 178
  term, 195
Breakage, 108
Bribery, 45, 46
Bureau of Export Administration
  (BXA), 166, 168, 169
Burundi, 257
Business class, 60
Business culture, 47–52
Business insurance, 133
Business license, 131
Business name, 130
Business Person's Guide to Africa,
  273
Business plan, 134–147
BXA, 166, 168, 169

C
C group, 26
Cables, 58

Calvert New Africa Fund, 268
Cameroon, 258
Cargo insurance, 102
Caribbean Basin Initiative (CBI),
  233
Caribbean Common Market
  (Caricom), 234
Caricom, 234
Caricom-Bolivia Free Trade
  Agreement, 234
Caricom-Venezuela Free Trade
  Agreement, 234
Carnet, 162
*Carnet: Move Goods Duty-Free
  Through Customs*, 64
Carnets, 63, 64, 289, 290
Catalog shows, 39
Cauris Investment, 270
CBI, 233
CDC, 272
Central African Republic, 258
Central America, 233, 234
Central American Common
  Market, 234
Certificate of manufacture,
  115, 118
Certificate of marine insurance,
  119, 120
Certificate of origin, 112, 113
CETRA, 279
Chad, 258
China, 277–280
China Business Guide, 279
Choice of product/service, 17, 18
CIA Fact Book, 74
CIBER, 74
CIF, 28
Cirrus Logic, Inc., 8, 9
Citizens Emergency Center, 60
Clean on board, 128
Clear Freight, 75
Collection documents, 111
  (*See also* Documentation)
COMAFIN, 268
COMESA, 272
Commerce Daily Bulletin, 86
Commercial attaché, 115

Commercial entry process, 179–187
Commercial invoice, 112, 114
Commercial News USA, 158
Commercial risk, 87–102
Commercial service centers, 152
Commercial Service International
    Contacts (CSIC), 158
Common Market of Eastern and
    Southern Africa (COMESA),
    272
Commonwealth Africa Investment
    Fund (COMAFIN), 268
Commonwealth Development
    Corporation (CDC), 272
Commonwealth of Independent
    States (CIS), 238, 239
Communications, 54–59
Company name, 130
*Complying with the Made in the
    U.S.A. standard*, 169
Conference lines, 106
Congo Republic, 258
Consignment, 89
Consular invoice, 112, 115–117
Contacts, 19–21
Continuous bonds, 195
Copyrights, 53
Cost elements, 30–34
Counterpurchase, 44, 45
Countertrade, 44
Covering, 104
Creative Tour Consultants, 8
Credit information, 101, 102
Crystal Treasures, 10
CSIC, 158
Culture, 46–52
Currency risk, 103, 104
Customs bonded warehouses,
    204–206
Customs house brokers, 177–179
Customs Service, 173–176
Customs Service Statistics, 160

D
D group, 26
DAF, 28
DBA, 130

DECs, 154
Definitions (glossary), 297–328
Democratic Republic of the Congo,
    258
*Destination Japan: A Business
    Guide for the 1990s*, 281
Developed countries, 18
Development Finance Company of
    Uganda, 269
Direct sales method, 38
*Directory of Manufacturers
    Agents*, 177
DISCs, 170
Distributors, 40–42, 104, 105
District export councils (DECs),
    154
Documentary credit, 91
    (*See also* Letter of credit [L/C])
Documentation, 110–128
    bill of lading, 121, 125–128
    certificate of manufacture,
        115, 118
    certificate of origin, 112, 113
    commercial invoice, 112, 114
    consular invoice, 112, 115–117
    inspection certificate, 115,
        118, 121
    insurance certificate, 115,
        119, 120
    packing list, 118, 122
    shipper's export declaration
        (SED), 118, 121, 123, 124
Domain name, 72
Domestic international sales
    corporations (DISCs), 170
Drawback, 178

E
E-commerce (*see* Internet)
E group, 26
E-mail, 76, 77
EAR, 164, 165
Economic Bulletin Board (EBB),
    157
Economic Community (ECC), 237
Economic Community of Central
    African States, 266

Economic Community of West
    African States (ECOWAS),
    266, 267
ECOWAS, 266, 267
Education, 49
EEA, 237
Egypt, 256
Eisenhower, Dwight, 134
*EMC-Your Export Department,
    The*, 161
EMCs, 161
Enterprise Fund, 271
Enterprise Fund-South Africa, 270
Entry process, 179–187
ETCA, 155
Ethiopia, 259
Euro, 245
Europages, 75
European Community (EC), 237
European Economic Area (EEA),
    237
European Patent Convention, 54
European Patent Organization, 54
European Union (EU), 6, 235–249
    common currency, 245
    customs duties, 241
    customs procedures, 241, 242
    distribution, 247
    EFTA, 237
    four freedoms, 236
    further reading, 249
    history, 237
    markings, 246
    national treatment, 240
    nonmember documentation, 242
    nonpreferential rules of origin,
        243, 244
    preferential rules, 243
    quality system registration, 246
    rules of origin, 242–244
    SEA, 240
    standards, 245, 246
    valuation, 241
    VAT harmonization, 244
Europeonline, 75
EXIMBank, 85, 86, 102, 103, 267
Expenses, 132

Export Administration
    Regulations (EAR), 164, 165
Export assistance centers (EACs),
    153, 154, 156
Export controls, 164–169
Export costing worksheet, 33
*Export-Import Bank of the United
    States*, 162
Export joint ventures, 155
Export license, 115, 164–169
*Export Programs: A Business
    Directory of U.S. Government
    Service*, 156
Export prospects, 157, 158
Export Statistics Profiles, 160
Export Trade Certificate of
    Review Program, 155
Export Trading Company Act
    (ETCA), 155
Exporter Yellow Pages, 161
Exporter's Encyclopedia (Annual),
    161
Exporting, 151–172
    export controls, 164–169
    freight forwarding, 162–164
    government export counseling,
        152–156
    information sources, 156–162
    Made in U.S.A., 169
    research checklist, 21–23
    tax incentives, 169–171
    unfair import practices,
        171, 172
Exposure, 104
EXW, 28
Eyebrows, 50

F
F group, 26
Facilitating payments, 45
Facsimile (fax), 55, 57
Factor, 84
FAS, 28
FCIA, 103
FCS, 152
Fictitious name, 130
Financial records, 131

Financing, 81–86
   Africa, 267–272
   AID, 86
   banker's acceptance, 83
   bank, 82–84
   EXIMBANK, 85, 86
   factors, 84
   IDCA, 86
   OPIC, 85
   PEFCO, 84
   SBA, 85
Follow-up communications, 55
Foreign Commercial Service
   (FCS), 152
Foreign Corrupt Practices Act
   (FCPA), 45
Foreign Credit Insurance
   Association (FCIA), 103
Foreign exchange risk, 103, 104
Foreign representative, 41
Foreign sales corporation (FSC),
   170, 171
Foreign trade zones (FTZs),
   199–204
Former Soviet states, 238, 239
Forward contract, 104
Forward rate, 104
Foul bill, 128
Free Trade Area of the Americas
   (FTAA), 215
Free trade zones, 198–204, 206
Freight forwarding, 162–164
FSC, 170, 171
FTAA, 215
FTZ success stories, 10, 11
FTZs, 199–204
Future exchange rate, 104

G
Gabon, 258
Gambia, 260
Gates, Bill, 66
General bonds, 195
General Information on Patents,
   52
General rules of interpretation
   (GRI), 187

General System of Preferences
   (GSP), 195
Ghana, 261
Ghana Venture Capital Fund
   (GVCF), 271
Global Electronic Commerce
   Korea, 75
Glossary, 297–328
Gold Key service, 159
Government-approved trade
   missions, 39
Government bookstore, 291–293
Government export counseling,
   152–156
Government procurement, 75, 76
Greater Horn Information
   Exchange, 273
GRI, 187
Grooming, 50
Group of Three, 234
GSP, 195
Guide to Documentary Operations,
   91
Guinea, 261
GVCF, 271

H
Harmonized Tariff Schedule
   (HTS), 187, 188
Harmonized Tariff System,
   187–195
Hedging, 104
Hong Kong, 279
Hotels, 61
How to Get the Most from
   Overseas Exhibitions, 160
HTML, 69–71
HTS, 187, 188
Humor, 51, 52

I
IA, 171, 172
IATA, 163
IBP, 159
ICP, 158
IDCA, 86
IEBB, 75

IMI, 157
Import Administration (IA), 171, 172
Import costing worksheet, 34
Import/export business, 3, 4
Import Export Bulletin Board (IEBB), 75
Import quotas, 195, 196
Importing, 173–207
 customs bonded warehouses, 204–206
 customs house brokers, 177–179
 entry process, 179–187
 free trade zones, 198–204, 206
 government support (Customs Service), 173–176
 Harmonized Tariff System, 187–195
 information sources, 176, 177
 quotas, 195, 196
 research checklist, 23, 24
 special regulations, 196–198
 tariffs, 179
Importing into the United States, 176
In-bond regions (free trade zones), 198–204
INCOTERMS, 26
INCOTERMS 2000, 26
Independent lines, 106
Indirect sales method, 38
Industry Sector Analysis (ISA), 157
Information sources (see Sources of information)
Initial quotations, 24–26
Inspection certificate, 115, 118, 121
Insurance, 102, 103, 133
Insurance certificate, 115, 119, 120
Intellectual property, 52–54
Intermodalism, 107, 108
International Air Transportation Association (IATA), 163
International Buyer Program (IBP), 159
International Company Profile (ICP), 158
International conferences, 21

International Convention for the Protection of Industrial Property, 54
International credit information, 99
International Development Cooperation Agency (IDCA), 86
International mailgrams, 58
International Market Insights (IMI), 157
International market research, 21–24
International time zones, 61, 62
International trade, 3
International Trade Administration (ITA), 152–154
Internet, 57, 58, 65–79
 Africa, 272, 273
 domain name, 72
 e-mail, 76, 77
 finding foreign buyers, 74, 75
 finding foreign markets, 74
 further reading, 78
 history, 58
 keeping in touch, 77
 marketing techniques, 76
 payment, 77
 search engines, 73
 software tools/suppliers, 70–72
 terminology (definitions), 326–328
 Web site design, 68–72
Introduction to the Overseas Private Investment Corporation (OPIC), 161
Introductory letter, 55, 56
Irrevocable credit, 93
ISA market research reports, 157
ISO standards, 18
ITA, 152–154

J
Japan:
 distribution/sales channels, 276, 277
 import policies, 275, 276

Japan (*Cont.*):
   information, 277
   JETRO, 276
   marketing strategy, 276
   penetrating foreign markets, 47
   role-play negotiation, 43
   taxes, 276
Japan External Trade
      Organization (JETRO), 276
Jokes, 51, 52
Jurisdictional clause, 105

K

Kenya, 259
Keys to success, 283–287

L

L/C (*see* Letter of credit [L/C])
Labeling, 109
LAIA, 234
Land bridges, 107
Land transportation, 107
Language, 47
Las Brisas Exports, 9
Latin American Integration
      Association (LAIA), 234
Least developed countries, 19
Legal environment, 48
Lesotho, 264
Letter of assignment, 100
Letter of credit (L/C), 91–100
   assignment of proceeds, 95, 96,
      98–100
   back-to-back L/C, 96, 98, 101
   charges, 92
   code of practice, 91
   issuing/confirming/advising, 93
   phases of documentary credit,
      93, 97
   sample, 96
   standby L/C, 91, 92
   transferable L/C, 95, 98
   types, 93
Letter of injury, 25
Letter of introduction, 55, 56
Liberia, 261
Libya, 257

Load center, 107
Logistics, 105–109

M

Macro, 36
Macrosegmentation, 37
Made in U.S.A., 169
Madrid Arrangement for
      International Registration of
      Trademarks, 54
Mali, 261
Maquiladora, 232, 233
Marginal cost pricing, 30
Marine cargo insurance, 102
Market channel, 29
*Market Guide of Mass
      Merchandisers*, 177
Market place, 35–42
Market research, 21–24
Market segmentation, 36, 37
Marketing contacts, 20, 21
Marking, 109, 110
Matchmaker trade delegations, 159
Mauritania, 261, 262
Mauritius Venture Capital Fund
      (MVCF), 269, 270
Mercosur, 234
Mexican Maquiladora Program,
      232
Micro, 37
Microbridge, 107
Microsegmentation, 37
MIGA, 273
Minibridge, 107
Modern Packaging Encyclopedia,
      108
Morgan Stanley Africa
      Investment Fund, 268, 269
Morocco, 257
Mozambique, 264
Multistate/catalog exhibitions, 159
MVCF, 269, 270

N

NAFTA, 217–232
   admission of goods, 219
   agriculture, 230

NAFTA (*Cont.*):
  automotive goods, 228
  business travelers, 218, 219
  certificate of origin, 220
  claiming NAFTA tariff, 223, 226
  content calculation, 228
  country-of-origin marking, 219, 220
  energy/basis petrochemicals, 229, 230
  financial services, 231
  government procurement, 230
  intellectual property, 231
  investment, 231
  key provisions, 217, 218
  national treatment, 218
  preference criteria, 226–228
  rules of origin (ROO), 220–223
  services, 231
  technical standards, 230
  telecommunications, 231
  temporary entry rules, 219
  textiles/apparel, 228, 229
  transformation of goods, 232
Namibia, 264
National Minority Business Council, 273
National Ship Building Company, 11
Negotiations, 42–46
NEOS, 75
New South Africa Fund, 269
Niger, 262
Nigeria, 262
NLR, 165
North American Free Trade Agreement (*see* NAFTA)

O

Ocean bill of lading, 127
Ocean freight forwarder, 163
Ocean service, 106
OETCA, 155
Office, 132
Office of Export Trading Company Affairs (OETCA), 155
Old West Exports, 8

Open account, 88, 89
OPIC, 85, 103, 254
Order bills of lading, 128
Organization of Eastern Caribbean States, 234
Overseas Private Investment Corporation (OPIC), 85, 103, 254
Overseas promotion, 158–162
Overseas Trade Promotions Calendar, 160

P

Pacific Basin, 280–282
Packaging, 108, 109
Packing list, 118, 122
Paris Union, 54
Partnership for Economic Growth and Opportunity in Africa, 253
Passport, 61
Patent Cooperation Treaty, 54
Patents, 53, 54
Payment, 87–99
PEFCO, 84
People's Republic of China (PRC), 277–280
Personal sales, 38
Physical distribution, 105–109
Political risk, 102, 103
PRC, 277–280
Price, 29, 30
Pricing model, 31
Private Export Funding Corporation (PEFCO), 84
Pro forma invoice, 25–27
Pro forma statements, 140–147
Product buyback, 44
Product standards, 18
Profit, 24
Protocol for Profit: A Manager's Guide to Competing Worldwide (Nelson), 256

Q

Quantitative quotas, 196
Quotas, 195, 196

R

Relationships, 47
Religion, 48
Republic of China (ROC), 279
Republic of the Congo, 258
Request for quotation (RFQ), 24
Research, 21–24
Revocable credit, 93
RFQ, 24
Risk, 86, 87
  (*See also* Avoiding risk)
RO/RO, 107
ROC, 279
ROO, 220–223
Rotswana, 264
Rules of origin (ROO), 220–223
Rules of Practice and Procedure,
  171
Russia, 247, 248
Rwanda, 259

S

SACU, 266
SAD, 242
SADC, 266, 273
SBA, 85
SBA Office for International
  Trade, 74
SBDCs, 155
SCORE, 155
SEA, 240
Search engines, 73
Secured financing, 82, 83
Segmenting the market, 36, 37
Seller's permit, 131
Seminar missions, 39
Senegal, 262
SENIVEST, 271
Service marks, 53
Shipper's export declaration
  (SED), 118, 121, 123, 124
Shipping, 105–109
Shipping documents, 111
  (*See also* Documentation)
Shipping risks, 102
Sierra Leone, 263
Sight draft, 88, 90

Single Administrative Document
  (SAD), 242
Single European Act (SEA), 240
Small Business Administration
  (SBA), 85
Small business development
  centers (SBDCs), 155
Smile, 50
Social organization, 49
Social stratification, 49
Societé Financiàre-SENIVEST,
  271
Somalia, 259
Sources of information:
  Africa, 272, 273
  credit information, 101, 102
  export license, 168, 169
  exporting, 156–162
  foreign travel information, 60
  importing, 176, 177
  Internet web sites, 74–77
  Japan, 277
  near east/Asia, 281, 282
Sourcing contacts, 19, 20
South Africa, 264, 265
South African Development
  Community (SADC), 273
South America, 233, 234
Southern Africa Fund, Inc., 269
Southern African Customs Union
  (SACU), 266
Southern African Development
  Conference (SADC), 266
Special immediate entry permit,
  183–185
Special missions, 39
Special tariff treatment programs,
  194
Specific delivery point, 29
Staging codes, 295
Standby L/C, 91, 92
Starting-up, 129–134
Straight bills of lading, 128
Success stories, 7–13
Success, keys to, 283–287
Sudan, 260
Surety bond, 178
Swaziland, 265

T

Taiwan, 279
Tanzania, 265
Tanzania Venture Capital Fund
  (TVCF), 270
Tariff-rate quotas, 196
Tariffs, 179
  (*See also* Harmonized Tariff
  System)
Tax incentives (exporting),
  169–171
Technical marketing decisions, 18
Technology, 49
Telecopier service, 55
Telegrams, 58
Telephone, 55
Telexes, 58
Term bonds, 195
Terminology, 16, 297–328
Terms of sale, 26–28
*Thomas Register of American
  Manufacturers*, 176
TIC, 156
Time draft, 88–90
Time zones, 61, 62
Togo, 263
TOP, 158
Trade Card, 214
Trade dress, 53
Trade fair certification, 159
Trade financing institutions,
  84, 85
Trade Information Center (TIC),
  156
Trade missions, 39
Trade name, 53
Trade opportunities Program
  (TOP), 158
Trade secrets, 53
Trade Show Central, 39, 75
Trade shows (fairs), 38, 39
Trademarks, 53, 54
Tradeport, 74
Trading regions:
  Africa, 251–273
  Americas, 215–234 (*See also*
  NAFTA)

Trading regions (*Cont.*):
  Europe, 235–249 (*See also*
  European Union [EU])
  near East/Asia, 275–282
Tramp vessels, 106
Transferable L/C, 95, 98
Travel, 59–64
Treaty for Enhanced East African
  Cooperation, 266
Treaty of Fusion, 237
Treaty of Paris, 237
Treaty of Rome, 237
Tunisia, 257

U

Uganda, 260
*Understanding United States
  Foreign Trade Data*, 160
Unfair import practices,
  171, 172
Uniform Customs and Practice for
  Documentary Credits, 91
U.S. (*see* NAFTA)
U.S. Customs Service, 173–176
*U.S. Export Management
  Companies (EMCs)*, 161
U.S. government bookstore,
  291–293
*United States Government
  Information: Publications,
  Periodicals, and Electronic
  Products*, 160, 161
Unsecured financing, 84
USAID, 254, 255

V

Value-added tax (VAT), 244, 245
Values, 48
VAT, 244, 245
Video/catalog exhibitions, 39
Visa, 61
Voice communications, 55

W

Walk on two legs, 82, 286
Water transportation, 106
Women, 51

World Intellectual Property
   Organization, 54
World Trade Center University
   (WTCU), 214
World trade centers, 6, 211–214
World Trade Centers Association
   (WTCA), 5, 6, 211
World Trade Organization (WTO), 5
World Wide Web, 66
   (*See also* Internet)

Written communication, 54–59
WTCA, 5, 6, 211
WTCU, 214
WTO, 5
www.AVGTSG.com, 77

Z

Zaire, 258
Zambia, 265
Zimbabwe, 265, 266

About the Author

Carl Nelson is a specialist in international trade and a professional writer, who is listed in *most* Who's Who in the World. Dr. Nelson is Professor of International Business at the International School of Management (San Diego), where he teaches undergraduate and graduate courses. He is also President of Global Business and Trade (GBT), an international business consulting and training company.

As a specialist in international business, he has more than 40 years of global experience in government and private business. He lived for two years in Japan and one year in South Vietnam, and is intimately knowledgeable on Hawaii, Guam, South Korea, Hong Kong, Australia, Philippines, New Zealand, and the Indian Ocean area. His experience includes economic development under the U.S. Agency for International Development (USAID) and participation in California/Mexico Maquiladora operations.

As a professional writer, Dr. Nelson has published seven nonfiction books as well as many short stories, articles, and technical papers. His first novel, titled *The Advisor (Cô-Vân)*, was published in 1999 by Turner Publishing Company. His second novel, *Secret Players*, will be published in the fall of 2000 by Olin Frederick. In 1989 he received the best fiction award at the first Southern California Writer's Conference and in 1995 was recognized for his nonfiction writing by the San Diego Book Awards Association. He is the immediate past president of the San Diego Writers/Editors Guild.

Dr. Nelson earned his Doctorate in Business Administration (D.B.A.), Finance, (emphasis on international finance and trade), from the United States International University in San Diego, California. He was recognized by USIU with its 1989 outstanding alumni award. He is also a graduate of the Naval War College, holds a Master of Science in Management (economics/systems analysis) from the Naval Post Graduate School in Monterey, California, and has an engineering degree from the United States Naval Academy in Annapolis, Maryland.